Hacking The Cyber Threat
A Cybersecurity Primer
for Business Leaders
and Executives

Pedro D. Cordero

CPA, CISSP, GPEN, GWAPT, GMOB, GNFA, GCIH

This publication is designed to provide accurate and authoritative information in regard to the subject matter covered. It is sold with the understanding that the publisher is not engaged in rendering professional services. If professional advice or other expert assistance is required, the services of a competent professional should be sought.

ISBN: 1985216477
ISBN 13: 9781985216471
Library of Congress Control Number: 2017914672
CreateSpace Independent Publishing Platform
North Charleston, South Carolina

DEDICATION

This book is dedicated to all IT cybersecurity professionals around the world whose job is to continually protect their organization's IT infrastructure, personnel, and operations; respond, mitigate and recover from all cyber security events and cyber incidents; and continually attempt to educate employees (including executive management) to protect the organization from the daily stream of cyber-attacks from today's global cyber threat actors. The cyber threat is a continuously evolving strategic threat. With the assistance of cyber-savvy business executives and leaders, the IT cybersecurity profession will appropriately address this strategic threat through dedicated efforts, appropriate strategic resources, and the best cybersecurity training. I hope this book will assist the IT cybersecurity profession in this strategic endeavor by providing a solid cybersecurity foundation to your respective business executives and leaders.

TABLE OF CONTENTS

ACKNOWLEDGMENTS

I acknowledge each FBI National Academy student in my undergraduate and graduate "Cyber Threat Landscape for Leaders/Executives" courses. They all have taught me about the cyber threat and its unique impact on them as executives and leaders as well as on their respective organizations. Their dedicated cyber warrior efforts and individual acceptance of the challenge to address the strategic cyber threat inspired me to write this book. I have been privileged to assist transforming executives with minimal or no understanding of the strategic cyber threat into cyber-savvy executives. These cyber warriors will change how our law-enforcement addresses the strategic cyber threat around the world. For this, I thank each one of you.

I also acknowledge and thank Techopedia for allowing me to use their cyber definitions throughout this book, as a glossary, and as a resource for my readers. I found Techopedia definitions user-friendly with easy-to-read explanations on many technical cyber topics.

I also acknowledge and thank seven cybersecurity vendors, (ISC)², CompTIA, ISACA, SANS Institute, Offensive Security, EC-Council, and Cisco, for granting me permission to use their cybersecurity training course descriptions for my book as a technical resource for my readers.

Finally, I thank my lovely wife Carrie and our beautiful children for their love, support, patience, and understanding for allowing me to use our family time to write this book. I love each of you with all my heart and thank you for your support in allowing me to write this book.

INTRODUCTION

Data breaches. Over the last few years, the private and public sector have suffered massive data breaches caused by unauthorized cyber intrusions. During 2013, the larger data breach victims included Adobe (38 million user accounts compromised) and Living Social (up to 50 million member accounts were put at risk). During 2014, the larger data breach victims included eBay (data loss of over 145 million records), J.P. Morgan Chase (76 million bank accounts accessed by cyber threat actors), and Home Depot (56 million credit and debit cards exposed due to point of sale cyber compromise). During 2015, the larger data breach victims included Anthem (over 80 million records), Premera Blue Cross (11 million records), the US Office of Personnel Management (OPM) (21.5 million entries in a government database), Sony Pictures (10 million records), and Experian T-Mobile customers (15 million records of potential T-Mobile customers). During 2016, the larger data breach victims included Mossack Fonseca (11.5 million encrypted documents of Panamanian law firm specializing in anonymous offshore companies), VTech (11.6 million records of customers), and Yahoo (suffered two data breaches of 500 million records in 2014 and one billion records in 2013 but not announced until 2016) (Albaugh, 2017). So far for 2017, the data breaches include Verizon (up to 14 million customer records), Bell Canada (1.9 million customer records), and Cellebrite (900 GB of sensitive corporate data) just to name a few (Whitaker, 2017). On September 8, 2017, the credit monitoring agency Equifax, announced it had suffered a massive data breach resulting in the exposure of up to 143 million American consumers personal information (Johnson, 2017). As any business executive can note, a tactical cyber breach can have significant operational and strategic consequences for any business organization.

The cyber threat has a *tactical, operational,* and *strategic* impact on any type of business organization.

For example, an employee of a medium-sized business organization opens a phishing e-mail and proceeds to click on and open an attachment with ransomware. The ransomware executes and proceeds to infect the employee's workstation. This is an example of a *tactical* cyber event.

The ransomware then successfully infects other workstations and servers throughout the entire business organization and encrypts the files on the workstations and servers, which impacts all employees of the business organization running daily operations. This is an example of the *operational* impact of this cyber threat to the business organization.

Business executives are then informed about this ransomware infection into its entire IT infrastructure, its direct impact on operations, and the accompanying extortion demand in a virtual currency by the cyber threat actor. The business executives then decide to hire a third-party cyber-response team to address the infection.

The third-party cyber-response team addresses the ransomware infection and determines (1) there have been additional undetected cyber intrusions, in which both customer credit card and employee personally identifying information (PII) have been compromised; (2) the organization IT infrastructure is extremely vulnerable due to age and unsupported operating systems and software and needs to be upgraded entirely; and (3) the organizational IT infrastructure backup systems did not work properly and organizational information will be lost unless the ransomware extortion is paid.

The business executives now have to consider how to strategically address (1) having to consider alterative courses of action, which include paying an extortion demand to possibly get the key to decrypt its files; (2) determine how to obtain the financial resources to upgrade its entire IT infrastructure and backup systems to improve its cybersecurity posture from future cyberattacks; (3) notify customers, employees, and possibly the public about the data breach; (4) prepare to spend financial resources to obtain multiyear credit monitoring for all impacted customers and employees; (5) prepare for potential legal liability due to abuse of the stolen credit card information and PII; (6) prepare for possible regulatory action due to these multiple cyber breaches; and (7) prepare strategic communications to advise the public about these cyber breaches. In addition, this IT infrastructure remediation will have a disruptive impact on daily operations for some time in the near term. Additional concerns will be the potential loss of customers and future revenues due to impacted customers no longer buying services or goods from the organization. This is an example of the *strategic* impact of the cyber threat.

Cybersecurity. How does a business organization define *cybersecurity*? Does cybersecurity mean hardening your organization's information-technology (IT) infrastructure with defense-in-depth best practices to protect against intrusions perpetrated by cyber threat actors? Does cybersecurity include information-security (InfoSec) training for all employees to protect the organization from phishing e-mails and other cyber threats? Does it entail obtaining the most-current cybersecurity training for the organization's IT staff to prevent, monitor, action, and investigate security events and reconstitute your organization's IT systems after a cyber incident? Does cybersecurity include considering the tactical, operational, and strategic costs associated with a data breach or another serious cyber incident? Does it involve obtaining cyber training for your organization's senior leadership, middle management, and first-line supervisors? Does cybersecurity involve providing continual and the most-current cyber training to all of your organization's employees? The simple answer to all these questions is yes.

Cybersecurity is a term that is very difficult to define because of the multiple facets of the cyber threat. Business executives have many responsibilities to their organization, their shareholders, their customers, the organization's employees and society. These responsibilities include leading employees to perform their best to meet the business organizations' short- and long-term goals and objectives to be a profitable organization that continues to provide the best products, at the most competitive price, with the best service to its customers. Another very important responsibility is for business executives to operate in an effective and efficient manner to reduce costs and maximize profits.

This book is designed for the non-cyber-savvy business leader or executive who does not understand the cyber threat landscape and all of its components. This book is designed to take a non-cyber-savvy business leader or executive and turn him or her into a cyber-savvy leader or executive with a foundational understanding of computer networks, computer network security, and the various elements that compose the cyber threat landscape.

For the purposes of this book, the author includes in the use of the term *executives* the chief executive officer, other c-suite executives, members of the corporate board of directors, audit committee members, and senior level executives in a position of organizational authority within a business organization. In addition, the author includes in the use of the term *leaders* the middle management, first-line supervisors, and other employees in leadership positions. The author will use the term *executives* to reflect both business *executives* and *leaders* during the remainder of the book.

This book will cover the following:

1. Understanding the Cyber Threat Landscape
2. The Basics of Information Technology
3. Understanding Malicious Software
4. Information Operations
5. Industrial Control Systems (ICS) and Critical Infrastructures
6. Wireless and Mobile Devices
7. Web Infrastructure Security and Third-Party Risk
8. Cybercrime and Hacktivism
9. The Cyber Underground
10. Cyber Defense and Liaison with IT Personnel
11. Incident Response and Digital Forensics
12. Cyber Training and Certifications
13. Private- and Public-Sector and Cybersecurity
14. Cyber Challenges for Business Executives

It should be noted that this book is not designed for IT security professionals, because there are several vendors—such as the SANS Institute, (ISC)², Offensive Security, CompTIA, ISACA, EC-Council, and CISCO—that provide some of the best cybersecurity training for IT security professionals.

A cyber-savvy business leader or executive can strategically support an organization's cybersecurity efforts by supporting his or her organization's chief information officer (CIO), chief information security officer (CISO), chief security officer (CSO), or IT director. In addition, a cyber-savvy executive will support his or her organization's IT security professionals from the executive leadership level of the organization.

ABOUT THE AUTHOR

Pedro D. Cordero has served as a special agent of the FBI for over twenty-six years. Mr. Cordero is currently a supervisory special agent and the cyber instructor for the FBI National Academy at the FBI academy located at Quantico, Virginia. Mr. Cordero is a certified public accountant (CPA) and certified information systems security professional (CISSP), and he holds multiple advanced SANS Global Information Assurance Certification (GIAC), cybersecurity certifications in penetration testing (GPEN, GMOB, GWAPT), network forensics and analysis (GFAN), and hacker techniques and incident response (GCIH). Mr. Cordero holds a bachelor's in business administration (BBA) in accoun-. tancy, from the University of Texas at El Paso (UTEP), and a master of science degree in national resource strategy, from the National Defense University (NDU) Eisenhower School–Industrial College of the Armed Forces (ICAF) war college, with a core concentration certification in information operations from the NDU College of Information and Cyberspace (formerly known as the Information Resources Management College).

The views expressed in the book do not necessarily represent the views of the US Department of Justice (DOJ), the FBI, or the United States.

INTEGRATING THE CYBER
THREAT IN STRATEGIC PLANNING
CHIEF EXECUTIVE OFFICER (CEO)

The chief executive officer (CEO) is the highest-ranking executive of a company whose primary responsibilities include making major corporate decisions, managing the overall operations and resources of the organization, and acting as the main point of communication between the Board of Directors and corporate operations (Investopedia, 2017). The CEO is also the strategic leader for an organization and responsible for strategically planning 5 to 10 years in the future in an uncertain world which is constantly changing. So why should a CEO should be concerned about cybersecurity?

As the highest-ranking business executive, a CEO needs to understand the cyber threat and how it impacts the organization strategically, operationally and tactically. Why should a CEO worry about tactical cybersecurity events when a CEO oversees an organization's long-term strategy? Because a data breach resulting in the public exposure of hundreds of thousands of customer's personally identifiable information (PII) or credit card information is a tactical event which has strategic consequences for any business organization.

An example of the impact and potential cost of a data breach in the corporate world is the September 22, 2016, announcement by Yahoo that it had suffered a data breach in which cyber threat actors stole the PII of more than five hundred million users. This data breach was announced after Yahoo had previously agreed to sell its core business to Verizon Communications Inc. for $4.8 billion (McMillan 2016). On October 6, 2016, media reports said that Verizon

Communications Inc. was pushing for a $1 billion discount off its pending $4.8 billion agreement to buy Yahoo (Atkinson 2016), because of the data breach. On December 14, 2016, Yahoo announced a second data breach that affected more than one billion accounts (Fiegerman 2016). As of February 21, 2017, Verizon and Yahoo have agreed to reduce the acquisition price by $350 million because of the two data breaches, and they have agreed to a new purchase price of $4.48 billion (Fiegerman 2017).

There are many cybersecurity questions a CEO must ask in today's environment with the various components of the cyber threat. Is the organization's IT infrastructure secure from cyberattacks? Is his or her organization's IT infrastructure being tested by penetration testers? Are all levels of the organization's leadership team cyber-savvy executives and cyber-savvy leaders? For the business executive, are the organization's most important assets such as Research and Development (R&D), Intellectual Property, and Strategic Business Development Plans secure from cyber threat actors? If the organization has implemented a strategic cybersecurity risk management program, how is the organization ensuring their strategic cybersecurity risk management program is actually working?

The chief information officer (CIO) is the organization's executive responsible for the management, implementation, and usability of information and computer technologies. A CIO analyzes how these technologies benefit the organization or improve an existing business process and then integrates a system to realize that benefit or improvement (Investopedia 2017). Some organizations may have a CIO, CISO, CSO, or IT director who has these same responsibilities. Does your organization's CIO, CISO, CSO, or IT director have all the necessary resources in terms of funding and personnel to secure your organization's IT infrastructure from the multiple aspects of the cyber threat? Are all of your organization's employees being trained in information security at least once per year and receiving monthly cybersecurity intelligence updates from the IT department? Has your organization reviewed the cybersecurity requirements of its day-to-day operations? If you have answered no to any of these questions, you may need to reevaluate your organization's strategic cybersecurity requirements to better protect your organization from the cyber threat.

How does a CEO ensure that the next generations of his or her organization's executive leadership are appropriately trained to deal with the cyber threat at the strategic, operational, and tactical levels and strategically lead the organization when the time comes? The cyber mind-set of the CEO must be to strategically protect, defend, react, and quickly recover from the cyber threat to keep the organization's IT infrastructure, operations, and personnel as secure as possible from the strategic cyber threat. A cyber-savvy CEO does this by countering the cyber threat at the strategic level by continually being aware of the ever-changing cyber threat landscape and, most important, by providing the organizational resources to continually counter the cyber threat at all levels. A cyber-savvy CEO will also serve as a model CEO to emulate for his or her organization's next generation of senior leaders.

Chief Financial Officer

The chief financial officer (CFO) is the senior executive responsible for managing the financial actions of an organization, which include tracking cash flow, financial planning, analyzing the organization's financial strengths and weaknesses, and proposing corrective actions. The CFO is like a treasurer or controller in smaller organizations because he or she is responsible for managing the finance and accounting divisions and for ensuring the financial reports are completed accurately and in a timely manner (Investopedia 2017). Is your organization's CFO a cyber-savvy executive who understands the cyber threat? Is he or she strategically resourcing this threat appropriately—that is, in conjunction with the CIO, CISO, CSO, or IT director? Or does your organization have a non-cyber-savvy CFO who is worried about cutting last year's cybersecurity funding by 15 percent to meet this year's goals for effectiveness and efficiency? Is your organization's non-cyber-savvy CFO a fiscally conservative executive who is exceptional at running the organization's fiscal matters in the most effective and efficient manner possible? If so, the cybersecurity of the organization may be in jeopardy.

CFOs must be trained as cyber-savvy executives to understand the strategic impacts of the various cyber events, such as a data breach, which can cause an organization to suffer significant losses and costs on multiple levels. A CFO only needs to realize how cyber is intertwined in the day-to-day operations of every level of an organization, including the C-Suite. A CFO only has to look in his or her respective office and see a computer workstation, possibly a laptop or tablet, and one or two smartphones. Now, if this is the case, there are at least four separate operating systems with various software programs, mobile applications, security software, log-in requirements, and so on. What does this mean? This means that cyber is here to stay and that planning for the strategic cyber threat must be treated similarly to a fixed cost. The strategic cyber threat must be incorporated as an integral part of an organization's strategic capital outlays each year, as compared with cyber expenses being treated as variable costs that can be continually reviewed for cost savings and cost efficiencies each quarter or each fiscal year.

A CFO must transition to a cyber-savvy CFO by obtaining cybersecurity training. A cyber-savvy CFO must incorporate the cost of cybersecurity into his or her strategic-, operational-, and tactical-level organizational investments. A cyber-savvy CFO is one who inquires as to which are the best cybersecurity programs, components, and services for the organization; obtains cost comparisons of the best cybersecurity products presented to him or her by the CIO, CISO, CSO, or IT director and to his or her staff; provides the funding and time required to have the most talented cybersecurity staff; and understands there is a significant investment—not expense—in keeping the organization secure from cyberattacks and cyber threat actors.

The cyber mind-set of the CFO must be to protect, defend, react, and re-cover by providing the organizational resources as requested by the CIO, CISO, CSO, and IT director, to keep the IT infrastructure secure, to have the best cybersecurity-trained IT staff, to provide continual information-security monitoring and training to all employees, and to conduct regularly scheduled vulnerability assessments and penetration tests of the IT infrastructure to con-tinually counter the cyber threat.

The one constant about cybersecurity is it is constantly evolving and be-coming more complex with the passage of time. A cyber-savvy CFO must look at a continuity of cyber investments to maintain the best organizational cybersecurity posture. The CIO, CISO, CSO, or IT director and his or her IT staff are constantly challenged in having to secure and update the orga-nization's IT infrastructure to defend against the most-sophisticated cyber threats. In addition, his or her cybersecurity responsibilities include keeping IT staff up to date in cybersecurity training and ensuring the organization's employees understand the most-current cyber threats with information-secu-rity training and timely cyber intelligence and threat alerts. To ensure that these responsibilities are fulfilled correctly at the strategic, operational, and tactical level, this strategic endeavor requires a significant investment of or-ganizational resources.

The non-cyber-savvy CFO who is reading this might be saying to himself or herself, "What I have just read in the preceding pages is just plain wrong. We can be effective and efficient in our cybersecurity expenses and keep our organization secure from cyberattacks." I have one response: consider the strategic costs of a data breach by a successful cyberattack that includes the public release of PII or an organization's customer's financial data.

What are an organization's costs due to this data breach and public release of PII or customer financial information? To start, here are just a few of the significant expenses an organization will have after suffering a data breach: irreparable reputational damage to the organization brand and its stock value (if publicly traded), costs associated with the data breach (legal, incident-response, mitigation, and post-incident-monitoring expenses), legal and civil liability, regulatory oversight and possible regulatory action against the organization, potential decline in revenues due to consumer concerns regarding the lack of cybersecurity of the organization's IT infrastructure, and new and significant costs associated with cybersecurity training and the implementation of costly IT cybersecurity solutions to prevent another data breach. These are only the initial costs of a data breach; other significant costs include the loss of organizational and employee productivity from the time of the data breach to the time at which the organization's IT infrastructure is made more secure.

According to the 2015 IBM and Ponemon Institute global study of the cost of a data breach of 350 companies in eleven countries (the United States, the United Kingdom, Germany, Australia, France, Brazil, Japan, Italy, India, the Arabian region [a consolidation of organizations in the United Arab Emirates and Saudi Arabia], and Canada), the average total cost of the data breach was $3.8 million, and the average consolidated cost for each stolen or lost record containing sensitive or confidential information was $154. This report cited three major reasons why these data-breach costs keep climbing: (1) cyberattacks are increasing in frequency; (2) customers are lost because of the breaches; and (3) victim companies are incurring higher forensic, investigative, and crisis-management costs because of the breaches (IBM 2015).

According to the 2016 IBM and Ponemon Institute global study of the cost of a data breach of 383 companies located in twelve countries (the United States, the United Kingdom, Germany, Australia, France, Brazil, Japan, Italy, India, the Arabian region [the United Arab Emirates and Saudi Arabia], Canada, and South Africa), the average total cost of a data breach in 2015 was $4 million, and the average cost for each stolen or lost record containing sensitive or confidential information was $158 (IBM 2016).

According to the 2017 IBM and Ponemon Institute global study of the cost of a data breach of 419 companies located in twelve countries (the United States, the United Kingdom, Germany, Australia, France, Brazil, Japan, Italy, India, the Middle East [including the United Arab Emirates and Saudi Arabia], Canada, and the ASEAN region [including Singapore, Indonesia, the Philippines, and Malaysia]), the average total cost of the data breach, which occurred in 2016, was $3.62 million, and the average cost for each stolen or lost record containing sensitive or confidential information was $141 (IBM 2017).

Now let's continue the data breach cost example by taking the incalculable costs of a significant data breach of an organization to the strategic level. Imagine your IT infrastructure is breached by a cyber threat actor and this cyber threat actor successfully compromises your organization's Research and Development (R&D) servers, which houses the organization's most valuable intellectual property for your organization's future products for the marketplace. Your organization has spent hundreds of millions of dollars in the development of these future products. This strategic investment accounts for one of the largest strategic capital investments by your organization. This intellectual property and future sales of the proposed final products are the future of your organization's future revenues for the next five to ten years.

Now imagine saving a few hundred thousand dollars by not investing in your CIO, CISO, CSO, or IT Director's recommended cybersecurity upgrades to protect your organization's IT infrastructure, operations and personnel and an unknown cyber threat actor exploits a vulnerability and commits a successful cyber intrusion into your IT infrastructure. The cyber threat actor then proceeds to steal your organization's prized intellectual property. Now fast forward 18 months, and suddenly a very similar product is introduced into the marketplace that looks quite a bit like your organization's planned future products. How does any organization calculate the strategic losses in clients, R&D costs, and lost future revenues due to the theft of an organization's intellectual property? How does an organization calculate the strategic, operational and tactical costs of the loss of your intellectual property due to a cyber breach? This scenario and this type of strategic cost can lead to devastating consequences to the organization.

So now reconsider the costs of not being a cyber-savvy CFO and failing to incorporate cybersecurity in all aspects of strategic, operational, and tactical financial planning.

A Cyber-Savvy Executive team

How does a CEO begin to transform the organization's executive team into a cyber-savvy executive team? This is where setting the example in leadership comes into play. Are you a cyber-savvy CEO? After purchasing and reading this book, I recommend each CEO take a five-day management course in cybersecurity training from such vendors as (ISC)² or the SANS Institute, which are two of the best providers in cybersecurity training in the world.

Why do I recommend that CEOs lead by example and take a five-day cyber course? It is for a few reasons. The five-day course is very intense, and the CEOs will learn to appreciate what an organization's IT staff must go through in time, attendance, and learning when they take those cybersecurity courses to improve their skills. It will also provide the CEO with an appreciation of why these courses are expensive and why they are well worth the cost. In addition, if the CEO obtains a cyber certification such as (1) the prestigious (ISC)² Certified Information Systems Security Professional (CISSP) certification or (2) the SANS Global Information Assurance Certification (GIAC) Security Leadership Certification (GSLC), the CEO will set the cyber standard for the organization's executive team. Your executive team will follow in your footsteps, and this then becomes the norm for your successor's executive-leadership teams. The first-generation leadership team (five years from taking over as the senior executives) and the second-generation leadership team (ten years from taking over as the senior executives) will follow the strategic example set by the current CEO and his or her executive team. By attending a five-day (ISC)² or SANS management course and by obtaining a high-level cybersecurity certification, such as the CISSP or GSLC, you will set an organizational strategy in motion. All three generations of your leadership (current, first generation, and second generation) will recognize the importance of strategic cyber threats and will follow in your footsteps. As the CEO, you will set an expectation with the first- and second-generation leaders that cybersecurity training is a strategic element to being a senior executive in your organization. In addition, the future senior executives will search for even more cybersecurity training as they continue their leadership journey to the senior-leadership level.

Train the Senior Executives and Midlevel Executives

For senior executives to understand the strategic importance and the strategic impact of cyber threats, they must be trained in cybersecurity. There is a significant difference between being briefed on tactical cyber threat issues and being trained to strategically understand the cyber threat and its impact.

Senior executives are constantly being provided business updates regarding the organizations' day-to-day operations. For many organizations, these updates also include cyber threat briefings. This allows the senior executives to have a general understanding of how cyber threats can impact their organizations' tactical, operational, and strategic activities.

Ask yourself how well you as a senior executive truly understand the cyber threat. Consider the following example. A simple computer network that includes modems, routers, servers, workstations, wireless access points, smartphones, laptops, tablets, and a remote log-in capability has numerous separate cyber threat intrusion vectors. Modems can be attacked by a denial of service (DoS) or war dialers; routers can be attacked by a DoS attack or unauthorized access due to an improper configuration; servers can be attacked with structured query language (SQL) injection attacks, cross-site scripting attacks, and command-injection attacks; workstations are vulnerable to malicious software (malware) and phishing e-mail attacks; wireless access points can be attacked by rogue access points and weak encryption attacks; smartphones and tablets are vulnerable to malicious mobile-application software, untested mobile applications, information and data leakage, unpatched operating systems; and the potential loss of sensitive intellectual property with the loss of an organization-issued smartphone; and remote log-ins can be compromised with stolen credentials. If this simple network example with its multiple threat vectors was something new for you as a senior executive, I will humbly state that as a senior executive, you do not understand the multiple facets of the cyber threat landscape.

Cyber leadership training for senior executives requires a time commitment from the senior executive and resources from the organization. There are various entities whereby an organization can obtain cybersecurity training or information-assurance training for its employees. An organization's training division can research entities such as cybersecurity vendors, local community colleges, universities, and online and in-person cybersecurity training.

Cyber leadership training for executives must be concise, strategic, and to the point. This expenditure should be an investment in creating the best cyber-savvy leaders for the organization. There is a shortage of cyber-savvy business executives, and there are many reasons for this. A few reasons are the following: (1) the mind-set that cyber is an IT problem, not a strategic leadership issue; (2) the cost of cybersecurity training; (3) the time commitment required for cyber-security courses and cyber certifications; (4) the fear and lack of understanding of the terms and language associated with the strategic cyber threat and cybersecurity; and, most important, (4) the lack of desire to learn a new and challenging cyber language and technical skill set that is required in today's strategic global environment.

What executive with today's hectic schedule has time to commit his or her precious time and resources to cyber leadership training? This is where the executive leadership of every business organization needs to change its mind-set. It should not be a question of which executive has time to take this cyber leadership training; rather, all executives in the organization should be required to obtain cybersecurity leadership training.

As noted above, one cyber-training organization that offers cyber-leadership, cybersecurity, and information-assurance training for executives is the SANS Institute. The SANS Institute uses various teaching methodologies in its various curricula of cybersecurity training, such as cyber conferences, on-demand training, private training, and community training. SANS offers a management curriculum, which includes level one (introductory), level two (intermediate), and level three (advanced) cyber-leadership security courses, in addition to specialty courses, such as the SANS Training Program for CISSP Certification (SANS Institute 2017). It should be noted these in-person courses are rather expensive, averaging about $5,000 per course (plus an additional cost for the certification exam), and they have an average duration of five days. The SANs course and certification cost do not include employee per diem, lodging, and travel expenses.

Cyber Is a Strategic Element, Not Just a Factor in Strategic Planning

As the CEO, being responsible for the success or failure of an organization is a herculean responsibility. How do you as the CEO ensure that the cyber threat is not only a factor but also a major element in your organization's strategic planning? One sure methodology is to have a cyber-savvy executive team assist you in your organization's strategic planning. A cyber-savvy executive team fully understands the strategic, operational, and tactical risks the cyber threat imposes on an organization. As the CEO, consider whether your executive team is cyber-savvy, or have they only been briefed on the tactical cyber threat, whereas some members of your executive team understand the basic elements of the cyber threat? If your executive team is not cyber-savvy, the responsibility lies squarely with you as the organization's CEO. As the CEO, you also have the power to transform your organization into a cyber-savvy organization, but it must start at the CEO level and flow down to the executive team and then into all levels of the organization.

1

UNDERSTANDING THE CYBER THREAT LANDSCAPE

The cyber threat landscape encapsulates the multitude of cyber threats and cyber threat actors that an organization faces in today's environment. Cyber threat actors include cybercriminals, hacktivist groups, nation-state actors, advanced-persistent-threat (APT) actors, transnational cybercriminal organizations, the cyber insider threat, the cyber underground, and other hackers. The cyber threat landscape comprises these various elements, which are currently targeting your organization's IT infrastructure. It does not matter if your organization is a law-enforcement agency, a government agency, a Fortune 500 corporation, or a limited-liability partnership—your IT infrastructure will be targeted and probably compromised by these cyber threat actors.

Is the cyber threat the responsibility of the information technology (IT) staff, or is cybersecurity the responsibility of an organization's executive leadership? The IT staff play a paramount and very important role in securing your organization's IT infrastructure, but the cyber threat is an executive-leadership issue that needs to be addressed at a strategic, operational, and tactical level by your organization's CEO and his or her senior executive leadership team.

The CIO, CISO, CSO, or IT director and IT staff play a very prominent role in protecting an organization's IT infrastructure but require strategic direction, support, and resourcing from the organization's senior executive leadership team. If your organization is allowing the IT staff to address the cyber threat at the strategic, operational, and tactical level, how will a non-cyber-savvy senior executive leadership team know whether they are strategically addressing the cyber threat properly in their strategic planning? How will this organization's senior-executive leadership team know whether they have done everything possible to ensure that their agency's information, PII, financial information, strategic-planning details, and other crown jewels of the organization are constantly protected from the various cyber threat actors that compose the cyber threat landscape?

A cyber-savvy business executive will understand the need for the necessary network security equipment, IT personnel, cybersecurity training and the funding that is required to keep the organization's information secure from cyber threat actors. A cyber-savvy business executive understands the strategic requirement to secure the organization's IT infrastructure to protect the organization's data, customer information, and intellectual property of the organization's next generation of products that are strategically projected to bring in the organization's next 5 years' worth of revenue.

Having a cyber-savvy executive-leadership team will allow these executives to engage with the CIO, CISO, CSO, or IT director and IT staff and to ask the right questions regarding what is required to continuously maintain the most secure IT infrastructure to prevent any type of intrusions, data breaches, or thefts of the organization's most-sensitive information and data. A cyber-savvy executive will understand that the cyber threat is here to stay and that it must be addressed as a strategic fixed cost and not a variable cost that is constantly subject to being reduced for the sake of efficiency and effectiveness.

2

THE BASICS OF INFORMATION TECHNOLOGY

Review the simple-network example previously noted in the book's introduction, the example that included modems, routers, servers, workstations, wireless access points, smartphones, laptops, tablets, and a remote log-in capability. This very simple network has numerous cyber threat intrusion vectors, which include denial of service (DoS), war dialers, and cross-site scripting.

Even if you as an executive do not know what a DoS, war dialer, or cross-site scripting attacks are, it is very apparent from this example that a simple computer network has numerous cyber threat intrusion vectors. This means there are numerous potential vulnerabilities throughout the IT infrastructure, personnel, and operations that can be exploited by malicious cyber threat actors. If malicious cyber threat actors are successful in exploiting these vulnerabilities, the results can include the following:

1. A compromised workstation or network, leading to unauthorized access to your entire network infrastructure
2. Theft of the organization's current intellectual property.
3. Data breach of personally identifiable information (PII), protected health information (PHI), or client financial data, such as credit-card data or bank-account data.
4. The organization's most sensitive future product(s) research and development projects designed for future strategic revenue generation for the next five to ten years.

There are so many facets regarding the cyber threat and cybersecurity that these two topics boggle the mind. Now, how does an executive begin to address the cyber threat at a strategic, operational, and tactical level? An executive begins to address the cyber threat by becoming a cyber-savvy executive.

Overview of Information Assurance, Operating Systems, Networks, Threats, and Vulnerabilities

Business executives must realize that there are fundamentals they must comprehend to fully understand what it means to secure information from the cyber threat. This foundational basis is a necessity to better understand cybersecurity and how an organization can better secure its IT infrastructure from the various cyber threat actors attacking today's IT infrastructure around the world.

Information assurance, in the simplest terms, is the process involved in protecting an organization's computer networks, computer systems, and IT infrastructure. Information assurance comprises five information-security principles: (1) availability, (2) integrity, (3) confidentiality, (4) authentication, and (5) nonrepudiation (Techopedia 2017).

Traditionally, there have been three security principles of information assurance: availability, integrity, and confidentiality, also known as the AIC triad or the CIA triad. Two additional principles, authentication and nonrepudiation, have been added as components of information assurance.

Availability refers to the "ability of a user to access information or resources in a specified location and in the correct format" (Techopedia 2017).

Availability means that your IT infrastructure works reliably and as designed, without any disruptions, and provides access to your organization's data to the appropriate personnel. It also means that if there is a disruption to your organization's IT infrastructure, it should recover quickly and smoothly and minimize any negative impact to business productivity and your organization's personnel, data, and resources.

Integrity refers to "methods of ensuring that data is real, accurate and safeguarded from unauthorized user modification" (Techopedia 2017).

Integrity is maintained when accuracy and reliability of your organization's data and IT infrastructure are not modified in any way.

Confidentiality "allows authorized users to access sensitive and protected data. Specific mechanisms ensure confidentiality and safeguard data from harmful intruders" (Techopedia 2017).

Confidentiality ensures that your organization's data is secure both at rest and during transport to and from your organization's IT infrastructure and that your organization's data is not breached through unauthorized disclosure from the use of authentication, role-based security, and access control.

Authentication "is a process that ensures and confirms a user's identity." Authentication involves ensuring that users are who they say they are by using such authentication methods as username, passwords, biometrics, tokens, and other devices (Techopedia 2017).

Nonrepudiation "is a method of guaranteeing message transmission between parties via digital signatures and/or encryption." Nonrepudiation is used in e-mail messages, signatures, and digital contracts (Techopedia 2017).

As a business executive, you may be asking yourself why availability, integrity, confidentiality, authentication, and nonrepudiation are so important to the strategic planning of your organization. These five principles of information assurance are required to ensure that your organization's IT infrastructure is secure and available to all of your organization's authorized employees. These five principles ensure the secrecy of your organization's data and information at all levels of communication, transport, and at rest; prevent, detect, react, and recover from any potential modification or negative impact to the integrity of your organization's IT infrastructure from cyber threat actors; ensure that only authorized individuals have access to your organization's IT infrastructure; and ensure that message transmissions between parties involve digital signatures, encryptions, or both.

It is important for an executive to understand the challenges facing your organization's CIO, CISO, CSO, or IT director in his or her attempt to find the right balance in providing information assurance to your organization. The challenges faced by him or her include providing the appropriate availability to your organization's customers and authorized employees; providing the appropriate level of integrity by providing security for your organization's IT infrastructure at all organizational levels (personnel, IT systems, customer data, intellectual property, information-security training, etc.); and providing confidentiality by using the best encryption systems to secure your organization's data and informational resources while at rest and while in transit through the network and across the Internet. The key for executives to understand these phenomenal challenges faced by the CIOs, CISOs, CSOs, or IT directors is to understand the cyber threat landscape and its components. By understanding the elements of the cyber threat landscape, you will better understand these challenges facing your CIO, CISO, CSO, or IT director, and you will become his or her advocate and ally in securing your organization's IT infrastructure and information.

The strategic impact of the CIO, CISO, CSO, or IT director trying to achieve the right balance of information assurance for your organization will be increased organizational costs and increased resources. These additional costs and resources are needed to continuously secure the organization's IT infrastructure. The reasons for these increased costs and resources are the continuous evolution of the various cyber threat actors and the increasing sophistication of their cyberattack methodology. For example, if a multinational law-enforcement operation is successful in taking down a botnet, a cyber-criminal forum, or a strain of ransomware, these cyber threat actors quickly learn how this was accomplished by law-enforcement. The cyber threat actors quickly adapt, change, and improve their cybercriminal techniques and tradecraft so that it is more difficult for law-enforcement to replicate the successful law-enforcement operation. Law-enforcement cyber investigators are constantly reacting and responding to these cyber threat actors and their criminal efforts. The strategic impact for the business executive is to better understand what creates these increased costs as relayed to you by the CIO, CISO, CSO, or IT director.

Operating Systems

As an executive, do you know what type of computer operating systems your organization uses? In today's environment, there are three main computer operating systems used:

1. Windows
2. Linux or UNIX
3. Apple Mac

We will review mobile operating systems in chapter 6, which covers wireless and mobile devices.

Each of these three operating systems has different and specific vulnerabilities that are exploited by cyber threat actors. It is important to understand whether your organization's IT infrastructure includes one or all three operating systems.

The Windows environment is the most popular computer operating system currently in use. The worldwide desktop operating systems market share for the Windows environment is 84.31 percent as of July 2017 (StatCounter GlobalStats 2017). The most current Windows operating system is Windows 10, and older Windows operating systems include Windows 8.1, Windows 8, Windows 7, Windows Vista, and Windows XP.

Apple products such as the MacBook, MacBook Air, and MacBook Pro use the Mac OS. The worldwide desktop operating systems market share for the Mac OS environment is 11.61 percent as of July 2017 (StatCounter GlobalStats 2017).

The Linux or UNIX environment has variations such as Red Hat Linux, Ubuntu, Debian, Fedora, and many others. The worldwide desktop operating systems market share for the Linux environment is 1.74 percent as of July 2017 (StatCounter GlobalStats 2017).

As one can see, an organization that uses more than one operating system in its IT infrastructure can increase the organization's attack surface and increase the likelihood of exploitation by cyber threat actors. To reduce these vulnerabilities, the organization must secure all operating systems; if the organization does not, it risks being exploited, possible data loss, and compromising the organization's IT infrastructure.

Networks and Network Components
To understand the cyber threat landscape, one must understand the basics of a network and its components, which will lead to understanding the various intrusion vectors that are available to cyber threat actors.

A basic network has several components. These network components include workstations, servers, transmission media (optical fiber, cable, etc.), network-interface cards, protocols, shared peripherals (printers, software, etc.), operating system (workstation), network operating system, hub, switch, bridge, local area network (LAN), wireless components, remote access, and routers.

Network-security components can include antivirus, antimalware, and antispyware programs. They also include firewalls, encryption, demilitarized zones (DMZ), intrusion-detection systems (IDS), intrusion-prevention systems (IPS), network-security managers (NSM), security information and event management (SIEM) systems, and mobile device management systems (MDM).

Network management of an organization's IT infrastructure includes the administration, operation, maintenance, and security of the IT infrastructure. The administration of the IT infrastructure includes maintaining the inventory of the network components and monitoring the network's hardware and software performances. The operation of the IT infrastructure ensures that the enterprise networks are working properly, efficiently, and effectively and addressing issues before they impact the enterprise users. Network maintenance includes repair and upgrades for all network components. Network security involves ensuring your organization's IT infrastructure is protected with policies, procedures, and security components that prevent cyber threat actors from gaining unauthorized access to, exploiting, modifying, or conducting successful denial-of-service attacks against the organization's IT infrastructure.

Threats and Vulnerabilities

Even the most basic network illustrates the challenges of cybersecurity. *Cybersecurity* as a term is very difficult to define for this very reason. If I were to ask a variety of business executives to define the term *cybersecurity*, I would probably receive numerous definitions, none of which would be the same.

As an example, we will use a simple computer network that includes modems, routers, firewalls, servers, workstations (operating systems and software applications), a wireless local area network, and remote access for mobile devices and laptops.

In this basic computer network and its components, there are various intrusion vectors that are present for cyber actors to exploit if the computer network is not secured. For instance, the wrong configuration on a router firewall can allow a cyber actor to gain access into your network by exploiting an open port. Using weak encryption on your router, such as Wired Equivalent Privacy (WEP), could provide a cyber actor unauthorized access into your network via your wireless router. Not having an enterprise-level patch-management program for your IT infrastructure (which ensures patching of computer operating systems, software applications, and third-party software applications) can provide a cyber actor unauthorized access to your IT infrastructure via exploitation of vulnerabilities in both the operating system and software applications. Remote access from home or by a smartphone used by the CEO or other senior business executives can be compromised by a remote-access Trojan (RAT), thereby allowing the cyber threat actor remote access to your organization's most-sensitive information and data.

As one can see, even the most basic computer network offers any CIO, CISO, CSO, or IT director a very serious challenge in providing information assurance. This serious challenge is never ending because protecting an organization's IT infrastructure from the various types of sophisticated cyber threat actors includes having your CIO, CISO, CSO, or IT director continuously monitor and constantly adjust to the sophisticated and ever-evolving cyber threat landscape.

The CIO, CISO, CSO, or IT director and his or her staff must constantly be aware of and understand the ever-evolving cyber threat landscape and must act quickly to pivot and address these security challenges with the best cyber personnel, the best IT infrastructure, the best network-security devices, and the appropriate strategic-funding resources. These strategic resources for funding and personnel are a strategic necessity for the CIO, CISO, CSO, or IT director to appropriately and continuously address cyber threats and protect the organization's IT infrastructure from them.

In summary, business executives who understand the principles of information assurance and the basics of networks and network security will be in a better position to understand the overall challenges posed by the cyber threat to his or her organization's CIO, CISO, CSO, or IT director and IT staff. A business executive who understands the cyber threat landscape will be an advocate and supporter of his or her CIO, CISO, CSO, or IT director's strategic challenge in (1) continually attempting to best secure the entire IT infrastructure and operations from unauthorized access or modification by the various cyber threat actors seeking to exploit any potential vulnerability in the IT infrastructure of the executive's organization, (2) keeping the organization's IT infrastructure running and available for all the employees and customers, (3) having the best-trained cybersecurity staff, and (4) keeping all employees regularly informed of the most-current cyber threats.

3

UNDERSTANDING MALICIOUS SOFTWARE

One important cyber-threat-landscape attack vector that every business executive should understand is malicious software, or malware. *Malicious software*, or *malware*, is "any software that brings harm to a computer system" (Techopedia 2017).

Malware comes in various forms: viruses, worms, rootkits, spyware, adware, bots, Trojan horses, and remote-access Trojans (RATs).

A *virus* is a type of malware comprising small pieces of code attached to legitimate programs. When the program runs, the virus runs (Techopedia 2017).

A *worm* is malware that replicates while moving across different computers, leaving copies of itself in the memory of each computer in its path (Techopedia 2017).

Spyware is malware that secretly infiltrates and monitors unsuspecting users. It enables a cyber threat actor to obtain sensitive information, such as log-in passwords and bank log-in credentials, from a user's computer (Techopedia 2017).

Adware is software that contains commercial advertisements that collect web-browser data to target advertisements, such as pop-ups. Adware programs can include games, desktop toolbars, or utilities (Techopedia 2017). Some adware uses invasive measures that can cause security issues.

Rootkits are malware used by cyber threat actors to gain administrator-level or backdoor access to a computer or computer network. A rootkit is typically installed by exploiting a computer system's vulnerability or by compromising log-in credentials without the victim's consent or knowledge. Rootkits can hide other malware including a keylogger, a program that records and tracks a victim's keystrokes on his or her keyboard, resulting in the compromise of sensitive information, such as bank log-in credentials (Techopedia 2017).

A *Trojan horse* is a seemingly benign program that when activated, operates as malware that causes harm to a computer system. A Trojan horse can download additional malware to provide access to a victim's computer at a later time via a backdoor, to provide remote access to the victim's computer so that it can be accessed by the cyber threat actor at any time, to destroy files on the victim's computer, and to allow a cyber threat actor to use the victim's computer as a proxy to conduct illegal activities from the victim's computer (Techopedia 2017).

Botnets are a network of compromised computers operated by cyber threat actors known as bot herders, and the botnets are used for malicious purposes. Each compromised computer that composes the botnet is called a bot. These bots form a network of compromised computers and are controlled by a bot herder using command-and-control (C2) servers. The cyber threat actor can use the botnet to transmit malware or spam or to launch a denial-of-service (DoS) or distributed-denial-of-service (DDoS) attack (Techopedia 2017).

A *denial of service* (DoS) is any type of attack where the cyber threat actors attempt to prevent legitimate users from accessing the service. In a DoS attack, the cyber threat actor "usually sends excessive messages asking the network or server to authenticate requests that have invalid return addresses. The network or server will not be able to find the return address of the attacker when sending the authentication approval, causing the server to wait before closing the connection. When the server closes the connection, the attacker sends more authentication messages with invalid return addresses." Hence, the process of authentication and waiting on the server is repeated over and over again, keeping the network or server busy and causing the service to be inaccessible to legitimate users (Techopedia 2017).

A *distributed denial of service* (DDoS) is a "type of computer attack that uses a number of hosts to overwhelm a server, causing a website to experience a complete system crash." Denial-of-service attacks are perpetrated by cyber threat actors "to target large-scale, far-reaching and popular websites in an effort to disable them, either temporarily or permanently." DDoS attacks overwhelm the targeted servers with information requests, which disable the main systems and prevent them from operating, leaving the site's legitimate users unable to access the targeted website. It should be noted that a DDoS attack differs from a DoS attack in that a DDoS uses several hosts to bombard a server, and in a DoS attack, only a single host is used (Techopedia 2017).

Two recent examples of a game-changing DDoS attack occurred on September 20, 2016, against the Krebs on Security website (http://krebsonsecurity.com/), which is operated by Brian Krebs, a cybersecurity author and investigative reporter. This DDoS is believed to have been a retaliatory attack for Brian Krebs's series on the takedown of the DDoS-for-hire service vDOS. This DDoS attack was a record-setting DDoS attack, ranging from 620 gigabytes per second to 665 gigabytes per second (Krebs 2016). One gigabyte per second is one billion bits per second.

A second example and the supposedly largest ever DDoS attack occurred on October 21, 2016; it targeted Dyn, a major domain-name server (DNS) and cloud-infrastructure provider. According to McAfee, an Internet security provider, the DDoS used a botnet comprising poorly secured Internet-of-things (IoT) devices infected with the Mirai botnet that generated 1.2 terabytes per second at its peak (McAfee 2017). This DDoS attack effectively shut down many well-known websites, such as Twitter, Netflix, CNN, and PayPal (Thielman and Johnston 2016). It should be noted that one terabyte per second equals one thousand gigabytes per second.

To compare these massive new DDoS attacks with previous DDoS attacks, during 2013, Spamhaus, an international nonprofit organization that tracks spam and other cyber threats, suffered what was considered to be the largest DDoS attack at the time, reaching four hundred gigabytes per second. The US financial sector suffered 140-gigabytes-per-second DDoS attacks from Iranian cyber threat actors from 2011 through 2013 (York 2016). These massive new DDoS attacks should be a warning to business organizations as to the magnitude of these potentially devastating attacks and their potential impact on business websites and their online businesses around the world.

Let's now look at the composition of malware. Although there are many types and variants of malware, malware commonly has the following six components:

1. Insertion—installs itself on the victim's IT infrastructure
2. Avoidance—uses methodology to avoid being detected by the IT infrastructure's security components.

3. Eradication—removes itself from the infected IT infrastructure after the payload has been executed
4. Replication—makes copies of itself and spreads and infects other components of the IT infrastructure
5. Trigger—uses an event, such as a specific time and date, to execute its payload.
6. Payload—carries out its malicious function (such as installation of a backdoor), wipes a master-boot record, exploits a known operating-system vulnerability, and so on (Harris and Maymi 2016)

Malware is used by cybercriminals, hacktivists, transnational criminal organizations, insiders, and nation-state actors. The spectrum of the potency of malware ranges from known malware that is identified by antivirus programs to such things as the Stuxnet worm, which was a very advanced and sophisticated zero-day exploit that targeted critical infrastructure.

A *zero-day* exploit is malware that has not been detected by any antivirus or antimalware-detection software. What this means is your business organization can already be infected by a zero-day exploit or multiple zero-day exploits if a successful cyberattack has already compromised your organization's IT infrastructure.

One must note that there are various subcomponents of each category of malware (viruses, for example, include polymorphic viruses, macro viruses, and tunneling viruses). A business executive does not need to understand the many different types of malware and their subcomponents but must understand that there are many and varied types of dangerous malware that can strategically impact the entire organization's IT infrastructure, personnel, and operations.

An important aspect to note regarding malware is that it can be inserted in numerous ways into an organization's IT infrastructure, including via malicious phishing e-mails opened by unsuspecting and untrained employees in an organization; via malware downloaded from visiting a compromised website; or via a cyber threat actor who has compromised the organization's IT infrastructure by exploiting a known software, hardware, or browser vulnerability.

In May 2016, Amazon users were advised of a massive phishing campaign targeting them. This phishing campaign included phishing e-mails with an attached blank Word document containing macros that ran the Locky ransomware. After being prompted to enable the contents of the document, the Locky ransomware would then encrypt the victim's files and demand payment in the Bitcoin virtual currency for the key to decrypt the encrypted files (Trend Micro 2016). This is just one example of the many phishing e-mails with ransomware that can target businesses, law-enforcement, and other organizations around the world.

In May 2017, the largest ransomware infection in history (to date) occurred when the WannaCry ransomware infected Microsoft operating systems, impacting over two hundred thousand people and many organizations in at least 150 countries around the world (Dwoskin and Adam 2017). This global ransomware attack targeted Windows environments, including the retired Windows XP operating systems. Microsoft took the unusual step of quickly issuing a security patch for its retired Windows XP operating system to protect against the WannaCry ransomware (Microsoft 2017). This is very important to note as Microsoft stopped supporting Windows XP on April 8, 2014, and advised it would no longer provide security updates or technical support for it. Microsoft recommended customers migrate to its most modern operating system, Windows 10 (Microsoft 2014).

So how does an organization protect itself from so many different types of malicious software? As one can see, there are multiple intrusion attack vectors for malware to compromise any organization's IT infrastructure. Executives must understand the methods of defense-in-depth to protect their organizations' IT infrastructures. Defense in depth is a strategy "for achieving Information Assurance in today's highly networked environments. It is a 'best practices' strategy in that it relies on intelligent application of techniques and technologies that exist today." The defense-in-depth strategy "recommends a balance between the protection capability and cost, performance, and operational considerations" (Citadel Information Group Inc. 2017). We will discuss defense-in-depth in more detail in chapter 10.

The most basic defense mechanisms include antivirus software at the enterprise level. *Antivirus software* is software that detects, prevents, and removes viruses, worms, and other malware from a computer. The majority of antivirus programs include an auto-update feature that permits the program to download signatures or profiles of new viruses, enabling the system to check for the most recently discovered threats (Techopedia 2017). The way an antivirus program works is the antivirus companies identify malware, and then a signature is derived from this malware. These signatures are then inputted into a database that is used by the antivirus scans to detect known malware samples. Business executives must understand that there are hundreds of millions of different types of malware that have been discovered to date, so their organizations' antivirus protection will only guard against known malware and will not protect their organizations from zero-day exploits.

Executives must understand the strategic impact of malware when it comes to addressing this cyber threat. To provide our business executives with a strategic perspective on the challenges posed by malware, during April 2015, CNN Money reported that more than 317 million new pieces of malware were created in 2014; nearly 1 million new malware threats were released every day during 2014, according to the Internet security teams from Symantec and Verizon (Harrison and Pagliery 2015). A more recent report from MacAfee Labs reported that there are over six hundred million samples of malware as of April 2017 (McAfee 2017).

Another security component for networks is a *firewall*. A firewall "is used to maintain the security of a private network. Firewalls block unauthorized access to or from private networks and are often employed to prevent unauthorized web users or illicit software from gaining access to private networks connected to the Internet" (Techopedia 2017). There are many types of firewalls an organization can implement to restrict access to the various components of its IT infrastructure. One important aspect to note regarding firewalls is their configuration, which allows or disallows access to a protected network in the organization's IT infrastructure. If a firewall is not configured correctly and securely, it can create vulnerabilities that can be exploited by the various cyber threat actors seeking to gain unauthorized access to your organization's IT infrastructure. So even if you have your network-security device in place, such as a firewall, an improper configuration of this device can give the cyber threat actor unauthorized access to your internal network's infrastructure.

A *white list* is a list of websites, e-mail addresses, or other entities approved for authorized access to a specific area in a computing environment. White-listing is considered a proactive security measure (Techopedia 2017).

In contrast, a *blacklist* is a list of websites, e-mail addresses, or domains that are blocked from being delivered into a computing environment. When using blacklisting, a user is unable to send messages to an intended recipient. The primary reason for using blacklisting is to block spam, but the challenge is to filter out the spam from the legitimate e-mails from authorized marketing entities (Techopedia 2017).

Another network-security component is an *intrusion-detection system* (IDS), which is software that is designed to automatically alert administrators when a cyber threat actor is attempting to compromise system information through malicious activities or through security-policy violations (Techopedia 2017). The IDS will flag such unauthorized cyber intrusions but will not stop them.

An *intrusion-prevention system* (IPS) monitors an organization's network infrastructure for malicious activities (such as security threats or policy violations) to identify suspicious activity, and then the IPS logs the relevant information, attempts to block the activity, and finally reports it (Techopedia 2017).

Another important component of network security is a *security incident and event management* (SIEM) system. A SIEM identifies, monitors, records, and conducts analyses of security events or incidents in a real-time IT environment. It provides a comprehensive and centralized view of the network's security status of an organization's IT infrastructure. A SIEM usually has the following six attributes:

1. Retention: This attribute is used for storing data (such as logging activity from network-security components) for extended periods of time to assist in analyzing security incidents from better data sets.
2. Dashboards: This attribute is used for analysis and visualization of data (such as network-security logs) to recognize patterns or concentrate on specific and unusual activity that does not fit the normal baseline activity of the IT infrastructure.
3. Correlation: This attribute sorts IT infrastructure data into similar groups that provide additional information for more intelligent insight into the IT infrastructure activity.
4. Alerting: When a potential security event is identified from data analysis or specific triggers, the SIEM can provide alerts of potential security events to IT personnel via various methods (text, e-mail, etc.).
5. Data Aggregation: Data is gathered from different network components of the IT infrastructure and consolidated prior to being analyzed and retained.
6. Compliance: SIEMs can be used to collect information for organization and the government's compliance requirements (Techopedia 2017).

There are multiple reasons for an executive to understand the different net-work-security components. When executives become familiar with the components and understand their differences, they will comprehend why these network-security devices are needed, which in turn will lead to asking the appropriate strategic questions, such as those posed in the second part of the following scenario:

A non-cyber-savvy business executive is advised by the CIO, CISO, CSO, or IT director that the organization plans on spending a large amount of money to acquire the next-generation enterprise network IDS. A non-cyber-savvy business executive will not know any pertinent questions regarding this next-generation IDS. As the CIO, CISO, CSO, or IT director proceeds to describe all the dangers and threats this new IDS will detect to protect the organization's IT infrastructure, the non-cyber-savvy executive will depend solely on his or her CIO, CISO, CSO, or IT director's recommendations to drive the strategic decision on how to best protect the organization's IT infrastructure, data, personnel, and operations.

Now let us change the situation to one where a cyber-savvy business executive is faced with this same scenario. The cyber-savvy executive asks the CIO, CISO, CSO, or IT director why the organization is acquiring an enterprise network IDS as opposed to the next-generation enterprise network IDS/IPS. The cyber-savvy executive will pose questions as to which are the best IDS/IPS available and why the selected IDS/IPS is the best for the protection of the organization's IT infrastructure, data, personnel, and operations. Other questions could include the following: What is the cost difference among the top-three options? What are the additional strategic costs in required IT personnel resources and cybersecurity training? What additional network-security equipment (i.e., SIEM) will be needed to adequately monitor the IDS/IPS and network-environment logs to ensure the organization is preventing, detecting, reacting, and recovering from the cyber threats against the organization's IT infrastructure? A cyber-savvy business executive does not need to know all the intricacies of network-security devices but must have a solid foundational understanding of computer networks and their network-security devices.

As one can see, having a foundational knowledge base of network-security components will assist a business executive in planning for the cyber threat at the strategic, operational, and tactical levels in his or her organization.

Vulnerability Exercise

Let's conduct an exercise by reviewing a few different types of vulnerabilities and their effects on computing hardware, operating systems, and software from the MITRE Common Vulnerabilities and Exposures (CVE) list. The MITRE CVE list was launched in 1999 and is a dictionary composed of publicly known cybersecurity vulnerabilities, and it is maintained by the MITRE Corporation. The CVE list provides one name and one standardized description for each identified cybersecurity vulnerability. The CVE is sponsored by the US Department of Homeland Security's US Computer Emergency Readiness Team (US-CERT). As of June 2017, there were a total of 87,001 CVEs in the MITRE CVE list (Mitre 2017).

A vulnerability is defined as (1) a flaw in a system that can expose the system to attack, (2) any type of weakness in the computer system itself, (3) any type of weakness in a set of procedures, or (4) anything that exposes information security to any cyber threat actor for possible exploitation (Techopedia 2017).

To compromise IT infrastructures, cyber threat actors create exploits and malware to target the known cybersecurity vulnerabilities. These exploited vulnerabilities and malware, if successful, can allow cyber threat actors unauthorized access to an organization's IT infrastructure.

Let us select and review some of the latest 2017 CVEs affecting some of the most commonly used software operating systems and applications around the world (Microsoft, Apple, and Adobe) and their potential impact on organizations if those cybersecurity vulnerabilities are successfully exploited by a cyber threat actor.

2017 Microsoft Product Vulnerabilities

1. **CVE-2017-0281, also known as the "Office Remote Code Execution Vulnerability"** (released on May 12, 2017, and revised on May 25, 2017), is a cybersecurity vulnerability that affects multiple Microsoft Office products (Microsoft Office 2007 SP3, Office 2010 SP2, Office 2013 SP1, Office 2016, Office Online Server 2016, Office Web Apps 2010 SP2, Office Web Apps 2013 SP1, Project Server 2013 SP1, SharePoint Enterprise Server 2013 SP1, SharePoint Enterprise Server 2016, SharePoint Foundation 2013 SP1, SharePoint Server 2010 SP2, Word 2016, and Skype for Business 2016) and "allow[s] a remote code execution vulnerability

when the software fails to properly handle objects in memory." This cybersecurity vulnerability has a severity rating of high. The intrusion access vector is network exploitable, meaning the victim must voluntarily interact with the attack mechanism to allow unauthorized disclosure of information, unauthorized modification, and disruption of service (National Vulnerability Database 2017).

2. **CVE-2017-0265, also known as the "Microsoft Office Memory Corruption Vulnerability"** (released on May 12, 2017, and revised on May 23, 2017), is a cybersecurity vulnerability that affects Microsoft PowerPoint for Mac 2011 and "allows a remote code execution vulnerability when the software fails to properly handle objects in memory." This cybersecurity vulnerability has a severity rating of high. The intrusion access vector is network exploitable, meaning the victim must voluntarily interact with the attack mechanism to allow unauthorized disclosure of information, unauthorized modification, and disruption of service (National Vulnerability Database 2017).

3. **CVE-2017-0204, also known as the "Microsoft Office Security Feature Bypass Vulnerability"** (released on April 12, 2017, and revised on April 20, 2017), is a cybersecurity vulnerability that affects multiple Microsoft Outlook products (Microsoft Outlook 2007 SP3, Microsoft Outlook 2010 SP2, Microsoft Outlook 2013 SP1, and Microsoft Outlook 2016) and "allow[s] remote attacks to bypass the Office Protected View via a specially crafted document." This cybersecurity vulnerability has a severity rating of medium. The intrusion access vector is network exploitable, meaning the victim must voluntarily interact with the attack mechanism to allow unauthorized modification (National Vulnerability Database 2017).

4. **CVE-2017-0194, also known as the "Microsoft Office Information Disclosure Vulnerability"** (released on April 12, 2017, and revised on April 20, 2017), is a cybersecurity vulnerability that affects Microsoft Excel and other programs (Microsoft Excel 2007 SP3, Microsoft Excel 2010 SP2, and Office Compatibility Pack SP2) and "allow[s] remote attackers to obtain sensitive information from process memory via a crafted Office document." This cybersecurity vulnerability has a severity rating of medium. The intrusion access vector is network exploitable, meaning the victim must voluntarily interact with the attack mechanism

to allow unauthorized disclosure of information (National Vulnerability Database 2017).

5. **CVE-2017-0266, also known as the "Microsoft Edge Remote Code Execution Vulnerability"** (released on May 12, 2017, and revised on May 23, 2017), is a remote code execution vulnerability that "exists in Microsoft Edge in the way affected Microsoft scripting engines render when handling objects in memory." This cybersecurity vulnerability has a severity rating of high. The intrusion access vector is network exploitable, meaning the victim must voluntarily interact with the attack mechanism to allow unauthorized disclosure of information, unauthorized modification, and disruption of service (National Vulnerability Database 2017).

2017 Adobe Product Vulnerabilities

1. **CVE-2017-3074** (released on May 9, 2017, and revised on June 30, 2017) is a cybersecurity vulnerability that affects Adobe Flash Player versions 25.0.0.148 and earlier, which "have an exploitable memory corruption vulnerability in the Graphics class. Successful exploitation could lead to arbitrary code execution." This cybersecurity vulnerability has a severity rating of critical. The intrusion access vector is network exploitable and allows unauthorized disclosure of information, unauthorized modification, and disruption of service (National Vulnerability Database 2017).

2. **CVE-2017-3071** (released on May 9, 2017, and revised on June 30, 2017) is a cybersecurity vulnerability that affects Adobe Flash Player versions 25.0.0.148 and earlier, which have "an exploitable use after free vulnerability when masking display objects. Successful exploitation could lead to arbitrary code execution." This cybersecurity vulnerability has a severity rating of critical. The intrusion access vector is network exploitable and allows unauthorized disclosure of information, unauthorized modification, and disruption of service (National Vulnerability Database 2017).

3. **CVE-2017-3067** (released on May 9, 2017, and revised on May 17, 2017) is a cybersecurity vulnerability that affects Adobe Experience Manager (AEM) Forms versions 6.2, 6.1, and 6.0, which "have an information disclosure vulnerability resulting from abuse of the prepopulation service in AEM Forms." This cybersecurity vulnerability has a severity rating of

high. The intrusion access vector is network exploitable and allows unauthorized disclosure of information (National Vulnerability Database 2017).

4. **CVE-2017-3065** (released on April 12, 2017, and revised on April 18, 2017) is a cybersecurity vulnerability that affects Adobe Acrobat Reader versions 11.0.19 and earlier, 15.006.30280 and earlier, and 15.023.20070 and earlier, which "have an exploitable memory corruption vulnerability in the font manipulation functionality. Successful exploitation could lead to arbitrary code execution." This cybersecurity vulnerability has a severity rating of high. The intrusion access vector is network exploitable, meaning the victim must voluntarily interact with the attack mechanism to allow unauthorized disclosure of information, unauthorized modification, and disruption of service (National Vulnerability Database 2017).

5. **CVE-2017-3066** (released on April 27, 2017, and revised on May 9, 2017) is a cybersecurity vulnerability that affects Adobe ColdFusion 2016 update 3 and earlier, ColdFusion 11 update 11 and earlier, and ColdFusion 10 update 22 and earlier, which "have a Java deserialization vulnerability in the Apache BlazeDS library. Successful exploitation could lead to arbitrary code execution." This cybersecurity vulnerability has a severity rating of critical. The intrusion access vector is network exploitable and allows unauthorized disclosure of information, unauthorized modification, and disruption of service (National Vulnerability Database 2017).

2017 Apple Product Vulnerabilities

1. **CVE-2017-6981** (released on May 22, 2017, and revised on May 30, 2017) is a cybersecurity vulnerability that affects Apple iOS before 10.3.2 and macOS before 10.12.5 and involves the iBooks app. "It allows attackers to execute arbitrary code in a privileged context via a crafted app that uses symlinks." This cybersecurity vulnerability has a severity rating of high. The intrusion access vector is network exploitable, meaning the victim must voluntarily interact with the attack mechanism, which provides administrator access; allows complete confidentiality, integrity, and availability violation; and allows unauthorized disclosure of information and disruption of service (National Vulnerability Database 2017).

2. **CVE-2017-6978** (released on May 22, 2017, and revised on May 30, 2017) is a cybersecurity vulnerability that affects the Apple macOS versions before 10.12.5 and "involves the 'Accessibility Framework' component. It allows attackers to execute arbitrary code in a privileged context or cause a denial of service (memory corruption) via a crafted app." This cybersecurity vulnerability has a severity rating of high. The intrusion access vector is network exploitable, meaning the victim must voluntarily interact with the attack mechanism, which allows unauthorized disclosure of information, unauthorized modification, and disruption of service (National Vulnerability Database 2017).

3. **CVE-2017-2546** (released on May 22, 2017, and revised on June 1, 2017) is a cybersecurity vulnerability that affects the Apple macOS versions before 10.12.5 and "involves the 'Kernel' component. It allows attackers to execute arbitrary code in a privileged context or cause a denial of service (memory corruption) via a crafted app." This cybersecurity vulnerability has a severity rating of high. The intrusion access vector is network exploitable, meaning the victim must voluntarily interact with the attack mechanism, which allows unauthorized disclosure of information, unauthorized modification, and disruption of service (National Vulnerability Database 2017).

4. **CVE-2017-6984** (released on May 22, 2017, and revised on June 30, 2017) is a cybersecurity vulnerability that affects multiple Apple products (iOS before 10.3.2, Safari before 10.1.1, iTunes before 12.6.1 on Windows, and tvOS before 10.2.1) and "involves the 'WebKit' component. It allows remote attackers to execute arbitrary code or cause a denial of service (memory corruption and application crash) via a crafted website." This cybersecurity vulnerability has a severity rating of high. The intrusion access vector is network exploitable, meaning the victim must voluntarily interact with the attack mechanism, which allows unauthorized disclosure of information, unauthorized modification, and disruption of service (National Vulnerability Database 2017).

5. **CVE-2017-2530** (released on May 22, 2017, and revised on June 30, 2017) is a cybersecurity vulnerability that affects multiple Apple products (iOS before 10.3.2, Safari before 10.1.1, iCloud before 6.2.1 on Windows, and tvOS before 10.2.1) and involves "the 'WebKit' component. It allows remote attackers to execute arbitrary code or cause a denial of service (memory corruption and application crash) via a crafted website." This

cybersecurity vulnerability has a severity rating of high. The intrusion access vector is network exploitable, meaning the victim must voluntarily interact with the attack mechanism, which allows unauthorized disclosure of information, unauthorized modification, and disruption of service (National Vulnerability Database 2017).

As one can see from this exercise, there are many cybersecurity vulnerabilities in even the most popular software applications used around the world today. This exercise provided fifteen examples of cybersecurity vulnerabilities currently in the MITRE CVE list for only a part of 2017. These cybersecurity vulnerabilities have severity ratings of medium, high, and critical and encompass various operating systems and software applications.

How many of today's global organizations utilize Microsoft, Adobe, and Apple products in their everyday business operations? It would be very difficult to find a business organization today that did not use at least one of these products.

Executives must also understand that these are only fifteen CVE examples from the 87,001 total CVEs as of July 2017 (Mitre 2017). These are the known and reported cybersecurity vulnerabilities affecting the various operating systems, software programs, browsers, and hardware that can be exploited by cyber threat actors who create malware. As noted before, executives must also remember that there are over six hundred million samples of malware as of April 2017 (McAfee 2017).

The AV-Test Institute, an independent IT-security institute for over fifteen years, registers over 390,000 new malicious programs every day (AV-Test 2017). In the AV-Test Security Report 2015/2016, the AV-Test Institute noted that the number of known malware for Windows PCs was at 578.7 million samples, with strong signs of continued growth. This report also noted that the top ten most widely distributed malware during 2015 were made up exclusively of worms, computer viruses, and specialized Trojans (AV-Test 2017).

Kaspersky Labs, another Internet security provider, reported in their 2016 Global Security Bulletin the following overall protection statistics from its Kaspersky Security Network during 2016: 31.9 percent of user computers had at least one malware-class web attack during the year; the network defended against 758,044,650 online attacks from around the globe; it identified 261,774,932 malicious URLs; it detected 69,277,289 unique malicious objects; it found that various ransomware and other encryptors targeted 1,445,434 unique computers; and it blocked online banking malware from stealing money from 2,871,965 devices (Kaspersky 2017).

According to the McAfee Labs Threats Report for April 2017, McAfee Global Threat Intelligence (GTI) provided the following daily protection statistics during quarter four: GTI received an average of 49.6 billion queries per day, protected against 66 million malicious URLs per day, protected against 71 million malicious files per day, protected against 37 million potentially unwanted programs per day, and protected against 35 million risky IP addresses per day (McAfee 2017).

A business executive must understand the strategic, operational, and tactical impacts this multitude of malware and vulnerabilities can have on an organization's IT infrastructure. This malware and vulnerability threat can impact various aspects of an organization's IT infrastructure, including operating systems, software applications, office suite programs, third-party applications (such as Adobe Flash Player and Java), and web browsers (such as Microsoft Edge, Internet Explorer, Safari, Opera, Chrome, and Firefox).

So what does this global malware threat mean to a business executive? It means you must understand the magnitude of the malware threat your organization is exposed to on a day-to-day basis, twenty-four hours a day, 365 days a year, and then you must strategically incorporate investments in cybersecurity protection against the global malware threat in your organization's strategic and operational planning.

Sophisticated Malware
Regin

Now that we have reviewed fifteen different types of vulnerabilities that impact Microsoft, Adobe, and Apple products, let's look at sophisticated types of malware that have been found by the antivirus community. Let's start off with Regin, an advanced spying tool that was discovered in 2014.

Regin is described as an advanced malware that was used in spying operations against governments, critical infrastructures, businesses, researchers, and private individuals. Some of Regin's abilities include the following:

1. It is a backdoor-type Trojan with a powerful framework for mass surveillance.
2. It is believed that this sophisticated malware took months, if not years, to create and that it is an advanced malware used by nation-state actors.

3. It is a multistage threat, where each stage is encrypted and hidden except for the first stage.
4. It has multiple infection vectors.
5. It has a modular approach with dozens of custom payloads to include capturing screenshots, taking control of one's mouse, stealing passwords and credentials, and monitoring network traffic.
6. It has an antiforensic capability, which is a technique used as a countermeasure to forensic analysis.

It is a very stealthy malware because even when its presence was detected, it was very difficult to ascertain what the malware was actually doing (Symantec 2014).

The Equation Group
In February 2015, Kaspersky Labs confirmed it had identified the Equation Group, a cyberespionage organization that has been active for almost twenty years.

The Equation Group has used many different types of sophisticated and advanced malware with the following capabilities:

1. Reprogramming of the hard-drive firmware (which means rewriting the operating system of the hard drive) of more than a dozen of the popular hard-disk-drive (HDD) brands.
2. A Fanny worm that had the capability to compromise air-gapped systems (isolated computer systems with no connection to any other network or to the Internet).
3. Intrusion vectors included classic spying techniques, such as receiving a CD-ROM copy of conference materials from a conference that included this sophisticated malware (Kaspersky Labs Securelist 2015).

The sophistication of this cyber threat actor should concern every business executive responsible for protecting his or her organization's information and data. A cyber-savvy business executive who understands his or her cyber threat adversaries understands the adversaries' capabilities and properly plans for the relevant types of cyber threats. Are all cyber threat actors this sophisticated? The answer is no, but a business executive must understand the strategic dangers these very sophisticated cyber threat actors pose to an organization and must properly prepare for the threats by providing the resources and personnel to his or her CIO, CISO, CSO, or IT director to prevent, detect, react, and recover from these types of sophisticated cyber threat adversaries.

Malware in Today's News

Today's cybersecurity news headlines have many examples of tactical-level malware attacks that have strategic impacts on the victim organizations. Two of these tactical-level malware attacks include the March 2016 cyberattack on the Bangladesh Bank and the February 2016 ransomware attack on the Hollywood Presbyterian Medical Center located in Los Angeles, California.

The March 2016 cyberattack against the Bangladesh Bank account at the Federal Reserve in New York involved cyberthieves who attempted to steal over $1 billion, but they were only successful in stealing a little over $81 million. In a report dated July 21, 2016, Reuters reported that the Bangladesh Bank "had not protected its computer systems with a firewall, and it had used second-hand $10 electronic switches to network computers linked to the SWIFT global payment system, according to Mohammad Shah Alam, head of the Forensic Training Institute of the Bangladesh police's criminal investigation department" (Das and Spicer 2016).

SWIFT is the Society for Worldwide Interbank Financial Telecommunication, a global member-owned cooperative used by over eleven thousand banking, security, and other institutions in more than two hundred countries and territories around the world (SWIFT 2017).

"According to investigative reports by cybersecurity company FireEye, seen by Reuters, is that someone obtained the computer credentials of a SWIFT operator at Bangladesh Bank, installed six types of malware on the bank's systems and began probing them in January. The hackers did a series of test runs, logging into the system briefly several times between January 24 and February 2. One day they left monitoring software running on the bank's SWIFT system; on another they deleted files from a database" (Das and Spicer 2016).

Another malware in today's news is ransomware. Ransomware is used by cyber threat actors "to deny access to systems or data." The cyber threat actor "holds systems or data hostage until the ransom is paid. After the initial infection, the ransomware attempts to spread to shared storage drives and other accessible systems. If the demands are not met, the system or encrypted data remains unavailable, or data may be deleted" (Federal Bureau of Investigation 2016).

An example of the strategic impact ransomware can have on an organization is the ransomware attack on Hollywood Presbyterian Medical Center, which occurred on February 5, 2016. Cyber threat actors used ransomware to infect the hospital's computer infrastructure, "preventing staff from being able to communicate from those devices." Allen Stefanek, chief executive of the Hollywood Presbyterian Medical Center, stated, "The malware locks systems by encrypting files and demanding ransom to obtain the decryption key. The quickest and most efficient way to restore our systems and administrative functions was to pay the ransom and obtain the decryption key…in the best interest of restoring normal operations, we did this." The hospital paid the ransom of forty Bitcoins, a virtual currency used by many cybercriminals, which was the equivalent of about $17,000 (Winton 2016).

In summary, business executives need to understand the different types of malware, including ransomware, and their varying impacts and overall risks to their organizations' IT infrastructures. Executives need to understand the strategic threats of sophisticated cyber threat actors who use the most-advanced malware to attack organizations around the world. Executives must understand the strategic and operational impact of Dos or DDoS attacks on an organization's IT infrastructure and prepare in advance for potential solutions to mitigate the attacks' impacts. Executives must be aware of and have a basic foundational understanding of the various types of network-security devices used by today's organizations to protect against strategic cyber threats. A cyber-savvy business executive with a solid understanding of the overall malware threat vector not only understands this constant and ever-evolving cyber threat his or her organization faces daily but also strategically supports the organization's efforts in what must be done to prevent, detect, react, and recover from this strategic threat.

4

INFORMATION OPERATIONS: COMPUTER NETWORK DEFENSE, COMPUTER NETWORK EXPLOITATION, COMPUTER NETWORK ATTACK, AND ADVANCED PERSISTENT THREAT

*I*nformation operations (IO) are an operational component of the US military, and the term is defined as "the integrated employment of the core capabilities of electronic warfare, computer network operations, psychological operations, military deception and operations security, in concert with specified supporting and related capabilities, to influence, disrupt, corrupt or usurp adversarial human and automated decision making while protecting our own. Also called IO" (US Department of Defense Joint Chiefs of Staff 2017).

A component of information operations is computer network operations. Computer network operations include computer network attack, computer network exploitation, and computer network defense.

The *computer network operations* (CNO) are "composed of computer network attack, computer network defense, and related computer network exploitation enabling operations. Also called CNO" (US Department of Defense Joint Chiefs of Staff 2017).

Computer network attack (CNA) are "actions taken through the use of computer networks to disrupt, deny, degrade, or destroy information resident in computers and computer networks, or the computers and networks themselves. Also called CNA" (US Department of Defense Joint Chiefs of Staff 2017).

Computer network exploitation (CNE) are "enabling operations and intelligence collection capabilities conducted through the use of computer networks to gather data from target or adversary automated information systems or networks. Also called CNE" (US Department of Defense Joint Chiefs of Staff 2017).

Computer network defense (CND) are "actions taken through the use of computer networks to protect, monitor, analyze, detect and respond to unauthorized activity within Department of Defense information systems and computer networks. Also called CND" (US Department of Defense Joint Chiefs of Staff 2017).

In a joint publication dated November 20, 2014, the US Department of Defense Joint Chiefs of Staff revised its definition of *information operations* (IO) to "the integrated employment, during military operations, of information-related capabilities in concert with other lines of operation to influence, disrupt, corrupt, or usurp the decision-making of adversaries and potential adversaries while protecting our own. Also called IO" (US Department of Defense Joint Chiefs of Staff 2014). In addition, *computer network attack, computer network exploitation,* and *computer network defense* (as given above) are terms that are no longer used in the US Department of Defense Joint Chiefs of Staff Information Operations terms and definitions (US Department of Defense Joint Chiefs of Staff 2014).

For simplicity and for the purposes of this book and its intended audience, the author will use the previous US military definitions of CNO, CNA, CNE, and CNA (given above).

Another term in today's cyber threat landscape that has been used synonymously with *nation-state actors* is the *advanced persistent threat* (APT). APT refers to

a cyber-attack launched by an attacker with substantial means, organization and motivation to carry out a sustained assault against a target. An APT is advanced in the sense that it employs stealth and multiple attack methods to compromise the target, which is often a high-value corporate or government resource. The attack is difficult to detect, remove, and attribute. Once the target is breached, backdoors are often created to provide the attacker with ongoing access to the compromised system. An APT is persistent because the attacker can spend months gathering intelligence about the target and use that intelligence to launch multiple attacks over an extended period of time. It is

> threatening because perpetrators are often after highly sensitive information, such as the layout of nuclear power plants or codes to break into US defense contractors. (Techopedia 2017)

In its simplest sense, an APT actor's objective is to compromise an organization's IT infrastructure by exploiting multiple vulnerabilities with multiple types of malware (including zero-day exploits) to establish persistence to conduct surveillance, to steal sensitive information and data, or to conduct sabotage through multiple footholds within the targeted organization's network topography.

In today's global environment, a business executive must understand the overall concept of computer network operations as it applies to global cyber threat actors and their attack vectors against organizations' IT infrastructures. As a business executive, how do you protect your organization's IT infrastructure against sophisticated APT and other sophisticated cyber threat actors conducting computer network operations against your organization? There is no one solution to protect your organization's IT infrastructure against the complex world of sophisticated APT. Executives must work with their executive team and their CIOs, CISOs, CSOs, or IT directors to understand this strategic cyber threat and plan for it accordingly at the strategic, operational, and tactical level.

During the January 2016 USENIX Enigma Conference, a San Francisco Bay Area–based conference about emerging cyber threats and novel attacks, Rob Joyce, chief of Tailored Access Operations at the US National Security Agency (NSA), provided a presentation explaining how a nation-state actor works to compromise and exploit a targeted IT infrastructure. This thirty-four-minute video is a great resource to assist in educating any executive on how a nation-state actor exploits common and known vulnerabilities in IT infrastructure for intelligence ("USENIX Enigma 2016—NSA TAO Chief on Disrupting Nation State Hackers" 2016).

Executives must understand there is no single silver-bullet solution to defend against computer network operations conducted by an APT or other sophisticated cyber threat actors. The reason this reality is so strategically important to understand as a business executive is that this is one of many reasons an executive must decide whether or not to invest in his or her organization's cybersecurity posture for both the short term and long term.

Business executives must understand the concept of computer network defense. As previously noted, even the simplest networks have multiple intrusion vectors for sophisticated cyber actors to exploit and take advantage of and compromise an organization's IT infrastructure.

Computer network defense is not only a necessity but a foundation that is required and one that is constantly evolving. There are various network-security components that must be implemented to secure IT infrastructure, as previously noted. But because of the constant evolution of the sophisticated cyber threat actors, they make advances once vulnerabilities are mitigated and IT infrastructure is made more secure.

Why is this concept of computer network defense so strategically important for a CEO to understand? As your organization's CEO, you are responsible for protecting data and IT infrastructure, so you will be asked by your CIO, CISO, CSO, or IT director to approve strategic enterprise funding for continually improving your organization's network security as the sophisticated cyber threat evolves.

So, if the CIO, CISO, CSO, or IT director approaches you and requests $2 million to improve the network-security components of your business organization's IT infrastructure, do not be surprised if six months later the CIO, CISO, CSO, or IT director returns with another request for $1 million to improve the network security of your business organization's IT infrastructure. These cyber-security-improvement requests are due in part to the continual evolution of the cyber threat actors like APT, to having to defend your IT infrastructure from millions of new variants of malware (including zero-day exploits), and to the speed at which overall technology is improving today.

Business executives must understand that the cyber threat must be factored into strategic-, operational-, and tactical-level planning. Keeping that in mind, a cyber-savvy business executive will be better positioned to ask the difficult questions regarding the various network-security components (such as which of the comparable products are better, the breakdown of the different costs, and what the personnel costs associated with this request are). On the other hand, a non-cyber-savvy business executive will try to save 10 percent of the organization's annual security budget to make the annual bonuses based on perceived effectiveness and efficiency.

A non-cyber-savvy business executive may save 10 percent and make his or her annual bonus but fail to adequately secure the organization's data and IT infrastructure. By failing to acquire the new network-security equipment, a known vulnerability (that could have been mitigated with the new network security requested) can be exploited and allow a sophisticated cyber threat actor to steal the organization's research and development of a new product line due for market release in the next three to five years. What would this strategically cost the organization in in future lost revenues? I bet it would be exponentially more than the 10 percent the non-cyber-savvy executive "saved" the organization! This is an example of how a cyber-savvy business executive is a strategic asset to the organization.

Penetration Testing

Another very important strategic component of computer network defense and securing an organization's IT infrastructure is to test the organization's IT infrastructure's security. This IT security testing is a process known as *penetration testing* (also known as pen testing). Penetration testing is a method of testing, measuring, and improving established security measures of IT infrastructure. Penetration testing is also known as *security assessment* (Techopedia 2017).

Penetration testing should not be confused with *vulnerability scanning*, which is a cybersecurity technique used to identify security weaknesses in IT infrastructure. Vulnerability scanning is used by IT staff for security purposes to identify known vulnerabilities to mitigate the identified vulnerabilities in operating systems, software, and hardware. It should be noted that cyber threat actors also use vulnerability scanners to identify and exploit vulnerabilities of target organizations to gain unauthorized access into an organization's IT infrastructure (Techopedia 2017).

Penetration testing is a process that simulates a cyberattack process utilized by sophisticated cyber threat actors. Penetration testing could include testing of an organization's networks, smartphones, mobile applications, remote access, wireless components, and web and web applications. Penetration testing can be conducted by either internal IT employees or outside professional cybersecurity vendors. At the end of the penetration test, a written report with an executive summary, a technical report, and a list of recommended actions based on the risk severity of vulnerabilities found is provided by the penetration tester to the organization's executive management.

One very important aspect when using outside vendors to conduct penetration testing is that the penetration test is an agreed-upon procedure by the organization's executive management and the penetration testers. There is a written agreement (referred to as the "get out of jail" agreement) that provides the scope of the activities authorized by the organization's executive management for the penetration testers to conduct against the organization's IT infrastructure and, most importantly, the authorization by the organization to conduct this type of security testing. The organization must agree to these procedures, understand the inherent risks of penetration testing, and provide authorization for penetration testers to obtain access to the organization's IT infrastructure.

There is a multistep process in conducting penetration testing. The first step in the penetration-testing process is to conduct reconnaissance of the targeted organization, which includes obtaining all open-source intelligence on the targeted organization, such as e-mail addresses, names of business executives, and known IP addresses—essentially, any information that can assist the penetration testers in identifying any vulnerability in the organization's IT infrastructure.

The second step is to use different penetration-testing tools to search the organization's IT infrastructure for known and unknown vulnerabilities that can be exploited. These tools are known as port scanners, vulnerability scanners, and mapping tools. Using these different tools during the second step assists the penetration tester in identifying potential vulnerabilities in the organization's network infrastructure, which assists the pen testers in the next step, exploitation.

In the third step, penetration testers attempt to exploit all the vulnerabilities found in the organization's IT infrastructure and determine whether these vulnerabilities provide the penetration tester with the initial unauthorized access into the organization's IT infrastructure.

In step four, the penetration tester will show the true value of a penetration test by taking it a step further from just exploiting the found vulnerabilities that allow the initial unauthorized access in step three. What this means is if, for example, the penetration tester sends a crafted phishing e-mail to an organizational employee and the employee clicks it, the malware should take control of the employee's workstation. If this employee happens to have administrative privileges (for Microsoft operating systems) or root privileges

(Linux operating systems)—that is, the highest permission levels that allow the user to install software and change configuration settings on a network—the penetration tester will exploit the administrative or root privileges to determine how much further unauthorized access into the organization's IT infrastructure can be obtained. This second round of exploitation makes it possible for the penetration tester to gain unauthorized access to servers containing strategic business plans, credit-card numbers, personally identifiable information (PII), protected health information (PHI), or intellectual property. It should be noted that the fourth step is the true value of a penetration test because it simulates a sophisticated real-world cyber threat actor compromising and obtaining unauthorized access to an organization's entire IT infrastructure. Upon the completion of this phase, a penetration-testing report is drafted with the discovered vulnerabilities and recommended solutions for executive management and their IT staff. Some of these discovered vulnerabilities could be rated as critical, high, medium, and low. These discovered vulnerabilities can be mitigated by simple means, such as applying a patch from a software vendor, or by complex means, such as by replacing an entire network of Windows XP systems to a more current operating system, like Windows 10.

The main purposes of a penetration test by qualified security professionals are to identify vulnerabilities throughout an organization's IT infrastructure and to secure or mitigate those vulnerabilities to reduce the likelihood of the relevant IT infrastructure's being compromised by malicious cyber threat actors. It must be noted that this penetration-test report is a snapshot in time as to the cybersecurity posture of the organization's IT infrastructure. Due to the constant change in personnel (e.g., new employees with computer access), technology (e.g., a new firewall that needs to be configured properly), and operations (e.g., a new virtual local-area network with SQL databases being added to assist a sales department), the cybersecurity posture of the organization's IT infrastructure will change even after a pen test has been conducted.

When considering to hire the services of a pen tester, a business executive must understand the qualifications of an outside vendor that conducts penetration testing. It is important to evaluate these outside vendors by reviewing their cybersecurity training and experience, and the review should look for penetration-testing certifications issued by recognized cybersecurity training institutions, such as the SANS Institute, Offensive Security, and the EC-Council. SANS Institute, Offensive Security, and EC-Council are private cybersecurity vendors that provide penetration-testing training and certification to participants who successfully complete the relevant training and rigorous certification exams.

Real-World Examples of Computer Network Operations
Saudi Aramco Malware Attacks, August 15, 2012 (Computer Network Attack)
On August 15, 2012, malware attacks were initiated against Saudi Aramco, the state-owned national oil company in Saudi Arabia and the world's largest exporter of crude oil. A group calling itself the Cutting Sword of Justice claimed responsibility for the attack, which only lasted a few hours. The devastating results of this destructive Shamoon, or Disttrack, malware included the partly wiping or totally destroying of the hard drives of thirty-five thousand Aramco computers, which took Aramco offline and affected the majority of its operations, including supply management, shipment tracking, and payment systems. The attackers compromised Aramco's IT infrastructure because an employee clicked on a link in a spear-phishing e-mail. Aramco had to use its private fleet of airplanes to fly employees directly to hard-drive factories in Southeast Asia, where those employees purchased fifty thousand drives, and it took five months to bring Aramco back online (Rashid 2015).

The Shamoon, or Disttrack, malware is a malware used against the energy sector. It is destructive malware that corrupts files on a compromised computer and overwrites the master boot record (MBR) to render a computer unusable (Symantec 2012). The MBR is "the very first sector found in computer mass storage media such as fixed disks and removable computer drives. The master boot record provides the information on loading the operating system and also on the partition of the hard disk. The programs residing in the master boot record help determine which partition needs to be used while booting" (Techopedia 2017).

The Shamoon malware has several components, including (1) a dropper, the main component and source of original infection, which drops additional modules; (2) a wiper, the module responsible for the destructive functionality of this malware; and (3) a reporter, the module responsible for reporting infection information back to the cyber threat actor (Symantec 2012).

US Charges Five Chinese Military Hackers with Cyberespionage (May 19, 2014) (Computer Network Exploitation)

On May 19, 2014, the United States charged five Chinese military hackers with computer hacking, economic espionage, and other offenses against six US victims in the US nuclear-power, metals, and solar-products industries. The five defendants were identified as Wang Dong, Sun Kailiang, Wen Xinyu, Huang Zhenyu, and Gu Chunhui, who were officers in Unit 61398 of the Third Department of the Chinese People's Liberation Army (PLA). The six US victims were identified as Westinghouse Electric Corporation (Westinghouse); US subsidiaries of SolarWorld AG (SolarWorld); the United States Steel Corporation (US Steel); Allegheny Technologies Inc. (ATI); the United Steel, Paper and Forestry, Rubber, Manufacturing, Energy, Allied Industrial and Service Workers International Union (USW); and Alcoa Inc.

The indictment alleged that the defendants conspired to hack into the victim's IT infrastructure, maintain unauthorized access to their computers, and steal information from the victims that was useful to their competitors in China, including state-owned enterprises (SOEs).

The following are summaries of the defendants' conduct, as described in the indictment.

In regard to the victim entity Westinghouse, while Westinghouse was building four AP1000 power plants in China and negotiating other terms of the construction with a Chinese SOE (SOE-1), defendant Sun stole confidential and proprietary technical and design specifications for pipes, pipe supports, and pipe routing within AP1000 power-plant designs. In addition, in 2010 and 2011, Sun stole sensitive, nonpublic, and deliberative e-mails belonging to senior decision makers responsible for Westinghouse's business relationship with SOE-1.

In regard to the victim entity SolarWorld, defendant Wen and at least one other unidentified coconspirator, using unauthorized access, stole thousands of files that contained information on cash flow, manufacturing metrics, production-line information, costs, and privileged attorney-client communications related to ongoing trade litigation, among other things.

In regard to the victim US Steel, defendant Sun sent spear-phishing e-mails to US Steel employees, resulting in malware installation in US Steel's IT infrastructure. Three days later, defendant Wang stole host names and descriptions of US Steel computers, including those that controlled physical access to company facilities and mobile-device access to company networks. Defendant Wang further identified and exploited additional vulnerable servers in US Steel's IT infrastructure.

In regard to the victim ATI, ATI was engaged in competition, a trade dispute, and a joint venture with SOE-2. Defendant Wen gained unauthorized access to ATI's IT infrastructure and stole network credentials for all of the ATI employees.

In regard to the victim USW, USW was involved in public-trade disputes over Chinese trade practices in two industries. At the time that USW issued public statements regarding these trade practices, defendant Wen obtained unauthorized access to USW's IT infrastructure and stole e-mails from senior USW employees containing confidential and nonpublic information about USW's trade-dispute strategies.

In regard to the victim ALCOA, defendant Sun sent a spear-phishing e-mail to Alcoa, acquired unauthorized access to ALCOA's IT infrastructure, and stole thousands of e-mails, including internal discussions regarding a joint partnership with SOE-3. This was just three weeks after ALCOA announced a partnership with a Chinese SOE-3 (Federal Bureau of Investigation 2014).

Sony Picture Entertainment Cyberattack (November 24, 2014) (Computer Network Attack)

On November 24, 2014, Sony Pictures Entertainment (SPE) was the victim of a cyberattack that used malware to destroy systems and large quantities of personal and computer data and to steal proprietary information and employees' identifiable information and confidential communications. It is believed the cyberattack was carried out as a response to SPE's film *The Interview*, which was to be released on Christmas Day 2014. The film featured a plot to assassinate Kim Jong-un, North Korea's leader.

According to Peter Elkind, "Before Sony's IT staff could pull the plug, the hackers' malware had leaped from machine to machine throughout the lot and across continents, wiping out half of Sony's global network. It erased everything stored on 3,262 of the company's 6,797 personal computers and 837 of its 1,555 servers. To make sure nothing could be recovered, the attackers had even added a little extra poison: a special deleting algorithm that overwrote the data seven different ways. When that was done, the code zapped each computer's startup software, rendering the machines brain-dead" (Elkind 2015).

Before the cyber threat actors destroyed the machines, they stole the data and proceeded to place "nine batches of confidential files onto public file-sharing sites: everything from unfinished movie scripts and mortifying e-mails to salary lists and more than 47,000 Social Security numbers." In addition, "Five Sony films, four of them unreleased, were leaked to piracy websites for free viewing. Then the hackers threatened a 9/11-style attack against theaters, prompting Sony to abandon *The Interview's* Christmas release" (Elkind 2015).

According to Elkind, "The studio was reduced to using fax machines, communicating through posted messages, and paying its 7,000 employees with paper checks" (Elkind 2015).

On December 19, 2014, the FBI announced, as a result of their investigation and in close coordination with other US government departments and agencies, that it had enough information to conclude that the North Korean government was responsible for the cyberattack on SPE (Federal Bureau of Investigation 2014).

On January 2, 2015, President Barack Obama of the United States signed an executive order authorizing additional sanctions on the Democratic People's Republic of Korea. This executive order was a response to the Democratic People's Republic of Korea government's actions, particularly its destructive and coercive cyberattack against Sony Pictures Entertainment and threats against movie theaters and moviegoers (The White House 2015).

United States Charges Syrian Hackers for Cyberattacks in United States (March 22, 2016) (Computer Network Exploitation and Computer Network Attack)

Three members of the Syrian Electronic Army (SEA)—Amad Umar Agha (also known as the Pro), Firas Dardar (also known as the Shadow), and Peter Romar (also known as Pierre)—were charged via criminal complaints by the United States in the Eastern District of Virginia with cybercrime offenses executed on behalf of SEA, a group of hackers that support the regime of Bashar al-Assad, the Syrian president.

The victims of the SEA hackers included (1) the unauthorized computer access of the Executive Office of the President, (2) the compromise of the Twitter account of a prominent US media organization and release of a tweet claiming that a bomb had exploded at the White House and injured the president, and

(3) the compromise of the US Marine Corps' recruiting websites and the posting of a message urging marines to "refuse their orders."

Defendants Agha and Dardar collected usernames and passwords, giving them access to and the ability to deface websites, redirect domains to sites controlled by the conspirators, steal e-mails, and hijack social-media accounts. The defendants also used spear-phishing techniques to trick victims who had privileged access to their organizations' websites and social-media channels into volunteering sensitive information by posing as a legitimate entity.

In addition, defendants Dardar and Romar extorted US businesses for profit by obtaining unauthorized access to the victims' IT infrastructures and then threatening not only to damage the victims' computers but also to delete or sell their data unless they, the conspirators, were paid a ransom (Federal Bureau of Investigation 2016).

US Charges Iranian Cyber Actors for Cyberattacks on US Financial Sector and Unauthorized Access to US Critical Infrastructure (March 24, 2016) (Computer Network Exploitation and Computer Network Attack)

On March 24, 2016, a US federal indictment was unsealed and charged the following seven Iranians with computer hacking charges: Ahmad Fathi, thirty-seven; Hamid Firoozi, thirty-four; Amin Shokohi, twenty-five; Sadegh Ahmadzadegan (also known as Nitr0jen26), twenty-three; Omid Ghaffarinia (also known as PLuS), twenty-five; Sina Keissar, twenty-five; and Nader Saedi (also known as Turk Server), twenty-six. These defendants were charged via an indictment by a grand jury in the Southern District of New York for their involvement in conspiracies to conduct a coordinated and systematic campaign of distributed-denial-of-service (DDoS) attacks against nearly fifty institutions in the US financial sector from 2011 to 2013. These attacks disabled banks' websites, prevented customers from accessing their accounts online, and cost the targeted US financial institutions tens of millions of dollars (US Department of Justice 2016).

In addition, Hamid Firoozi was charged with obtaining unauthorized access during 2013 to the supervisory control and data acquisition (SCADA) systems of Bowman Dam computer systems, located in Rye, New York. Although the defendant never gained control of the dam, Firoozi did access critical information about Bowman Dam's operations, including information about the gates that control water levels and flow rates. This unauthorized access would have permitted unauthorized personnel to remotely operate and manipulate the Bowman Dam's sluice gate. The defendant did not have this remote-operation capability because the sluice gate was manually disconnected for maintenance at the time of the computer intrusion (US Department of Justice 2016).

Per the indictment, each of these defendants was employed as a manager or employee of either the ITSecTeam or Mersad Company, both of which were private computer-security companies based in Iran and performed work on behalf of the Iranian government and the Iranian Islamic Revolutionary Guard Corps (Federal Bureau of Investigation 2016).

Grizzly Steppe—Russian Malicious Cyberactivity (December 29, 2016) (Computer Network Exploitation)

On December 29, 2016, the FBI and DHS provided a joint-analysis report regarding the tools and infrastructure used by Russia's civilian and military intelligence services (RIS) to compromise IT infrastructures associated with the US election of 2016 and other government and private-sector entities. This was the first joint-analysis report to provide public attribution against a specific country (Russia) based on technical indicators from the US intelligence community (FBI and DHS 2016). This joint-analysis report expanded on the October 7, 2016, joint statement released by the Office of the Director of National Intelligence and DHS, and the statement identified the Russian government as directing the compromise of e-mails of both US people and political organizations (DHS and ODNI 2016).

The RIS malicious cyberactivity included masquerading as third parties and using spear-phishing campaigns targeting government organizations, critical infrastructure entities, think tanks, universities, political organizations, and corporations, which resulted in theft of information (FBI and DHS 2016).

Regarding the US political party, the RIS actors, identified as advanced persistent threat (APT) 29, first compromised this US political party's IT infrastructure during the summer of 2015. APT 29 conducted a spear-phishing campaign that targeted over one thousand recipients, which included US government victims. After successfully compromising this US political party's infrastructure, APT 29 established persistence and escalated privileges on the IT infrastructure, which resulted in the theft and exfiltration of data, which included e-mails from several victims of this US political party (FBI and DHS 2016).

A second RIS actor, identified as APT 28, compromised the US political party's infrastructure during the spring of 2016 by the use of another spear-phishing campaign, which tricked victims into changing their passwords. These credentials were then harvested by APT 28 and used to gain access, resulting in the theft and exfiltration of information from multiple senior party members. The stolen information was subsequently leaked to the press and publicly disclosed (FBI and DHS 2016).

During December 2016, Burlington Electric in Vermont detected the malicious code associated with Grizzly Steppe in one of its laptops. This laptop was not connected to Burling Electric's electrical grid systems. Although the RIS did not actively use this malicious code to disrupt operations, it showed the potential vulnerabilities of the US electrical grid and raised questions as to RIS's intent in targeting critical US infrastructure (Eilperin and Entous 2016).

United States Charges Two Russian Federal Security Service (FSB) Officers for Hacking Five Hundred Million Yahoo Accounts and Yahoo Network (March 15, 2017) (Computer Network Exploitation)
On March 15, 2017, a federal grand jury in the Northern District of California indicted Dmitry Aleksandrovich Dokuchaev, thirty-three, a Russian FSB officer, national, and resident; Igor Anatolyevich Sushchin, forty-three, a Russian FSB officer, national, and resident; Alexsey Alexseyevich Belan, also known as "Magg" twenty-nine, a Russian national and resident; and Karim Baratov, also known as "Kay," "Karim Taloverov," and "Karim Akehmet Tokbergenov," twenty-two, a Canadian national and resident of Canada, for computer hacking, economic espionage, and other charges in connection with a conspiracy to access Yahoo's networks and steal information from at least five hundred million Yahoo accounts.

After using information obtained from the unauthorized access to Yahoo's network and web-mail accounts, the defendants then obtained unauthorized access to other provider web-mail accounts, which included accounts of US and Russian government officials, Russian journalists, and employees of financial, transportation, and other private-sector companies. In addition, one of the defendants searched the Yahoo accounts for credit-card and gift-card account numbers, redirected Yahoo web traffic to make commissions, and stole the contacts of at least thirty million Yahoo accounts to facilitate a spam campaign (US Department of Justice 2017).

Operation Cloud Hopper—APT10 Sustained Global Cyberespionage against Managed IT Service Providers (MSPs) (April 2017) (Computer Network Exploitation)

PricewaterhouseCoopers's (PwC) UK cybersecurity practice worked closely with BAE Systems and collaborated with the United Kingdom's National Cyber Security Centre (NCSC) to uncover and disrupt what is thought to be one of the largest ever sustained global cyberespionage campaigns—the operation referred to as Operation Cloud Hopper.

Since late 2016, PwC and BAE Systems have been collaborating to research the threat, brief the global-security community, and assist known victims. The China-based threat actor assessed to be behind the campaign is widely known within the security community as "APT10," referred to within PwC UK as "Red Apollo." This PWC and BAE Systems study shows that APT10 has targeted, compromised, and exfiltrated a high volume of data from managed IT service providers (MSPs), providing APT10 unprecedented access to the most-sensitive data and computer networks of these MSPs and their clients globally. It is believed that APT10 began this sustained campaign against MSPs in early 2014. MSPs are responsible for the remote management of customer IT and end-user systems, and the remote management allows the MSPs unfettered and direct access to their clients' networks. In addition, MSPs store significant quantities of their customers' data on their own internal IT infrastructure.

The sectors targeted by APT10 in Operation Cloud Hopper included the engineering and construction sector, public sector, pharmaceuticals and life-science sector, technology sector, business and professional services sector, energy and mining sector, metals sector, industrial-manufacturing sector, and retail and consumer sector. The countries targeted by APT10 in Operation Cloud Hopper included the United States, Canada, Brazil, the United Kingdom, France, Switzerland, Sweden, Finland, Norway, India, South Africa, Thailand, South Korea, Japan, and Australia.

This indirect approach to reaching many through only a few targets demonstrates a new level of maturity in cyberespionage (PwC 2017).

In summary, business executives need to have a foundational understanding of information operations, the three components (CNA, CNE, CND) of computer network operations, and the global use of information operations by nation-state actors against organizations around the world. Executives can see from these multiple law-enforcement actions and private-sector cybersecurity efforts that computer network operations conducted by nation-state actors are a very real and strategic cyber threat. Business executives must understand that their organizations can be targeted by nation-state actors or their proxies to conduct computer network exploitation or computer network attacks. Business executives must anticipate this sophisticated, strategic cyber threat actor when strategically planning their computer network defenses at the strategic, operational, and tactical levels.

5

CRITICAL INFRASTRUCTURE AND INDUSTRIAL CONTROL SYSTEMS (ICS)

Imagine a scenario where the electric power grid ceased to function and all electricity stopped flowing into your community. Have you ever imagined how much electricity use is intertwined in our daily lives? Without electricity, there would be no lighting in our homes, and appliances such as the washing machines, dishwashers, dryers, garage-door openers, and home alarm systems would not function. Now imagine driving to the grocery store (with no functioning traffic lights) to purchase groceries without the use of the point-of-sale terminals, without the ability to withdraw cash at your local bank's ATM, or without being able to fill your gas tank at your local gas station by using a debit or credit card. Now imagine this nightmare scenario lasting for days or even weeks in your community and surrounding communities. Ask yourself how long it would take before a civilized society would begin to break down into chaotic disaster.

Does this scenario seem impossible? On December 23, 2015, three Ukrainian regional energy-distribution companies experienced unscheduled power outages caused by a remote cyberattack on their IT infrastructures and their industrial control systems (ICS). The cyberattack caused approximately 225,000 customers to lose power across various areas for six hours.

This cyberattack in Ukraine was the first publicly acknowledged cyber incident against civilian critical infrastructure that resulted in power outages.

A team of US ICS experts from the US Department of Homeland Security (DHS), National Cybersecurity and Communications Integration Center (NCCIC), Industrial Control Systems Cyber Emergency Response Team (ICS-CERT), the US Computer Emergency Readiness Team (US-CERT), the FBI, the Department of Energy, and the North American Electric Reliability Corporation traveled to Ukraine and worked with the Ukrainian government to study and assess the cyberattack. The team assessed that the cyberattack was caused by external cyber threat actors.

The sophisticated cyberattacks against the three energy companies occurred within thirty minutes of each other, and the actions of the cyber threat actor included the following:

1. Infection of each company's IT infrastructure with the Black Energy malware, which was delivered via spear-phishing e-mails and assessed to have been used as the initial intrusion vector to acquire credentials
2. Extensive reconnaissance of the victim networks prior to the cyberattack
3. Acquirement of legitimate user credentials to remotely control the industrial control systems (ICS) including the supervisory control and data acquisition (SCADA) systems as part of the cyberattack
4. Wiping of some of the computer systems (including human-machine interfaces [HMIs] embedded in remote terminal units) with destructive malware after the cyberattack, leaving these systems inoperable
5. Corruption of the firmware of devices at substations, rendering these devices inoperable and useless
6. Scheduling of disconnects of servers' uninterruptable power supplies (UPS) via the UPS remote interface to interfere and disrupt restoration efforts (US Department of Homeland Security 2016)

In addition, the cyber threat actors conducted a denial-of-service (DoS) attack on the telephone system of the energy companies' call centers to prevent legitimate callers from getting through to the utilities (Zetter 2016).

On July 8, 2017, it was reported that the US National Security Agency (NSA) had detected that the Russian intelligence service, FSB, had conducted successful cyber intrusions into US nuclear-power and energy companies and had stolen network log-in and password information, in efforts to assess those networks. US officials advised there was no evidence of a breach or disruption of core systems that controlled the operations of the nuclear and energy facilities. This Russian FSB cyber-intrusion campaign was the first time that Russian hackers were known to have compromised US nuclear-company networks (Nakashima 2017). These extremely dangerous cyber intrusions by the Russians might have been a reconnaissance of US critical infrastructure to prestage and conduct catastrophic cyberattacks aimed at creating domestic chaos, in case of war with the United States in the future.

These real-world examples have made what was formerly only a myth of possible attack on the energy sector into a real-world reality today. Those two very successful, multifaceted, and tactical cyberattacks showed the strategic danger that cyber threat actors pose to all critical infrastructure sectors.

Why is this successful cyberattack on the civilian energy sector so important to comprehend as a business executive? A business executive must (1) understand whether their organization is part of the sixteen identified US critical infrastructure sectors, (2) possess a foundational knowledge regarding ICS, and (3) know whether your organization utilizes these ICS in any part of your organization's IT infrastructure.

If your organization operates in any of these sixteen (16) critical infrastructure sectors, it is incumbent upon your executive team to be familiar not only with your organization's processes but the cybersecurity challenges facing your specific critical infrastructure sector.

How does an executive team obtain a foundational knowledge regarding the cyber threats facing their respective critical-infrastructure sectors in their area of responsibility? There are three great resources when it comes to obtaining a foundational knowledge of ICS, of how to secure ICS, and of the cyber threats these ICS systems face in today's cyber threat landscape.

The first resource is the US Presidential Policy Directive–21 (PPD-21), issued in 2013, which identified the sixteen critical-infrastructure sectors in the United States, as well as the sector-specific agency responsible for each sector.

The second resource is the US Department of Homeland Security (DHS), which, according to PPD-21, "shall provide strategic guidance, promote a national unity of effort, and coordinate the overall Federal effort to promote the security and resilience of the Nation's critical infrastructure" (The White House 2013).

The third resource is the US Department of Commerce's National Institute of Standards and Technology (NIST) Special Publication 800–82 Revision 2, the "Guide to Industrial Control Systems (ICS) Security," which "provides guidance for establishing secure industrial control systems (ICS)" (National Institute of Standards and Technology 2015).

US Critical Infrastructure

In February 2013, "Presidential Policy Directive–Critical Infrastructure Security and Resilience," also known as PPD-21, was issued by the US White House. PPD-21 identified sixteen critical-infrastructure sectors in the United States. The US Department of Homeland Security (DHS) defines these sixteen critical-infrastructure sectors as "whose assets, systems, and networks, whether physical or virtual, are considered so vital to the United States that their incapacitation or destruction would have a debilitating effect on security, national economic security, national public health or safety, or any combination thereof" (US Department of Homeland Security 2017).

This detailed DHS information is provided by the author to give business executives a broad foundational understanding (background, subsectors, and interconnectivity with other critical infrastructures) of each of the sixteen US critical-infrastructure sectors. DHS identifies the sixteen US critical-infrastructure sectors and their respective sector-specific agencies (SSAs) (US Department of Homeland Security 2017) as follows:

1. Chemical Sector (SSA is the Department of Homeland Security)

   "The Chemical Sector is an integral component of the US economy that manufactures, stores, uses, and transports potentially dangerous chemicals upon which a wide range of other critical infrastructure sectors rely. Securing these chemicals against growing and evolving threats requires vigilance from both the private and public sector" (US Department of Homeland Security 2017).

"The Chemical Sector—composed of several hundred thousand US chemical facilities in a complex, global supply chain—converts various raw materials into more than 70,000 diverse products that are essential to modern life. Based on the end product produced, the sector can be divided into five (5) main segments, each of which has distinct characteristics, growth dynamics, markets, new developments, and issues:

- Basic chemicals
- Specialty chemicals
- Agricultural chemicals
- Pharmaceuticals
- Consumer products" (US Department of Homeland Security 2017).

2. Commercial Facilities Sector (SSA is the Department of Homeland Security)

"The Commercial Facilities Sector includes a diverse range of sites that draw large crowds of people for shopping, business, entertainment, or lodging. Facilities within the sector operate on the principle of open public access, meaning that the general public can move freely without the deterrent of highly visible security barriers. The majority of these facilities are privately owned and operated, with minimal interaction with the federal government and other regulatory entities" (US Department of Homeland Security 2017).

"The Commercial Facilities Sector consists of eight subsectors:

- Entertainment and Media (e.g., motion picture studios, broadcast media).
- Gaming (e.g., casinos).
- Lodging (e.g., hotels, motels, conference centers).
- Outdoor Events (e.g., theme and amusement parks, fairs, campgrounds, parades).

- Public Assembly (e.g., arenas, stadiums, aquariums, zoos, museums, convention centers).
- Real Estate (e.g., office and apartment buildings, condominiums, mixed use facilities, self-storage).
- Retail (e.g., retail centers and districts, shopping malls).
- Sports Leagues (e.g., professional sports leagues and federations)" (US Department of Homeland Security 2017).

3. Communications Sector (SSA is the Department of Homeland Security)

"The Communications Sector is an integral component of the US economy, underlying the operations of all businesses, public safety organizations, and government. Presidential Policy Directive 21 identifies the Communications Sector as critical because it provides an 'enabling function' across all critical infrastructure sectors. Over the last 25 years, the sector has evolved from predominantly a provider of voice services into a diverse, competitive, and interconnected industry using terrestrial, satellite, and wireless transmission systems. The transmission of these services has become interconnected; satellite, wireless, and wireline providers depend on each other to carry and terminate their traffic, and companies routinely share facilities and technology to ensure interoperability" (US Department of Homeland Security 2017)

"The Communications Sector is closely linked to other critical infrastructures including:

- The <u>Energy Sector</u>, which provides power to run cellular towers, central offices, and other critical communications facilities and also relies on communications to aid in monitoring and controlling the delivery of electricity.

- The <u>Information Technology Sector</u>, which provides critical control systems and services, physical architecture, and Internet infrastructure, and also relies on communications to deliver and distribute applications and services.
- The <u>Financial Services Sector</u>, which relies on communications for the transmission of transactions and operations of financial markets.
- The <u>Emergency Services Sector</u>, which depends on communications for directing resources, coordinating response, operating public alert and warning systems, and receiving emergency 9-1-1 calls.
- The <u>Transportation Systems Sector,</u> which provides the diesel fuel needed to power backup generators, and relies on communications to monitor and control the flow of ground, sea, and air traffic" (US Department of Homeland Security 2017).

4. Critical Manufacturing Sector (SSA is the Department of Homeland Security)

"The Critical Manufacturing Sector is crucial to the economic prosperity and continuity of the United States. A direct attack on or disruption of certain elements of the manufacturing industry could disrupt essential functions at the national level and across multiple critical infrastructure sectors. The Critical Manufacturing Sector identified several industries to serve as the core of the sector:

- Primary Metals Manufacturing
  - Iron and Steel Mills and Ferro Alloy Manufacturing
  - Alumina and Aluminum Production and Processing
  - Nonferrous Metal Production and Processing
- Machinery Manufacturing
  - Engine and Turbine Manufacturing

- Power Transmission Equipment Manufacturing
- Earth Moving, Mining, Agricultural, and Construction Equipment Manufacturing
  - Electrical Equipment, Appliance, and Component Manufacturing
    - Electric Motor Manufacturing
    - Transformer Manufacturing
    - Generator Manufacturing
  - Transportation Equipment Manufacturing
    - Vehicles and Commercial Ships Manufacturing
    - Aerospace Products and Parts Manufacturing
    - Locomotives, Railroad and Transit Cars, and Rail Track Equipment Manufacturing

Products made by these manufacturing industries are essential to many other critical infrastructure sectors" (US Department of Homeland Security 2017).

5. Dams Sector (SSA is the Department of Homeland Security)

"The Dams Sector delivers critical water retention and control services in the United States, including hydroelectric power generation, municipal and industrial water supplies, agricultural irrigation, sediment and flood control, river navigation for inland bulk shipping, industrial waste management, and recreation. Its key services support multiple critical infrastructure sectors and industries. Dams Sector assets irrigate at least 10 percent of US cropland, help protect more than 43 percent of the US population from flooding, and generate about 60 percent of electricity in the Pacific Northwest" (US Department of Homeland Security 2017).

"There are more than 87,000 dams in the United States—approximately 65 percent are privately owned, and approximately 80 percent are regulated by state dams safety offices. The Dams

Sector has interdependencies with a wide range of other sectors, including:

- Communications—Communications networks enable remote Dams Sector operations and control.
- Energy—Hydropower dams provide critical electricity resources and black start capabilities.
- Food and Agriculture—Dams Sector assets provide water for irrigation and protect farmland from flooding.
- Transportation Systems—Navigation lock systems in the Dams Sector enable all inland and intracoastal waterway freight movements. Major roads may traverse dams.
- Water—Dams Sector assets provide drinking water supplies and pumping capabilities" (US Department of Homeland Security 2017).

6. Defense Industrial Base Sector (SSA is the Department of Defense)

"The Defense Industrial Base Sector is the worldwide industrial complex that enables research and development, as well as design, production, delivery, and maintenance of military weapons systems, subsystems, and components or parts, to meet US military requirements. The Defense Industrial Base partnership consists of Department of Defense components, more than 100,000 Defense Industrial Base companies and their subcontractors who perform under contract to the Department of Defense, companies providing incidental materials and services to the Department of Defense, and government-owned/contractor-operated and government-owned/government-operated facilities. Defense Industrial Base companies include domestic and foreign entities, with production assets located in many countries. The sector provides products and services that are essential to mobilize, deploy, and sustain military operations. The Defense Industrial Base Sector does not include the commercial infrastructure of providers of services such as power, communications, transportation, or utilities that the Department of Defense uses to meet military operational requirements. These commercial infrastructure assets are addressed by other Sector-Specific Agencies" (US Department of Homeland Secuity 2017).

7. Emergency Services Sector (SSA is the Department of Homeland Security)

"The Emergency Services Sector (ESS) is a community of millions of highly skilled, trained personnel, along with the physical and cyber resources, that provide a wide range of prevention, preparedness, response, and recovery services during both day-to-day operations and incident response. The ESS includes geographically distributed facilities and equipment in both paid and volunteer capacities organized primarily at the federal, state, local, tribal, and territorial levels of government, such as city police departments and fire stations, county sheriff's offices, Department of Defense police and fire departments, and town public works departments. The ESS also includes private sector resources, such as industrial fire departments, private security organizations, and private emergency medical services providers" (US Department of Homeland Security 2017).

"The mission of the Emergency Services Sector is to save lives, protect property and the environment, assist communities impacted by disasters, and aid recovery during emergencies. Five distinct disciplines compose the ESS, encompassing a wide range of emergency response functions and roles:

- Law Enforcement
- Fire and Rescue Services
- Emergency Medical Services
- Emergency Management
- Public Works" (US Department of Homeland Security 2017).

"The ESS also provides specialized emergency services through individual personnel and teams. These specialized capabilities may be found in one or more various disciplines, depending on the jurisdiction:

- Tactical Teams (i.e., SWAT)
- Hazardous Devices Team/Public Safety Bomb Disposal
- Public Safety Dive Teams/Maritime Units
- Canine Units
- Aviation Units (i.e., police and medevac helicopters)
- Hazardous Materials (i.e., HAZMAT)
- Search and Rescue Teams
- Public Safety Answering Points (i.e., 9-1-1 call centers)
- Fusion Centers
- Private Security Guard Forces
- National Guard Civil Support" (US Department of Homeland Security 2017).

8. Energy Sector (SSA is the Department of Energy)

"The US energy infrastructure fuels the economy of the 21st century. Without a stable energy supply, health and welfare are threatened, and the US economy cannot function. Presidential Policy Directive 21 identifies the Energy Sector as uniquely critical because it provides an 'enabling function' across all critical infrastructure sectors. More than 80 percent of the country's energy infrastructure is owned by the private sector, supplying fuels to the transportation industry, electricity to households and businesses, and other sources of energy that are integral to growth and production across the nation" (US Department of Homeland Security 2017).

"The energy infrastructure is divided into three interrelated segments: electricity, oil, and natural gas. The US electricity segment contains more than 6,413 power plants (this includes 3,273 traditional electric utilities and 1,738 nonutility power producers) with approximately 1,075 gigawatts of installed

generation. Approximately 48 percent of electricity is produced by combusting coal (primarily transported by rail), 20
percent in nuclear power plants, and 22 percent by combusting natural gas. The remaining generation is provided by hydroelectric plants (6 percent), oil (1 percent), and renewable
sources (solar, wind, and geothermal, 3 percent). The heavy
reliance on pipelines to distribute products across the nation
highlights the interdependencies between the Energy and
Transportation Systems Sector" (US Department of Homeland
Security 2017).

"The reliance of virtually all industries on electric power and fuels means that all sectors have some dependence on the Energy
Sector. The Energy Sector is well aware of its vulnerabilities
and is leading a significant voluntary effort to increase its planning and preparedness. Cooperation through industry groups
has resulted in substantial information sharing of best practices
across the sector. Many sector owners and operators have extensive experience abroad with infrastructure protection and have
more recently focused their attention on cybersecurity" (US
Department of Homeland Security 2017).

9. Financial Services Sector (SSA is the Department of Treasury)

"The Financial Services Sector represents a vital component of
our nation's critical infrastructure. Large-scale power outages,
recent natural disasters, and an increase in the number and sophistication of cyberattacks demonstrate the wide range of potential risks facing the sector" (US Department of Homeland
Security 2017).

"The Financial Services Sector includes thousands of deposi-
tory institutions, providers of investment products, insurance
companies, other credit and financing organizations, and the
providers of the critical financial utilities and services that
support these functions. Financial institutions vary widely

in size and presence, ranging from some of the world's largest global companies with thousands of employees and many billions of dollars in assets, to community banks and credit unions with a small number of employees serving individual communities. Whether an individual savings account, financial derivatives, credit extended to a large organization, or investments made to a foreign country, these products allow customers to:

1. Deposit funds and make payments to other parties
2. Provide credit and liquidity to customers
3. Invest funds for both long and short periods
4. Transfer financial risks between customers" (US Department of Homeland Security 2017).

10. Food and Agriculture Sector (SSA is the US Department of Agriculture and Department of Health and Human Services)

"The Food and Agriculture Sector is almost entirely under private ownership and is composed of an estimated 2.1 million farms, 935,000 restaurants, and more than 200,000 registered food manufacturing, processing, and storage facilities. This sector accounts for roughly one-fifth of the nation's economic activity. The Food and Agriculture Sector has critical dependencies with many sectors, but particularly with the following:

- <u>Water and Wastewater Systems</u>, for clean irrigation and processed water
- <u>Transportation Systems</u>, for movement of products and livestock
- <u>Energy</u>, to power the equipment needed for agriculture production and food processing
- <u>Chemical</u>, for fertilizers and pesticides used in the production of crops" (US Department of Homeland Security 2017).

11. Government Facilities Sector (SSA is the Department of Homeland Security and General Services Administration)

"The Government Facilities Sector includes a wide variety of buildings, located in the United States and overseas, that are owned or leased by federal, state, local, and tribal governments. Many government facilities are open to the public for business activities, commercial transactions, or recreational activities while others that are not open to the public contain highly sensitive information, materials, processes, and equipment. These facilities include general-use office buildings and special-use military installations, embassies, courthouses, national laboratories, and structures that may house critical equipment, systems, networks, and functions. In addition to physical structures, the sector includes cyber elements that contribute to the protection of sector assets (e.g., access control systems and closed-circuit television systems) as well as individuals who perform essential functions or possess tactical, operational, or strategic knowledge" (US Department of Homeland Security 2017).

"The Education Facilities Subsector covers prekindergarten through 12th grade schools, institutions of higher education, and business and trade schools. The subsector includes facilities that are owned by both government and private sector entities. The National Monuments and Icons Subsector encompasses a diverse array of assets, networks, systems, and functions located throughout the United States. Many National Monuments and Icons assets are listed in either the National Register of Historic Places or the List of National Historic Landmarks" (US Department of Homeland Security 2017).

12. Healthcare and Public Health Sector (SSA is Department of Health and Human Services)

"The Healthcare and Public Health Sector protects all sectors of the economy from hazards such as terrorism, infectious disease outbreaks, and natural disasters. Because the vast majority of the sector's assets are privately owned and operated, collaboration and information sharing between the public and private sectors is essential to increasing resilience of the nation's Healthcare and Public Health critical infrastructure. Operating in all US states, territories, and tribal areas, the sector plays a significant role in response and recovery across all other sectors in the event of a natural or manmade disaster. While healthcare tends to be delivered and managed locally, the public health component of the sector, focused primarily on population health, is managed across all levels of government: national, state, regional, local, tribal, and territorial" (US Department of Homeland Security 2017).

"The Healthcare and Public Health Sector is highly dependent on fellow sectors for continuity of operations and service delivery, including Communications, Emergency Services, Energy, Food and Agriculture, Information Technology, Transportation Systems, and Water and Wastewater Systems" (US Department of Homeland Security 2017).

13. Information Technology Sector (SSA is the Department of Homeland Security)

"The Information Technology Sector is central to the nation's security, economy, and public health and safety as businesses, governments, academia, and private citizens are increasingly dependent upon Information Technology Sector functions. These virtual and distributed functions produce and provide hardware, software, and information technology systems and services, and—in collaboration with the Communications Sector—the Internet. The sector's complex and dynamic environment makes identifying threats and assessing vulnerabilities difficult and requires that these tasks be addressed in a collaborative and creative fashion" (US Department of Homeland Security 2017).

"Information Technology Sector functions are operated by a combination of entities—often owners and operators and their respective associations—that maintain and reconstitute the network, including the Internet. Although information technology infrastructure has a certain level of inherent resilience, its interdependent and interconnected structure presents challenges as well as opportunities for coordinating public and private sector preparedness and protection activities" (US Department of Homeland Security 2017).

14. Nuclear Reactors, Materials, and Waste Sector (SSA is the Department of Homeland Security)

"Nuclear power accounts for approximately 20 percent of our nation's electrical generation, provided by 99 commercial nuclear plants. The sector includes:

- Nuclear power plants
- Nonpower nuclear reactors used for research, testing, and training
- Manufacturers of nuclear reactors or components
- Radioactive materials used primarily in medical, industrial, and academic settings.
- Nuclear fuel cycle facilities
- Decommissioned nuclear power reactors
- Transportation, storage, and disposal of nuclear and radioactive waste" (US Department of Homeland Security 2017).

The sector is interdependent with other critical infrastructure sectors:

- Chemical Sector, as a consumer of chemicals through the nuclear fuel cycle and at reactor sites.
- Energy Sector, as a supplier of electricity to our nation's electrical grid.

- <u>Healthcare and Public Health Sector</u>, as a supplier of nuclear medicine, radiopharmaceuticals, and in the sterilization of blood and surgical supplies.
- <u>Transportation Systems Sector</u>, through the movement of radioactive materials" (US Department of Homeland Security 2017).

15. Transportation Systems Sector (SSA is the Department of Homeland Security and Department of Transportation)

"The Department of Homeland Security and the Department of Transportation are designated as the Co-Sector-Specific Agencies for the Transportation Systems Sector. The nation's transportation system quickly, safely, and securely moves people and goods through the country and overseas" (US Department of Homeland Security 2017).

"The Transportation Systems Sector consists of seven key subsectors, or modes:

- **Aviation** includes aircraft, air traffic control systems, and about 19,700 airports, heliports, and landing strips. Approximately 500 provide commercial aviation services at civil and joint-use military airports, heliports, and sea plane bases. In addition, the aviation mode includes commercial and recreational aircraft (manned and unmanned) and a wide-variety of support services, such as aircraft repair stations, fueling facilities, navigation aids, and flight schools.
- **Highway and Motor Carrier** encompasses more than 4 million miles of roadway, more than 600,000 bridges, and more than 350 tunnels. Vehicles include trucks, including those carrying hazardous materials; other commercial vehicles, including commercial motor coaches and school buses; vehicle and driver licensing systems; traffic management systems; and cyber systems used for operational management.

- **Maritime Transportation System** consists of about 95,000 miles of coastline, 361 ports, more than 25,000 miles of waterways, and intermodal landside connections that allow the various modes of transportation to move people and goods to, from, and on the water.
- **Mass Transit and Passenger Rail** includes terminals, operational systems, and supporting infrastructure for passenger services by transit buses, trolleybuses, monorail, heavy rail—also known as subways or metros—light rail, passenger rail, and vanpool/rideshare. Public transportation and passenger rail operations provided an estimated 10.8 billion passenger trips in 2014.
- **Pipeline Systems** consist of more than 2.5 million miles of pipelines spanning the country and carrying nearly all of the nation's natural gas and about 65 percent of hazardous liquids, as well as various chemicals. Aboveground assets, such as compressor stations and pumping stations, are also included.
- **Freight Rail** consists of seven major carriers, hundreds of smaller railroads, over 138,000 miles of active railroad, over 1.33 million freight cars, and approximately 20,000 locomotives. An estimated 12,000 trains operate daily. The Department of Defense has designated 30,000 miles of track and structure as critical to mobilization and re-supply of US forces.
- **Postal and Shipping** moves about 720 million letters and packages each day and includes large integrated carriers, regional and local courier services, mail services, mail management firms, and chartered and delivery services" (US Department of Homeland Security 2017).

16. Water and Wastewater Systems Sector (SSA is Environmental Protection Agency)

"Safe drinking water is a prerequisite for protecting public health and all human activity. Properly treated wastewater is vital for preventing disease and protecting the environment. Thus, ensuring the supply of drinking water and wastewater treatment and service is essential to modern life and the Nation's economy" (US Department of Homeland Security 2017).

"There are approximately 153,000 public drinking water systems and more than 16,000 publicly owned wastewater treatment systems in the United States. More than 80 percent of the US population receives their potable water from these drinking water systems, and about 75 percent of the US population has its sanitary sewerage treated by these wastewater systems. The Water and Wastewater Systems Sector is vulnerable to a variety of attacks, including contamination with deadly agents; physical attacks, such as the release of toxic gaseous chemicals; and cyberattacks. The result of any variety of attack could be large numbers of illnesses or casualties and/or a denial of service that would also impact public health and economic vitality. The sector is also vulnerable to natural disasters. Critical services, such as firefighting and healthcare (hospitals), and other dependent and interdependent sectors, such as Energy, Food and Agriculture, and Transportation Systems, would suffer negative impacts from a denial of service in the Water and Wastewater Systems Sector" (US Department of Homeland Security 2017).

If you are a business executive in any of these sixteen critical infrastructure sectors, it is imperative you understand the cyber threat against your specific sector.

DHS has sector-specific Information Sharing and Analysis Centers (ISACs) that can assist business executives and their organizations in better understanding the various threats to their specific critical-infrastructure sectors including cyber threats. These ISACs are nonprofit, member-driven organizations formed by critical-infrastructure owners and operators to share information between the government and the private sector (US Department of Homeland Security 2017).

The DHS National Cybersecurity and Communications Integration Center (NCCIC) is a "key part of the DHS mission to create shared situational awareness of malicious cyber activity" (US Department of Homeland Security 2017). The NCCIC "is a 24 x 7 cyber situational awareness, incident response, and management center that is a national nexus of cyber and communications integration for the Federal Government, intelligence community, and law enforcement. The NCCIC shares information among public- and private-sector partners to build awareness of vulnerabilities, incidents, and mitigations. Users of cyber- and industrial-control systems can subscribe to information products, feeds, and services at no cost" (US Department of Homeland Security 2017)

The NCCIC comprises four branches:

1. NCCIC Operations and Integration (NO&I)
2. United States Computer Emergency Readiness Team (US-CERT)
3. Industrial Control Systems Cyber Emergency Response Team (ICS-CERT)
4. National Coordinating Center for Communications (NCC) (US Department of Homeland Security 2017).

DHS describes NO&I as its entity that "engages in planning, coordination, and integration capabilities to synchronize analysis, information sharing, and incident response efforts across the NCCIC's branches and activities" (US Department of Homeland Security 2017).

DHS describes the US-CERT as its entity that "brings advanced network and digital media analysis expertise to bear on malicious activity targeting our nation's networks." The US-CERT also "develops timely and actionable information for distribution to federal departments and agencies, state and local governments, private sector organizations, and international partners." The US-CERT also operates the National Cybersecurity Protection System (NCPS), which "provides intrusion detection and prevention capabilities to covered federal departments and agencies" (US Department of Homeland Security 2017).

DHS describes ICS-CERT as its entity that

> works to reduce risks within and across all critical infrastructure sectors by partnering with law-enforcement agencies and the intelligence community and coordinating efforts among federal,

state, local, and tribal governments and control systems owners, operators, and vendors. Cybersecurity and infrastructure protection experts from ICS–CERT provide assistance to owners and operators of critical systems by responding to incidents and helping restore services, and by analyzing potentially broader cyber or physical impacts to critical infrastructure. (US Department of Homeland Security 2017)

The ICS-CERT also "collaborates with international and private sector Computer Emergency Response Teams (CERTs) to share control systems-related security incidents and mitigation measures" (US Department of Homeland Security 2017).

DHS describes the NCC as its entity that "leads and coordinates the initiation, restoration, and reconstitution of National Security and Emergency Preparedness telecommunications services or facilities under all conditions. The NCC leverages partnerships with government, industry and international partners to obtain situational awareness and determine priorities for protection in response" (US Department of Homeland Security 2017).

Industrial Control Systems (ICS)

What is an ICS, and why should business executives be concerned about cyber threats to ICS? The US Department of Commerce National Institute of Standards and Technology (NIST) defines *industrial control system* (ICS) as a "general term that encompasses several types of control systems, including Supervisory Control and Data Acquisition (SCADA) systems, Distributed Control Systems (DCS), and other control system configurations such as Programmable Logic Controllers (PLC) often found in the industrial sectors and critical infrastructures" (National Institute of Standards and Technology Computer Security Division Computer Resource Center 2015).

An ICS consists of combinations of control components (e.g., electrical, mechanical, hydraulic, pneumatic) that act together to achieve an industrial objective (e.g., manufacturing, transportation of matter or energy). The part of the system primarily concerned with producing the output is referred to as the process. The control part of the system includes the specification of the desired output or performance. Control can be fully automated or may include a human in the loop. Systems can be configured to operate open-loop, closed-loop, and manual mode. In open-loop control systems the output is controlled by established settings. In closed-loop control systems, the output has an effect on the input in such a way as to maintain the desired objective. In manual mode, the system is controlled completely by humans. The part of the system primarily concerned with maintaining conformance with specifications is referred to as the controller (or control). A typical ICS may contain numerous control loops, Human Machine Interfaces (HMIs), and remote diagnostics and maintenance tools built using an array of network protocols. ICS control industrial processes are typically used in electrical, water and wastewater, oil and natural gas, chemical, transportation, pharmaceutical, pulp and paper, food and beverage, and discrete manufacturing (e.g., automotive, aerospace, and durable goods) industries. (National Institute of Standards and Technology Computer Security Division Computer Resource Center 2015)

There is terminology related to ICS that a business executive may not be familiar with. The following terms are necessary for business executives to develop a foundational knowledge of ICS.

Supervisor control and data acquisition (SCADA) is a "generic name for a computerized system that is capable of gathering and processing data and applying operational controls over long distances. Typical uses include power transmission and distribution and pipeline systems. SCADA was designed for the unique communication challenges (e.g., delays, data integrity) posed by the various media that must be used, such as phone lines, microwave, and satellite" (US National Institute of Standards and Technology 2015).

SCADA systems utilize human-machine interfaces (HMI). *Human-machine interfaces* (HMI) are

software and hardware that allow human operators to monitor the state of a process under control, modify control settings to change the control objective, and manually override automatic control operations in the event of an emergency. The HMI also allows a control engineer or operator to configure set points or control algorithms and parameters in the controller. The HMI also displays process status information, historical information, reports, and other information to operators, administrators, managers, business partners, and other authorized users. Operators and engineers use HMIs to monitor and configure set points, control algorithms, send commands, and adjust and establish parameters in the controller. The HMI also displays process status information and historical information. (US National Institute of Standards and Technology 2015)

SCADA systems are used in

distribution systems such as water distribution and wastewater collection systems, oil and natural gas pipelines, electrical utility transmission and distribution systems, and railway and other public transportation systems. SCADA systems integrate data acquisition systems with data transmission systems and HMI software to provide a centralized monitoring and control system for numerous process inputs and outputs. SCADA systems are designed to collect field information, transfer it to a central computer facility, and display the information to the operator graphically or textually, thereby allowing the operator to monitor or control an entire system from a central location in near real time. Based on the sophistication and setup of the individual system, control of any individual system, operation, or task can be automatic, or it can be performed by operator commands. (US National Institute of Standards and Technology 2015)

A *distributed control system* (DCS), as it relates to a control system, "refers to control achieved by intelligence that is distributed about the process to be controlled, rather than by a centrally located single unit" (US National Institute of Standards and Technology 2015).

A *programmable logic controller* (PLC) is a "small industrial computer originally designed to perform the logic functions executed by electrical hardware (relays, switches, and mechanical timers/counters). PLCs have evolved into controllers with the capability of controlling complex processes, and they are used substantially in SCADA systems and DCS. PLCs are also used as the primary controller in smaller system configurations. PLCs are used extensively in almost all industrial processes" (US National Institute of Standards and Technology 2015).

Programmable logic controllers are used in both SCADA and DCS systems as the control components of an overall hierarchical system to provide local management of processes through feedback control. In the case of SCADA systems, PLCs may provide the same functionality of remote terminal units (RTUs). When used in a DCS, PLCs are implemented as local controllers within a supervisory control scheme (US National Institute of Standards and Technology 2015).

A *remote terminal unit* (RTU) is a "special purpose data acquisition and control unit designed to support DCS and SCADA remote stations. RTUs are field devices often equipped with network capabilities, which can include wired and wireless radio interfaces to communicate to the supervisory controller. Sometimes PLCs are implemented as field devices to serve as RTUs; in this case, the PLC is often referred to as an RTU" (US National Institute of Standards and Technology 2015).

Why do business executives need to understand ICS? ICS are used in all of the sixteen US critical-infrastructure sectors, and many of these ICS networks are now connected to the Internet. There are SCADA systems, DCS, and PLCs that control (1) the distribution of your local area's electricity, (2) the proper combinations in creating chemicals or pharmaceuticals, (3) the mixing of complex chemicals, (4) the various chemicals and their exact mixture used to convert wastewater into drinkable water, and (5) automated industrial processes in manufacturing plants. Because of the Internet connectivity of today's ICS networks, these ICS networks are now exposed to the cyber threat landscape and all the cyber threat actors.

Every local community has financial institutions, water utilities, electrical utilities, hospitals, public-gathering facilities, various transportation modes, and various private- and public-sector entities that are members of each of the sixteen critical infrastructures. Many businesses in the sixteen critical infrastructure sectors already have liaison with local law enforcement agencies regarding the physical and terrorist threat against critical infrastructure. Business executives need to add the cyber threat discussion to their ongoing dialogue of other security topics. This dialogue should include discussions regarding the organization's cybersecurity posture and cyber-response capabilities.

It is strategically important for both business and law enforcement executives to understand ICS security, because local law-enforcement departments will have to handle the public reaction to a potential ICS failure caused by a cyberattack. The December 2015 cyberattack on the Ukraine power grid affected 225,000 customers. Imagine what would happen if this same scenario occurred in the United States and if there was no electricity for a few days or even a couple of weeks in your local metropolitan area. Imagine what would happen if a cyberattack on the critical industrial-control systems of your local energy company shut off the electricity in your area. As noted previously, we depend on electricity in our daily lives for a myriad of things, such as the use of bank ATMs and gas stations, so there is a good possibility that chaos would erupt after such a cyberattack. Local law-enforcement agencies would have the responsibility of maintaining public order during the response to this type of potential crisis and it is imperative for the business community in these sixteen critical infrastructure sectors to maintain an ongoing and regularly scheduled dialogue with local law enforcement regarding the cyber threat.

Industrial Control System (ICS) Vulnerability Exercise
Let us conduct another exercise by reviewing different types of known ICS vulnerabilities and their effects on industrial-control systems by reviewing the US Department of Homeland (DHS) ICS-CERT Alerts website (https://ics-cert.us-cert.gov/alerts) and the DHS ICS-CERT Advisories website (https://ics-cert.us-cert.gov/advisories).

The DHS ICS-CERT Alerts website provides timely notification to critical-infrastructure owners and operators regarding threats and activities that have the potential to affect critical-infrastructure computing networks (US Department of Homeland Security 2017).

The DHS ICS-CERT Advisories website provides to the public timely notification concerning current security issues, vulnerabilities, and exploits (US Department of Homeland Security 2017).

Let's review the following nine ICS-CERT advisories and one ICS-CERT alert and their respective vulnerabilities and potential effects, as well as the critical-infrastructure sectors where these industrial control systems and software are used:

1. Advisory (ICSA-17-187-01) Siemens OZW672 and OZW772 Vulnerability (Original release date: July 6, 2017)

Summary: A security researcher discovered and reported this vulnerability to Siemens. The vulnerability can be remotely exploited, allowing cyber threat actors to access and modify historical measurement data. Siemens has provided mitigation strategies to protect against this threat, and ICS-CERT has provided recommendations of defensive measures to protect from this vulnerability.

The affected Siemens OZW672 and OZW772 products are used for monitoring building controller devices worldwide in the Commercial Facilities critical infrastructure sector (US Department of Homeland Security 2017).

2. Advisory (ICSA-17-187-04) Schneider Electric Wonderware ArchestrA Logger Vulnerabilities (Original release date: July 6, 2017)

Summary: A security researcher discovered and reported these vulnerabilities to Schneider Electric. These vulnerabilities included (1) a stack-based buffer-overflow vulnerability that, if successfully exploited, could allow a remote attacker to execute arbitrary code in the context of a privileged account; (2) an uncontrolled-resource-consumption vulnerability that, if successfully exploited, could allow an attacker to exhaust memory resources and cause a denial of service; and (3) a null-pointer-deference vulnerability that, if successfully exploited, could allow an attacker to crash the logger process, causing a denial of service. Schneider Electric has provided a mitigation to protect against this threat, and ICS-CERT has provided recommendations of defensive measures to protect from this vulnerability.

This affected Schneider Electric Wonderware product is used worldwide in the critical manufacturing, dams, defense industrial base, energy, food and agriculture, government facilities, nuclear reactors, materials, and in waste, transportation systems, water and wastewater systems critical-infrastructure sectors (US Department of Homeland Security 2017).

3. Advisory (ICSA-17-180-01) Siemens SIMATIC Industrial PCs, SINUMERIK Panel Control Unit, and SIMOTION P320 Vulnerability (Original release date: June 29, 2017)

Summary: A security researcher discovered and reported these vulnerabilities to Intel. These vulnerabilities were found in the Siemens products that use Intel processors: Intel Core i5, Intel Core i7, and Intel XEON. If successfully exploited, it would allow a remote attacker with a low skill level to gain system privileges. Siemens has provided a mitigation to protect against this threat, and ICS-CERT has provided recommendations of defensive measures to protect from this vulnerability.

The affected Siemens products—Industrial PCs, SINUMERIK Panel Control Unit, and SIMOTION P320—are used worldwide in the chemical, commercial facilities, critical manufacturing, energy, food and agriculture, and water and wastewater systems critical infrastructure sectors (US Department of Homeland Security 2017).

4. Advisory (ICSA-17-171-01) Ecava IntegraXor Vulnerability (Original release date: June 20, 2017)

Summary: A security company reported this vulnerability and tested the patch. A SQL-injection vulnerability was found in the 5.2.1231.0 and prior versions of the Ecava IntegraXor, a web SCADA/HMI solution. If successfully exploited, this vulnerability could allow unauthenticated remote-code execution by an attacker with a low skill level. Ecava has provided a mitigation to protect against this threat, and ICS-CERT has provided recommendations of defensive measures to protect from this vulnerability.

The Ecava IntegraXor is used in the Critical Manufacturing, Energy, and Water and Wastewater Systems critical-infrastructure sectors and is deployed in the United Kingdom, United States, Australia, Poland, Canada, and Estonia (US Department of Homeland Security 2017).

5. Advisory (ICSA-17-166-01) Cambium Networks ePMP Vulnerabilities (Original release date: June 14, 2017)

Summary: A security researcher identified these vulnerabilities that affect all models of the Cambium ePMP network access control products. The vulnerabilities include an improper access-control vulnerability and an improper privilege-management vulnerability that, if successfully exploited, could allow an attacker with a low skill level to access device configurations and to make unauthorized changes to the products' configurations. Cambium has provided a mitigation to protect against this threat, and ICS-CERT has provided recommendations of defensive measures to protect against this vulnerability.

Cambium Networks ePMP network access control products are found in the information technology critical-infrastructure sector worldwide (US Department of Homeland Security 2017).

6. Advisory (ICSA-16-224-01) Rockwell Automation MicroLogix 1400 SNMP Credentials Vulnerability (Original release date: August 11, 2016)

Summary: A security research group reported to Rockwell that an undocumented and privileged Simple Network Management Protocol (SNMP) community string exists in the MicroLogix 1400 programmable logic controllers. This vulnerability can be exploited remotely and can enable an attacker to make unauthorized changes to the product's configuration, including firmware updates. Rockwell has released mitigation strategies to protect against this threat, and ICS-CERT has provided risk assessment and recommendations of defensive measures to protect against this vulnerability.

The affected Rockwell Automation products, MicroLogix, are programmable logic controllers deployed in several critical-infrastructure sectors to include chemical, critical manufacturing, food and agriculture, water and wastewater systems, and others, and these PLCs are used all over the world (US Department of Homeland Security 2017).

7. Advisory (ICSA-16-215-02) Siemens SINEMA Server Privilege Escalation Vulnerability (Original release date: August 02, 2016)

Summary: A security researcher working with a security company identified a privilege-escalation vulnerability in all versions prior to V13 SP2 of the Siemens SINEMA server. Successful exploitation of this vulnerability could enable users, authenticated via the operating system, to escalate their privileges under certain conditions. Siemens has provided a mitigation to protect against this threat, and ICS-CERT has provided risk assessment and recommendations of defensive measures to protect from this vulnerability.

The affected Siemens product, SINEMA, is a network-management appliance for industrial applications and allows network monitoring, diagnostics, and reporting functions to be integrated into supervisory control and data acquisition (SCADA) systems. This Siemens product is deployed in several critical-infrastructure sectors, including chemical, commercial facilities, critical manufacturing, energy, government facilities, water and wastewater systems, and others, and this product is used worldwide (US Department of Homeland Security 2017).

8. Advisory (ICSA-16-196-01) Schneider Electric Pelco Digital Sentry Video Management System Vulnerability (Original release date: July 14, 2016)

Summary: Schneider Electric has identified a hard-coded credential vulnerability in the Schneider Electric Pelco Digital Sentry Video Management System, and it can be exploited remotely and can enable an attacker to gain access to and execute code on the affected system. Schneider Electric has produced new firmware to mitigate this vulnerability, and ICS-CERT has provided recommendations of defensive measures to protect against this vulnerability.

The affected Schneider product is a video-recording system and is deployed in several critical-infrastructure sectors, including Commercial Facilities, and is used worldwide (US Department of Homeland Security 2017).

9. Advisory (ICSA-16-194-02) GE Proficy HMI SCADA CIMPLICITY Privilege Management Vulnerability (Original release date: July 12, 2016)

Summary: A security researcher identified an improper privilege-management vulnerability and released an exploit code for the GE Proficy HMI/SCADA CIMPLICITY application. Exploits that target this vulnerability are publicly available. Successful exploitation of this vulnerability can enable an authenticated user on the system to modify the configuration of the CIMPLICITY service and launch any executable on the system as a service. GE has produced a new version to mitigate this vulnerability, and ICS-CERT has provided recommendations of defensive measures to protect against this vulnerability.

The affected GE product is a client or server-based human-machine interface and supervisory-control and data-acquisition (HMI/SCADA) application that is deployed across several critical infrastructure sectors (US Department of Homeland Security 2017).

10. Alert (ICS-ALERT-15-041-01) Microsoft Security Bulletin MS15-011 JASBUG (Original release date February 10, 2015)

Summary: ICS-CERT issued this alert due to a Microsoft Windows critical-security update in the Microsoft Security Bulletin MS 15-011. This vulnerability impacts control-system owners using a domain-configured system. Exploitation of this vulnerability can enable a remote attacker to take complete control of an affected Windows system, which could then allow the attacker to install programs; view, change, or delete data; or create new accounts with full user rights.

The impacted Windows systems include Windows Server 2003, Windows Vista, Windows Server 2008, Windows 7, Windows Server 2008 R2, Windows 8, Windows Server 2012, Windows RT, Windows 8.1, Windows Server 2012 R2, and Windows RT 8.1.

It should be noted there are not updates available for this vulnerability for Windows XP, Windows Server 2003, or Windows 2000 (US Department of Homeland Security 2017).

Judging by these ten examples of ICS-vulnerability exercises, business executives should see that there are very serious known vulnerabilities affecting several types of ICS and a major operating system used across the various critical-infrastructure sectors worldwide. Both law-enforcement and business executives must understand the strategic impact these ICS vulnerabilities can potentially have on their respective critical infrastructures' ICS in the case of their being exploited by cyber threat actors.

In summary, business executives must have a foundational understanding of all sixteen US critical-infrastructure sectors and the various components of ICS, and they must understand that both critical infrastructures and their ICS networks are targets of cyber threat actors. Executives should review the critical-infrastructure resources available to them (PPD-21, DHS, and the NIST *Guide to ICS Security*) and understand the strategic impact cyber threat actors can have on critical infrastructures in their organizations. Business executives should consider establishing (or improving) liaisons with their local law enforcement in their respective locales for law enforcement to better understand the cyber-security posture, cyber-response capabilities, and cybersecurity assets of the local critical infrastructures. Business executives should also consider adding cyberattack tabletop exercises involving DHS; all local-area federal, state, and local law-enforcement; and local critical-infrastructure stakeholders to map out possible joint responses to a simulated successful cyberattack on local critical infrastructure.

6

WIRELESS AND MOBILE DEVICES

A business executive must understand all of the potential vulnerabilities in his or her organization's IT infrastructure to properly secure it. Business executives must understand the potential intrusion vectors associated with wireless and mobile devices, those through which attackers can negatively impact their organizations' IT infrastructure and the organization itself.

Wireless devices and mobile devices can remotely access an organization's IT infrastructure in numerous ways—for example, using wireless access points, gaining remote access via a remote-access protocol (such as Windows Remote Desktop Protocol), and through gaining authentication with usernames and passwords via encrypted channels with a virtual private network (VPN).

These remote accesses also provide cyber threat actors opportunities to exploit an organization's IT infrastructure. Vulnerabilities such as using weak encryption on a wireless access point or having a smartphone infected with malware can enable cyber threat actors to gain unauthorized access to an organization's IT infrastructure.

Business executives need to have a basic understanding of the various key aspects of wireless to include such things as wireless access points, service-set identifiers, wireless local-area networks (WLAN), wireless authentication, and the types of Wi-Fi security-encryption protocols.

In addition, any business executives contemplating allowing mobile devices (smartphones, tablets, laptops, etc.) to access their IT infrastructures need to have a basic understanding of such things as the various mobile-device operating systems, the multitude of mobile malware, mobile-application security processes, secure containers, and the use of mobile-device management systems to secure the mobile environments and their connection to the relevant organizations' IT infrastructures.

Wireless
Wireless Access Points

Business executives must understand a few concepts regarding wireless and mobile devices. Executives must be able to distinguish between a LAN and WLAN and understand the importance of wireless access points, SSIDs, wireless encryption, wireless protocols, and new wireless technologies, in the context of securing their organizations' IT infrastructures.

A *local-area network* (LAN) is a computer network within a small geographical area such as an office building. A LAN comprises interconnected workstations and personal computers that are each capable of accessing and sharing data and devices, such as printers, scanners, and data-storage devices anywhere on the LAN (Techopedia 2017).

A *wireless local-area network* (WLAN) is a "wireless distribution method for two or more devices that use high-frequency radio waves and often include access points to the Internet. A WLAN allows users to move around the coverage area while maintaining a network connection" (Techopedia 2017).

A *wireless access point* (WAP) is a "hardware device or configured node on a local area network (LAN) that allows wireless capable devices and wired networks to connect through a wireless standard, such as Wi-Fi or Bluetooth. WAPs feature radio transmitters and antennae, which facilitate connectivity between devices and the Internet or a network. A WAP is also known as a hotspot" (Techopedia 2017).

A wireless access point is another potential intrusion vector that cyber threat actors can exploit for unauthorized access into an organization's IT infrastructure.

Service Set Identifier (SSID)

A *service set identifier (SSID)*, also known as a network name, is a "type of identifier that uniquely identifies a wireless local area network (WLAN)" (Techopedia 2017). The SSID is required when a wireless device wants to authenticate to a wireless access point.

Wireless Fidelity or Wi-Fi

The Institute of Electrical and Electronics Engineers (IEEE) 802.11 standards refer to the "set of standards that define communication for wireless LANs (wireless local area networks or WLANs)." Wireless Fidelity, better known as Wi-Fi, is the branding of the technology behind the 802.11 standards. There is only one standard IEEE 802.11-2007, but it has many amendments, including 802.11a, 802.11b, 802.11g, and 802.11n (Techopedia 2017).

Wi-Fi is a wireless-network technology used for connecting to the Internet, and it uses 2.4-gigahertz or 5-gigahertz frequencies to ensure no interference with cellular traffic, radio, and two-way radios. "Wi-Fi is basically just radio waves broadcast from a Wi-Fi router, a device detecting and deciphering the radio waves, and then sending back data to the router" (Techopedia 2017).

Wireless Encryption

There are three types of wireless encryption: (1) Wired Equivalent Privacy (WEP), (2) Wi-Fi Protected Access (WPA), and (3) Wi-Fi Protected Access II (WPA2).

Wired Equivalent Privacy (WEP) was the first wireless encryption, released in 1999 as a portion of the IEEE 802.11 standard (Techopedia 2017).

There are two main types of wireless authentication for a wireless access point using the WEP protocol: open-system authentication and shared-key authentication (Harris and Maymi 2016). In many cases, the nonencrypted or *open-system authentication* only requires the correct SSID or network name for authentication. Open-system authentication does not require a wireless device to prove to the wireless access point that it has a specific cryptographic key for authentication purposes. Nonencrypted authentication means all transactions are in cleartext, which can enable a cyber threat actor to sniff the traffic, capture the necessary steps of authentication, and walk through the same steps to be authenticated and associated with the access point (Harris and Maymi 2016).

When a wireless access point is configured to use an encrypted authentication with *shared-key authentication* (SKA), the access point sends a random value to the wireless device. The device encrypts this value with its cryptographic key and returns it. The access point then decrypts and extracts the response, and if it is the original value, the wireless device is authenticated to the access point because it proved it had the necessary encryption key (Harris and Maymi 2016).

WEP was found to have three major security flaws that caused WEP's security to be vulnerable and decipherable. The three major security flaws were

(1) the use of static encryption keys (poor authentication), (2) the ineffective use of initialization vectors (which did not provide the necessary degree of randomness), and (3) the lack of packet-integrity assurance (which caused a lack of data integrity) (Harris and Maymi 2016). What this means is WEP has been broken, is crackable with available hacker tools, and should not be used in any business organization's IT infrastructure.

Wi-Fi Protected Access (WPA) was released in 2003 and is a "security standard to secure computers connected to a Wi-Fi network. Its purpose is to address the serious weaknesses in the previous system, the Wired Equivalent Privacy (WEP) standard" (Technopedia 2017).

Wi-Fi Protected Access II (WPA2) was released in 2004 and is a "security standard to secure computers connected to a Wi-Fi network. Its purpose is to achieve complete compliance with the IEEE 802.11i standard, only partially achieved with WPA, and to address the security flaw in the 128-bit 'temporary key integrity protocol (TKIP)' in WPA by replacing it with CCMP." WPA and WPA2 are concurrent security standards since WPA2 will not work in some older network cards (Techopedia 2017).

Another standard component of the IEEE 802.11 framework is IEEE 802.1X, which enhances wireless network security. "The IEEE 802.1X controls access to wireless or virtual local area networks (VLAN) and applies traffic policies based on user identity and credentials. IEEE 802.1X ensures a user authentication framework where network access is denied upon failed authentication" (Techopedia 2017).

Organizations should never use WEP and should use WPA2 wireless encryption to ensure the strongest wireless-encryption protection available.

Additional Wireless Concerns

There are wireless technologies that business executives need to understand since those technologies are being used in today's smartphones and will only grow in use in the future. Two of these wireless technologies are Bluetooth and near-field communication.

Bluetooth wireless technology is based on a portion of the 802.15 standard. It has a transfer rate of one to three megabytes per second and works in ranges of approximately one, ten, and one hundred meters. Security risks exist when transferring unprotected data via Bluetooth in a public area because any device within a certain range can capture this type of data transfer (Harris and Maymi 2016).

Near-field communication (NFC) is a

wireless technology that allows a device to collect and interpret data from another closely located NFC device or tag. NFC employs inductive-coupling technology, in which power and data are shared through coupled inductive circuits over a very close proximity of a few centimeters. NFC is often employed through mobile phones or credit cards, where information may be read if it is passed very close to another such device or NFC tag. (Techopedia 2017)

NFC technology is similar to radio-frequency identification (RFID) tags, but the contactless way in which NFC devices interact also bears similarity to Bluetooth. Near-field communication is not yet widely used, but it can be employed in contactless payment systems. It also provides a compact way to communicate information, which may be used for advertising or social media purposes" (Techopedia 2017). As some organizations' employees are using contactless payment systems, it is important for business executives to note the possible security concerns for NFC users, which include eavesdropping, data corruption or modification, interception attacks, and physical theft of a NFC-enabled smartphone. ("Security Concerns with NFC Technology" 2017)

Wireless Attacks

There are numerous wireless attacks that can impact the wireless environment of any organization. Wireless attacks can be categorized as follows:

Access-Control Attacks

Access-control attacks attempt to penetrate a network by using wireless or evading WLAN access-control measures. Examples of access-control attacks include the following:

- Rogue access point—A rogue access point refers to when the cyber threat actor installs an unsecure access point inside the firewall, creating an open backdoor into an organization's IT network ("A List of Wireless Network Attacks" 2017).

- War driving—War driving refers to discovering wireless local-area networks (WLANs) by listening to beacons or sending probe requests, thereby providing a possible intrusion vector for the cyber threat actor to initiate further attacks ("A List of Wireless Network Attacks" 2017).

Confidentiality Attacks

Confidentiality attacks attempt to intercept private information communicated over wireless channels, either in cleartext or encrypted traffic. Examples of confidentiality attacks include the following:

- WEP-key cracking—WEP-key cracking refers to when the cyber threat actor captures wireless data to recover the WEP key by using brute-force cryptanalysis ("A List of Wireless Network Attacks" 2017).
- Evil-twin access point—Evil-twin access point refers to when the cyber threat actor masquerades a rogue wireless access point as an authorized wireless access point for the targeted organization by beaconing the organization's WLAN's service set identifier (SSID) to lure users ("A List of Wireless Network Attacks" 2017).

Integrity Attacks

Integrity attacks refer to when cyber threat actors "send forged control, management or data frames over wireless to mislead the recipient or to facilitate another type of attack," such as a denial-of-service (DoS) attack. An example of an integrity attack is the following:

- 802.11 Frame Injection—802.11 Frame Injection refers to when the cyber threat actor crafts and sends forged 802.11 frames to the targeted organization's wireless environment ("A List of Wireless Network Attacks" 2017).

Authentication Attacks

Authentication attacks refer to when the cyber threat actors steal authorized user credentials to access the target organization's wireless infrastructure. An example of an authentication attack is the following:

- Shared-key guessing—Shared-key guessing refers to when the cyber threat actor attempts to gain 802.11 shared-key authentication with guessed keys, vendor default keys, or cracked WEP keys ("A List of Wireless Network Attacks" 2017).

Availability Attacks

Availability attacks by the cyber threat actor impede the delivery of wireless services to authorized users of the target organization by denying these authorized users access or crippling the organization's WLAN resources. An example of an availability attack is the following:

- 802.11 beacon flood—An 802.11 beacon flood refers to when the cyber threat actor generates thousands of counterfeit 802.11 beacons, making it difficult for stations to find legitimate wireless access points ("A List of Wireless Network Attacks" 2017).

Business executives must understand the various potential exploits and intrusion vectors that exist because of the wireless capabilities in the organizations' IT infrastructure. Transmitting in cleartext without encryption, the use of weak encryption (such as WEP), rogue access points, and other wireless attacks are just some of the potential security vulnerabilities facing today's organizations that use wireless capabilities. As one can see, there are quite a few wireless vulnerabilities that can be exploited by the cyber threat actor.

Mobile Devices and Mobile-Device Operating Systems

Mobile devices are integral and necessary in today's organizations. Many organizations issue mobile devices to allow their employees to communicate and access the Internet and the organizations' IT infrastructure while away from their offices.

These conveniences also allow cyber threat actors to exploit vulnerabilities associated with mobile devices. Some of these vulnerabilities are unpatched operating systems, malicious mobile applications, and mobile malware. Business executives need to understand the cyber threats targeting mobile devices and mobile-device vulnerabilities in order to strategically protect the organization and its IT infrastructure.

In November 2007, Google introduced the Android mobile-operating system. The Android mobile-operating system is the most popular mobile-operating system in use around today's world (Android, The World's Most

Popular Mobile Platform 2017). There have been numerous Android versions introduced in the marketplace since its introduction in 2008. The previous Android versions include Android 1.5 Cupcake (2009), Android 1.6 Donut (2009), Android 2.0–2.1 Eclair (2009), Android 2.2 Froyo (2010), Android 2.3 Gingerbread (2010), Android 3.x Honeycomb (2011), Android 4.0 Ice Cream Sandwich (2011), Android 4.1–4.3 Jelly Bean (2012), Android 4.4 KitKat (2013), Android 5.0 Lollipop (2014), Android 6.0 Marshmallow (2015), and the latest version is Android 7.0 Nougat (2016) (Hildenbrand 2016).

Android is an open-source platform that allows original equipment manufacturers (OEMs) to customize their Android operating system and allows carriers to install their own software onto these Android devices. This has caused security concerns due to the various Android operating system versions used by various OEMs that have installed their own software onto these Android devices. This open-source platform customization is very different in comparison with Apple's iOS walled-garden infrastructure, which does not allow for any customization of the Apple iOS or Apple updates (Smith 2015).

This Android customization feature allows for a disparity when it comes to applying Android security patches. If an OEM or carrier customizes the Android operating system, any security patches issued by the Android security team must be tested by the OEM and carrier to determine whether the security patch will work on its mobile devices. Sometimes this Android security patch does not work on these customized Android operating systems and cannot be pushed out to the devices with a security vulnerability, thus leaving the mobile user and mobile device with a vulnerable Android operating system that is potentially open to exploitation by a cyber threat actor.

In comparison, Apple has full control of its applications, content, and media and restricts convenient access to nonapproved applications or content. But this may be changing, as noted in an announcement by Apple on June 13, 2016, in which Apple stated it is opening up Maps, Siri, and Messages to other software developers (Olson 2016).

In January 2016, Duo Security conducted an analysis of over one million mobile devices and determined that 90 percent of Android devices are running out-of-date versions of the Android operating system. In addition, similar analyses of Apple iOS devices revealed that 50 to 80 percent of Apple iPhones were out of date (Seals 2016). These analyses were particularly concerning for Android users, as the "Stagefright" vulnerability affected Android version 4.0 (Ice Cream Sandwich) and older Android operating system versions at the time.

When it was discovered during 2015, the Stagefright vulnerability on Android operating systems had impacted over 950 million vulnerable Android devices worldwide. This vulnerability resided in Stagefright, an Android code library that processes several widely used media formats. Stagefright had an exploit where all the cyber threat actor needed was a victim's telephone number to send a malicious message via a multimedia message format. The surreptitious, malicious code would then execute on the vulnerable Android device with no action required by the victim (Goodin 2015).

As a result of the Stagefright vulnerability, Google began to provide monthly Android security updates in September 2015, but there was still no scalable update system to provide these updates to all the various Android device users (Amadeo 2015). As of July 2017, the Android security team was providing security patches for Android versions 4.4 (KitKat) and above. This left older Android versions without security patches from Android Security.

Although the fragmentation of the various Android mobile-operating systems has caused security concerns, it should be noted that Google is addressing and improving the security of the Android mobile-operating system. The latest version, Android 7.0 (Nougat), has a number of security features that include strong encryption, permission sharing between apps that is not easy to enable, an "always-on VPN" feature for encrypting Internet browsing and app data, and quicker updates (Bapna 2017).

As of July 2017, the Android Dashboard Platform Versions (which monitors the Android versions used globally) noted that 11.5 percent of all Android users in the world are using Android 7.0 (Nougat), 31.8 percent of global Android users are using Android 6.0 (Marshmallow), 30.1 percent of global Android users are using Android 5.0 (Lollipop), 17.1 percent of global Android users are using Android 4.4 (KitKat), and the older Android versions (Jelly Bean, Ice Cream Sandwich, and Gingerbread) account for 9.5 percent of global Android users (Android 2017).

As of May 2017, Android has more than two billion monthly active devices in use around the world (Popper 2017).

If Apple users thought they were safe from a Stagefright-type vulnerability, this changed in July 2016, when Cisco researchers unveiled a similar vulnerability that affected the Apple OS X and iOS operating systems. This vulnerability made it possible for the cyber threat actor to get hold of a user's password and files simply by sending a spoofed file. By sending a specially crafted image file to the iPhone user via iMessage, a cyber threat actor could achieve remote-code execution on the vulnerable Apple devices, since iMessage was tuned to automatically render images when they were received by the Apple device. Apple issued a patch to fix this vulnerability (Ungureanu 2016).

During July 2017, both Google and Apple issued Android and iPhone security patches to address a vulnerability impacting Wi-Fi on both mobile platforms. Security researcher Nitay Artenstein found a vulnerability called Broadpwn in a Wi-Fi chip that impacted billions of Android and iPhone devices. This vulnerability allowed cyber threat actors to come within Wi-Fi range not only to hack into the Android or iPhone device but also to turn these devices into rogue access points that would in turn be used to infect nearby phones (Greenberg 2017).

Apple iOS and Android are not the only mobile operating systems impacted by malware. Other mobile-device platforms, such as Windows Phone and BlackBerry, are also impacted by mobile malware and can be exploited by the cyber threat actor.

Mobile Malware

Today's smartphones can be a treasure trove for the cyber threat actor. Each smartphone stores a great amount of the user's personal information. This single point of access includes not only personal information but also financial data, personal and business calendars, personal and business e-mails, photos, and other personal or business-related documents. Therefore, smartphones are an attractive target for cyber threat actors. The following are statistics reported during 2015 and 2016 on the tremendous growth of mobile vulnerabilities and malware impacting the various mobile-device operating systems in today's mobile environment.

During 2015, Symantec identified the following mobile malware risks to Apple iOS: (1) nine new Apple iOS threat families, (2) a compromised iOS developer software kit known as XcodeGhost that infected as many as four thousand Apple iOS apps, (3) the YiSpecter malware that was able to bypass the Apple App Store by using the enterprise app provisioning framework, (4) a software known as Youmi that was used to display advertising in 256 iOS apps but also sent out personal information, and (5) vulnerabilities in Apple's AirDrop wireless file-transfer system that could enable an attack to install malware on an Apple device (Symantec 2016).

During 2016, Kaspersky Lab detected 8,526,221 malicious mobile malware installation packages, 128,886 mobile banker Trojans, and 261,214 mobile ransomware Trojans (Kaspersky Lab 2017).

In the April 2017 Symantec Internet Security Threat Report, Symantec reported that 290 new iOS mobile vulnerabilities and 316 new Android mobile vulnerabilities had been detected during 2016. Symantec also reported that four new Android mobile malware families with 3,600 new Android malware variants had been detected during 2016 (Symantec 2017).

Mobile Applications

In addition to mobile operating-system vulnerabilities and mobile malware, business executives must understand the dangers of mobile applications used by mobile devices that may connect to their organizations' IT infrastructures. Mobile applications that have not been vetted through a security process may have installed features that can cause unauthorized data leakage, introduce mobile malware, or provide unauthorized access to an organization's information or PII.

To provide business executives a perspective on the various vulnerabilities in the mobile-application environment, let us look at the Open Web Application Security Project's (OWASP) Mobile Security Project (OWASP 2017). The OWASP's Mobile Security Project provides mobile-device penetration testers a baseline checklist for checking the security of mobile applications. This baseline checklist lists ninety-one different vulnerability checks and tests, which include everything from SQL injection, applications vulnerable to cross-site scripting (XSS), weak password policy, cleartext passwords in response, and others. This means there are many potential vulnerabilities in a mobile application (OWASP 2017).

The 2016 OWASP Mobile Top Ten mobile-application security concerns included

1. Improper platform usage
2. Insecure data storage
3. Insecure communication
4. Insecure authentication

5. Insufficient cryptography
6. Insecure authorization
7. Client code quality
8. Code tampering
9. Reverse engineering
10. Extraneous functionality

This OWASP Mobile Top Ten list of mobile-application security concerns indicates the different areas of a mobile application that can potentially be compromised by cyber threat actors (OWASP 2017).

Any business organization that has implemented the use of mobile devices and mobile applications needs to have all mobile applications reviewed through a detailed security process and approved by certified mobile-device penetration testers prior to being implemented in the organization's IT infrastructure.

In further consideration of securing their organizations' IT infrastructures, business executives must consider the use and implementation of a mobile-applications store for their organizations' employees. This mobile-applications store should offer employees only authorized mobile applications that have been reviewed thoroughly by the business organization through a detailed security process by certified mobile-device penetration testers. In addition, the use of security containers is recommended. *Security containers* are authenticated and encrypted areas in mobile devices that separate an organization's sensitive and confidential information from users' personal data and personal applications. The purpose of security containers is to prevent malware, cyber threat actors, system resources, and other applications from interacting with the secured application and associated organization's confidential information and data (Techtarget 2017).

Business executives need to also consider the implementation of an *enterprise mobility-management suite* to control and reduce the exploitation of potential vulnerabilities of all aspects of mobile-device and mobile-application security. These enterprise mobility-management suites include the use of secure containers, mobile-device management, mobile-application management, mobile-content management, mobile e-mail management, and remote capability to wipe untrusted devices.

There are several vendors of enterprise mobility-management suites that include VMware AirWatch, BlackBerry's Good Secure EMM Suite, MobileIron, Sophos Mobile Control EMM, and the Citrix XenMobile Enterprise Mobility Management Suite.

One firm that conducts an analysis of the various enterprise mobility-management suites is Gartner, one of the world's leading information and technology research and advisory companies (Gartner 2017).

Business executives must understand the risks involved in implementing both mobile devices and mobile applications in their organizations' IT infrastructures. Business executives must weigh the different mobile-device and mobile-application security factors in deciding on whether to secure mobile devices and mobile applications as a part of their organizations' IT infrastructures. Some of these cybersecurity factors include (1) not issuing mobile devices to their employees and allowing employees to access the organization's IT infrastructure with their own insecure and unpatched mobile devices, (2) the increasing mobile malware threat against all mobile-operating-system platforms, and (3) the hundreds of potential vulnerabilities currently found in mobile applications. As one can see, it is imperative for all business executives to secure their organizations' IT infrastructures from these mobile-device and mobile-application security vulnerabilities. The use of an enterprise mobility-management suite by business organizations is a must in assisting business executives in protecting their data, organizational information, and IT infrastructures.

In summary, business executives need to understand the strategic impact that cyber threat actors will have on the mobile and wireless systems within their organizations' IT infrastructures. Business executives must consider several factors in strategically addressing the cybersecurity posture of their organizations' wireless capability to include protection against unauthorized access, weak encryption, rogue access points, various types of wireless attacks, and the potential security vulnerabilities of the different wireless protocols now in use, such as near-field communication and Bluetooth. Business executives must also consider several factors in strategically addressing the cybersecurity posture of their organizations' mobile-device capability to include vulnerable mobile operating systems, mobile malware, insecure mobile applications, and the use of enterprise mobility management suites to integrate and manage their mobile devices in their IT infrastructures. Serious consideration should also be given to having regularly scheduled penetration tests by qualified security professionals to ensure the security of the organizations' wireless, mobile-device, and mobile-application environments.

7

WEB INFRASTRUCTURE SECURITY AND THIRD-PARTY RISK

Web Infrastructure Security

As a business executive, do you know what port 80 and port 443 are? Port 80 is the computer port that one uses to communicate with the World Wide Web, and port 443 is the port that one uses to communicate with the World Wide Web securely over an encrypted channel.

Does your business organization use the World Wide Web for its business purposes? Is your business organization an e-commerce business offering its services and products online which require customers to provide personally identifying information (PII) and sensitive credit card or debit card information to purchase your products? Does your business organization have a website which provides the public information about your company, its executives, its product lines and other information? If you answered yes to any of these questions, you, as a business executive, need to understand the attack vectors utilized by cyber threat actors to conduct web attacks. These web attacks include website defacement, SQL injections, cross-site scripting (XSS), and web-server intrusions that can potentially provide the cyber threat actor complete control of your organization's web servers and IT infrastructure.

As an executive, have you ever wondered what's behind the process of surfing the Internet? Have you ever wondered what makes these Internet searches possible from the browser to the web page and to the user interaction allowed by a web application?

The following is some background on the World Wide Web and how it functions, and the information should provide business executives a foundational understanding of the World Wide Web, web servers, and web exploits.

The *World Wide Web* (WWW) is "what most people think of as the Internet. It is all the web pages, pictures, videos and other online content that can be accessed via a web browser. The Internet, in contrast, is the underlying network connection that allows us to send e-mail and access the World Wide Web" (Techopedia 2017).

A more technical definition of the World Wide Web is that it is a network of online content that is formatted in hypertext markup language (HTML) and accessed via hypertext transfer protocol (HTTP). Many readers will start to disengage from understanding the cyber threat when terms and acronyms such as HTML and HTTP are mentioned. Such acronyms can be difficult to understand even when they are spelled out completely.

Now that we have defined the World Wide Web, let's define a web address. A web address is known as the uniform resource locator (URL), which is displayed on a web page in the address bar. The following is an example of a URL:

http://www.hackingthecyberthreat.com/index.html

A typical URL could have the following format:

1. A protocol (which is *http*)
2. A host name (which is *hackingthecyberthreat.com*)
3. A file name (which is *index.html*)

A *protocol* is defined as "a set of rules and guidelines for communication data. Rules are defined for each step in process during communication between two or more computers. Networks have to follow these rules to successfully transmit data" (Techopedia 2017).

Two examples of protocols used to communicate in the World Wide Web are hypertext transfer protocol (HTTP) and hypertext transfer protocol secure (HTTPS).

Hypertext transfer protocol (HTTP) uses the client-server model, where the web browser is the client and communicates with the web server that is hosting the website (Techopedia 2017). HTTP transmits data in cleartext without encryption. The URL **http**://www.hackingthecyberthreat.com is an example of the use of the HTTP protocol.

Hypertext transfer protocol secure (HTTPS) "adds a layer of security to the data it is transmitting through a secure socket layer (SSL) or transport layer security (TLS) protocol connection which enables encrypted communication between the remote user and the web server" (Techopedia 2017). The URL **https**://www.hackingthecyberthreat.com is an example of the use of the HTTPS protocol.

One can distinguish HTTP from HTTPS while browsing on the World Wide Web, as HTTPS is designated by a lock image on the address bar. For example, when a user using the Google Chrome browser searches for the Google home page, the user will notice there is a lock icon and "Secure" to the right of the URL **https**://www.google.com in his or her address bar, which indicates an encrypted connection using HTTPS.

Let's discuss web browsers. Most computer users are familiar with the most popular browsers, such as Microsoft's Edge and Internet Explorer, Google's Chrome, Apple's Safari, Mozilla's Firefox, and the Opera browser.

But what is a web browser and what does a web browser do? A *web browser* is a software application used to locate, access, and display content on the World Wide Web, including web pages, images, video, and other files. Browsers are used primarily for displaying and accessing websites on the Internet and other content created using hypertext markup language (HTML), extensible markup language (XML), and so on (Techopedia 2017).

The World Wide Web provides visually engaging web pages and user interfaces for web applications. To better understand how the World Wide Web does this, we must first understand some of the technologies used to provide these features to users.

A *web-based application* refers to "any program that is accessed over a network connection using HTTP, rather than existing within a device's memory. Web-based applications often run inside a web browser. However, web-based applications also may be client-based, where a small part of the program is downloaded to a user's desktop, but processing is done over the Internet on an external server. Web-based applications are also known as web apps" (Techopedia 2017).

A *web server* is a "system that delivers content or services to end users over the Internet. A web server consists of a physical server, server operating system (OS) and software used to facilitate HTTP communication" (Techopedia 2017).

A *static web page* is "just a simple purveyor of information. Designers often use a combination of text and images, controlled by HTML tags, to render something that is a lot like a newspaper page. It has typesetting and layout, but it does not change from one load to another" (Techopedia 2017). In contrast, a *dynamic web server* serves both static and active content.

HTML, CSS, and JavaScript

Hypertext markup language (HTML), *cascading style sheets* (CSS), and *JavaScript* are three of the main technologies utilized by the World Wide Web to provide users a visually engaging experience. Let's further explain these three technologies.

Hypertext markup language (HTML) is the major markup language used to display web pages on the Internet. Web pages are composed of HTML, which is used to display text, images, or other resources through a web browser. All HTML is plaintext, meaning it can be read by humans (Techopedia 2017). To better understand HTML, surf the Internet to your favorite web page. Using the mouse, right-click and select the option to "View page source" or press the "ctrl" key and the letter "U" at the same time on your keyboard to view the HTML source code.

Cascading style sheets (CSS) is the standard for describing the formatting of markup-language pages (such as HTML). CSS defines the various elements for headings, subheadings, sub-subheadings, and so forth, in addition to providing element options for color, font, emphasis, size, and so on (Techopedia 2017). CSS provides a very similar functionality to how a word processor allows an individual to change the font and font size and add some headings and paragraphs to a document.

JavaScript is a scripting language primarily used on the World Wide Web. It is used to enhance HTML pages and is commonly found embedded in HTML. JavaScript renders web pages in an interactive and dynamic fashion. This allows the pages to react to events, exhibit special effects, accept variable text, validate data, create cookies, and detect a user's browser (Techopedia 2017). Business executives should understand cyber threat actors create malware using JavaScript to conduct web-based attacks.

Cookies are text files that a web browser stores on a user's machine. Cookies are used by websites for authentication, storing website information or preferences and other browsing information, and anything else that can help the web browser while accessing web servers (Techopedia 2017). Cookies assist websites in providing customized web pages for its customers, based on their browsing-history profile or preferences.

A *session* refers to a certain time frame for communication between two devices, two systems, or two parts of a system. For example, one of the most common is a client-server session between a server and a personal computer (or other device) accessing the server. Developers have developed session protocols for handling these interactions between systems. These session protocols cover all the many interactions required for browsing the World Wide Web and for sending and receiving e-mails from various e-mail clients. The common user does not recognize that these sessions are occurring and are actively hidden from the end user (Techopedia 2017).

Web-Application-Security Testing

As we have covered in previous chapters, the penetration-testing process also applies to web applications, websites, and web servers. The following paragraphs will help executives understand today's current methodology in the use of web-application-security testing.

As noted previously, the Open Web Application Security Project (OWASP) is a worldwide, not-for-profit, and charitable organization focused on improving the security of software, and the organization has a mission to make software security visible so that organizations and individuals can make informed decisions. All the OWASP materials are available under a free and open software license to anyone interested in improving application security (OWASP 2017).

Web-application-security testing "focuses only on evaluating the security of a web application. The process involves an active analysis of the application for any weaknesses, technical flaws, or vulnerabilities. Any security issues that are found will be presented to the system owner, together with an assessment of the impact, a proposal for mitigation or a technical solution" (OWASP 2017).

In "Web Application Security Testing," the fourth chapter of the fourth version of the *OWASP Testing Guide* (last updated April 2016), one will find one hundred different vulnerability-testing steps listed in the following areas:

4.1 Introduction and Objectives
4.2 Information Gathering (10 tests)
4.3 Configuration and Deployment Management testing (8 tests)
4.4 Identity Management testing (7 tests)
4.5 Authentication testing (10 tests)
4.6 Authorization testing (4 tests)

This OWASP guide is very detailed and covers these eleven different areas in web-application-security testing. What this means to a business executive is that there are dozens of potential vulnerabilities in an organization's use of web infrastructure and web applications that a cyber threat actor can exploit.

Let's review some of the more common threats to the web environment to gain a better understanding of how these web vulnerabilities can be exploited.

Information Gathering

Information gathering refers to when the cyber threat actor attempts to gather enough information to compromise the web environment. A cyber threat actor can use search engines like Google to obtain and aggregate information against the intended target. Many times, it is the web developer or web administrator who unintentionally leaves valuable information, such as administrative usernames, passwords, detailed comments in HTML, and indexes never meant to be accessed by the public but are accessible to the cyber threat actor with the use of certain tools.

Input Validation

One of the most common security weaknesses in web applications today is the failure to properly validate input coming from the client or from the environment before using it. This weakness leads to almost all the major vulnerabilities in web applications, such as SQL injection, cross-site scripting, buffer overflows, file system attacks, and more (OWASP 2017).

Input validation, also known as *data validation*, is a "process that ensures the delivery of clean and clear data to the programs, applications and services using it. It checks for the integrity and validity of data that is being inputted to different software and its components." Data validation ensures that the data sent to connected applications is complete, accurate, secure, and consistent. Input validation is achieved through data-validation checks and rules that check for the validity of the data (Techopedia 2017).

SQL Injection

If a web application is written to access a relational database, such as a Structured Query Language (SQL) database, there is a threat of SQL injection.

Structured Query Language (SQL) is a "standard computer language for relational database management and data manipulation. SQL is used to query, insert, update and modify data" (Techopedia 2017).

An *SQL-injection* attack is when the cyber threat actor uses SQL commands in malicious code and inputs this malicious code in a poorly designed application that is then passed to the back-end database. The malicious code then produces database-query results or actions that should have never been executed (Techopedia 2017).

By entering the "wrong" input, the unintentional results to this query can provide the cyber threat actor with SQL-database information, such as customer names, credit-card numbers, PII, PINs, and so on, and can have further devastating consequences if the cyber threat actor adds SQL statements, such as "DROP" and "DELETE," which will erase content in the SQL databases within the organization's IT infrastructure.

Cross-Site Scripting (XSS)

Cross-site scripting (XSS) is the process of a cyber threat actor adding malicious code, such as JavaScript, into a vulnerable website to gather web users' information, with malicious intent. These XSS cyberattacks are possible because of security vulnerabilities found in web applications and are commonly exploited by injecting a client-side script (Techopedia 2017).

There are three types of cross-site scripting vulnerabilities:

1. *Nonpersistent XSS vulnerabilities, or reflected XSS vulnerabilities,* occur when a cyber threat actor tricks the victim into processing a web address (URL) programmed with a malicious script to steal the victim's sensitive information, such as the victim's cookie or session ID. The principle behind this attack is exploiting the lack of proper input or output validation on dynamic web servers (Harris and Maymi 2016).

2. *Persistent XSS vulnerabilities*, or *stored XSS vulnerabilities*, are used in targeted websites that allow users to input data that is stored in forums, message boards, and other types of databases. The cyber threat actor posts some text that includes malicious JavaScript, and when other users view the posts later, their browsers render the page and execute the malicious JavaScript (Harris and Maymi 2016).

3. *Document object model* (DOM) *XSS* is the standard structure layout for representing HTML in the browser. In this XSS attack, the document components, such as form fields and cookies, can be referenced through JavaScript. The cyber threat actor uses this DOM environment to modify the original client-side JavaScript with malicious JavaScript and execute it on the victim's browser (Harris and Maymi 2016).

Cross-Site Request Forgery (CSRF)

Cross-site request forgery (CSRF) is a website exploit attack that is executed by issuing unauthorized commands from a trusted website user. To make a comparison, the CSRF exploits a website's trust for a particular user's browser; cross-site scripting (XSS) exploits the user's trust for a website (Techopedia 2017).

Command Injection

Command injection is an attack in which the cyber threat actor's goal is to execute arbitrary commands on the operating system of the web-server host via a vulnerable application. Command-injection attacks are possible when an application passes unsafe user-supplied data, such as cookies or forms. In this attack, the attacker-supplied operating-system commands are usually executed with the privileges of the vulnerable application. This attack is largely due to insufficient input validation (OWASP 2017).

Web-Security Tools

After assessing and synthesizing the foundational background of the World Wide Web, its associated technologies, and the dozens of potential web-environment threats that an organization faces in today's cyber environment, business executives need to understand how to protect their business organizations' IT web infrastructures from cyber threat actors.

There are many aspects to having a secure web environment. One important cybersecurity step in protecting an organization's web infrastructure is to have professional penetration testers who specialize in web-infrastructure and web-application-security penetration testing conduct a web-security penetration test of the organization's web environment. These specially trained penetration testers will assist the organization in identifying the possible vulnerabilities impacting the organization's web environment and mitigating these vulnerabilities from being exploited.

Another step in protecting an organization's web infrastructure is to have the relevant cybersecurity-trained IT staff use automated web-testing tools, also known as web-security proxies. A *web proxy* is a "piece of software installed on a system that is designed to intercept all traffic between the local web browser and the web server" (Harris and Maymi 2016). The use of web-security proxies allows cybersecurity-trained IT staff to identify web vulnerabilities and mitigate those vulnerabilities before cyber threat actors find and exploit them. There are various web-security proxies available to your cybersecurity-trained IT staff, including Portswigger's Burp Suite Professional and OWASP's Zed Attack Proxy (ZAP) Project.

Burp Suite Professional is a web proxy with integrated tools that work together to support the entire testing process from mapping, analyzing the attack surface, and finding and exploiting security vulnerabilities (Portswigger Web Security 2017).

The OWASP Zed Attack Proxy (ZAP) Project is one of the world's most popular free security tools and supported by hundreds of volunteers worldwide. This free web proxy is designed to find security vulnerabilities in an organization's web applications (OWASP 2017).

In summary, business executives need to understand how the World Wide Web, web applications, and web-focused cyber threats impact an organization's IT infrastructure. By understanding the basics of web servers, web browsers, HTML, JavaScript, CSS, HTTP, HTTPS, and other web topic areas, business executives will be better prepared to understand these web-focused threats to their organization's web infrastructure. Cyber-savvy business executives are better prepared to strategically resource and prepare their organizations in countering such web-environment threats as information gathering and input validation, as well as web attacks, such as cross-site scripting (XSS), cross-site request forgery (CSRF), command injection, and SQL-injection attacks. Business executives must consider web-application security and understand that there are dozens of known vulnerabilities impacting web applications. Business executives need to consider implementing proactive strategies to provide the best cybersecurity posture for their organizations' web infrastructures. Such proactive strategies include having regularly scheduled web-security penetration tests by qualified security professionals and the use of web proxies to assist in identifying and mitigating web-application vulnerabilities.

Third-Party and Vendor Risk

In both the public and private sector, organizations may allow vendors and third parties to connect to the organization's IT infrastructure. Such third parties could include points of sale, basic utilities, cloud storage, and managed service providers (MSPs) who manage an organization's application, network, and system infrastructure. These third-party network connections can provide cyber threat actors another intrusion vector into your organization's most sensitive data.

A 2016 survey of over 200 IT and security C-Level executives, directors and managers at enterprise-level companies determined that only two percent of respondents consider third-party secure access a top priority despite the strategic cyber threat of third-party risk. This survey determined:

1. Third-party access was not an IT priority, yet third-party access was a major source of data breaches
2. Respondents believed their own organizations were secure from third-party data breaches but thought their competitors were vulnerable to them
3. Providing third-party access was complex and tedious and has many moving parts and
4. IT professionals take data breaches personally but are not worried about losing their jobs due to a breach (Soha Systems 2016).

Business executives need to understand the strategic impact of a third-party data breach whose long-term effects include expensive forensic response and investigative services, legal liability from impacted parties (including customers), strategic damage to an organization's brand and reputation, and costly remediation of the organization's IT infrastructure to improve its cybersecurity posture.

A notable example of the dangers of third-party risk is described in the April 2017 PwC Operation Cloud Hopper report where an established China-based

APT actor targeted MSPs allowing unprecedented potential access to the most sensitive data of those MSPs and their global clients. This APT actor targeted multiple sectors including the engineering and construction sector, retail and consumer sector, energy and mining sector, industrial manufacturing sector, public sector, pharmaceuticals and life science sector, technology sector, metals sector, and business and professionals sectors. These multiple sectors were in multiple countries including the US, Canada, Brazil, Finland, Norway, UK, France, Switzerland, India, South Korea, South Africa, Australia, Japan, and Thailand (PwC 2017).

Business executives of these impacted victim organizations must now meet with their respective MSPs to review and determine the strategic impact of this unauthorized access and possible theft of their critical data, such as intellectual property. The MSPs executives also have the strategic responsibility to identify what client data was accessed and possibly compromised, and provide this information to all victim clients to assist these victim clients to determine how they strategically proceed with the incredible impact of this strategic cyber breach. This is a very sobering responsibility for the business executives of these victim client organizations. These business executives now must attempt to determine the future course of their organization's strategic direction based on the impact of this incredible breach, especially if their intellectual property for future and next generation products has been compromised by this China-based APT actor.

Some notable data breaches over the last few years include the December 2013 Target breach where cyber threat actor's obtained unauthorized access into Target's IT infrastructure by illegally obtaining the credentials of a third-party heating, ventilation, and air conditioning (HVAC) vendor which had an external connection with Target for electronic billing, contract submission, and project management (Mlot 2014). Because of this unauthorized cyber intrusion, approximately 40 million credit and debit card accounts were stolen which has cost Target $202 million as of May 2017 (Ramakrishnan and Bose 2017). During the September 2014 Home Depot data breach, cyber threat actors illegally used a third-party vendor log-on credentials to gain unauthorized access to Home Depot's IT infrastructure and steal 56 million credit and debit cards and 53 million e-mail addresses in the U.S. and Canada (Winter 2014). As of March 2017, based on a review of court records, this data breach has cost Home Depot at least $179 million (Roberts 2017).

Business executives need to ensure their CIO, CISO, CSO or IT director (1) identify all third-party connections to their organization's IT infrastructure and (2) conduct a strategic risk assessment as to the necessity of the third-party access connections to the organization's IT infrastructure. If the risk assessment identifies alternative non-IT connectivity methods or processes which meet the organization's objectives with the third-party, these alternate non-IT connected methods should be considered to minimize the cyber threat risk of third-party vendors. These risk assessments should also consider whether the cybersecurity posture of all necessary third-party vendor's meet or exceed, the high cybersecurity standards of your respective organization. If these third-party vendors do not meet your organization's high cybersecurity standards, thoughtful consideration should be made in finding alternative third-party vendors whose cybersecurity posture meets or exceeds your organization's high cybersecurity standards.

In summary, business executives need to work with their CIO, CISO, CSO or IT director to strategically identify all third-party vendor connections to the organization's IT infrastructure. The CIO, CISO, CSO or IT Director must conduct a strategic risk assessment as to the necessity of this third-party vendor access and ensure all necessary third-party vendor risk is minimized by requiring the highest cybersecurity posture to have the privilege to have secure access to the organization's IT infrastructure.

8

CYBERCRIME AND HACKTIVISM

What do Cryptowall ransomware, Locky ransomware, business e-mail compromise (BEC), Zeus financial malware, distributed-denial-of-service (DDOS) and denial-of-service (DOS) attacks, Tor, and Bitcoin have in common? These are just some of the tools used by today's cybercriminals to commit cybercrime.

Business executives do not need to understand the intricacies of the various cybercriminal tools or the details of the difference between Cryptowall ransomware and Locky ransomware. But business executives do need to understand that ransomware and other cybercrime vectors used by cybercriminals can cause strategic chaos for a business organization and can cause a very significant and negative impact on the organizations' IT infrastructures.

A business organization can suffer a cyberattack through financial malware or a phishing e-mail, such as a business e-mail compromise in which an unauthorized wire transfer is initiated and money is sent to overseas banks, where the cybercriminals quickly cash out.

On May 4, 2017, the FBI's Internet Crime Complaint Center (also known as IC3) posted a public service announcement (PSA) titled "Business E-mail Compromise: The 5 Billion Dollar Scam." In it, the center defined *business e-mail compromise* as a "sophisticated scam targeting businesses working with foreign suppliers and/or businesses that regularly perform wire transfer payments. The E-mail Account Compromise (EAC) component of BEC targets individuals that perform wire transfer payments."

This PSA describes five different types of BEC/EAC scenarios in use by cybercriminals at the time this PSA was published:

1. Business Working with a Foreign Supplier;
2. Business Executive Receiving or Initiating a Request for a Wire Transfer;
3. Business Contacts Receiving Fraudulent Correspondence through Compromise E-mail;
4. Business Executive and Attorney Impersonation; and
5. Data Theft.

> The BEC/EAC scam is carried out when a cyber threat actor compromises legitimate business e-mail accounts through social engineering or computer intrusion techniques to conduct unauthorized transfers of funds. (Federal Bureau of Investigation Internet Crime Complaint Center 2017)

IC3 advised that from October 2013 to December 2016, there were 40,203 BEC/EAC domestic and international incidents with a totaled combined exposed dollar loss of $5.3 billion. IC3 combined these statistics for this same time period from multiple sources including IC3 victim complaints and complaints filed with international law-enforcement agencies and financial institutions. During this same time period, there were 22,292 US victims with a total combined exposed dollar loss of almost $1.6 billion and 2,053 non-US victims with a total combined exposed dollar loss of almost $627 million, which were reported to IC3 via victim complaints (Federal Bureau of Investigation Internet Crime Complaint Center 2017).

On June 23, 2015, IC3 issued a PSA regarding cybercriminals continuing to defraud and extort funds from victims using ransomware schemes, specifically Cryptowall ransomware. This malware would be executed when a victim clicked on an infected e-mail or attachment and then would infect the victim's device. Once the victim's device was infected with the ransomware, the victim's files would become encrypted. For the victims to decrypt and regain access to their files, cybercriminals demanded a ransom payment of some type of virtual currency, which made it more difficult for law-enforcement agencies to track (Federal Bureau of Investigation Internet Crime Complaint Center 2015).

There has been a significant increase in the number of victims of ransomware during 2016. On April 29, 2016, the FBI published a PSA titled "Incidents of Ransomware on the Rise." This PSA indicated that law-enforcement agencies, state and local governments, school districts, hospitals, and small and large businesses were some of the entities victimized by ransomware (Federal Bureau of Investigation 2016).

Once a victim is infected with the ransomware by either clicking an e-mail with an infected attachment or a URL that directs the victim to a website with the malicious software that then infects his or her computer, the ransomware begins to encrypt files and folders located on local drives, attached drives, and other computers on the same network as the victim computer. A message is then shown on the victim's computer screen, advising of the ransomware attack and encryption of his or her files and folders, and demands a ransom payment in exchange for the decryption key. This message also includes payment instructions, usually in a virtual currency (such as Bitcoin), because of the anonymity this virtual currency provides (Federal Bureau of Investigation 2016).

This cyber threat vector has only increased during 2017. Ransomware has now grown to the point that it has had a global impact. As mentioned previously, the May 12, 2017, WannaCry ransomware attack had an immediate and global impact on over 150 countries, impacting hundreds of thousands of people. This was soon followed by the powerful and massive global cyberattack of the Petya (also known as Petrwrap) ransomware, which impacted dozens of countries but had the greatest impact on the country of Ukraine, where the ransomware targeted government ministries, banks, utilities, and private-sector companies nationwide (Roth and Nakashima 2017).

A list of the twelve types of ransomware described as the worst types of ransomware (as of July 2017) included

1. GoldenEye
2. WannaCry
3. CryptoLocker
4. Locky
5. Petya
6. Crysis
7. zCrypt
8. PowerWare

9. HydraCrypt
10. Cerber
11. RAA Ransomware
12. Cryptowall (Dunn 2017)

A strategic impact of ransomware on the business community is the destruction of sensitive organizational and customer data due to a ransomware infection. It is incumbent on business executives to ensure that their organization have multiple backups of this sensitive data so that it can be restored properly in the case that the organization's servers containing this sensitive data are compromised with ransomware.

Business executives need to understand that the ransom payment is not the only tactical cost when an organization suffers from a ransomware cyberattack. In addition to the possible payment of the ransom (due to lack of proper backups), an organization may suffer strategic costs such as public humiliation and damage to the organization's brand if this ransomware attack becomes public, a negative impact on its stock price (if publicly traded), loss of customers, mitigation costs, legal fees, costs to upgrade network security and the IT infrastructure, loss of productivity, and if customer PII is compromised, the cost for credit monitoring services for exposed customers and potential legal liability.

Types of Cybercrime Schemes

The FBI's IC3 has identified some of the most popular Internet-cybercrime schemes and has provided summary explanations of each of the following cybercrime schemes:

1. *Auction fraud*—"Auction fraud involves fraud attributable to the misrepresentation of a product advertised for sale through an Internet auction site or the nondelivery of products purchased through an Internet auction site" (Federal Bureau of Investigation Internet Crime Complaint Center 2017).
2. *Counterfeit cashier's check*—"The counterfeit cashier's check scheme targets individuals that use Internet classified advertisements to sell merchandise. Typically, an interested party located outside the United States contacts a seller. The seller is told that the buyer has an associate

in the United States that owes him money. As such, he will have the associate send the seller a cashier's check for the amount owed to the buyer. The amount of the cashier's check will be thousands of dollars more than the price of the merchandise, and the seller is told the excess amount will be used to pay the shipping costs associated with getting the merchandise to his location. The seller is instructed to deposit the check and, as soon as it clears, to wire the excess funds back to the buyer or to another associate identified as a shipping agent. In most instances, the money is sent to locations in West Africa (Nigeria). Because a cashier's check is used, a bank will typically release the funds immediately, or after a one or two day hold. Falsely believing the check has cleared, the seller wires the money as instructed. In some cases, the buyer is able to convince the seller that some circumstance has arisen that necessitates the cancellation of the sale, and is successful in conning the victim into sending the remainder of the money. Shortly thereafter, the victim's bank notifies him that the check was fraudulent, and the bank is holding the victim responsible for the full amount of the check" (Federal Bureau of Investigation Internet Crime Complaint Center 2017).

3. *Credit-card fraud*—"The Internet Crime Complaint Center has received multiple reports alleging foreign subjects are using fraudulent credit cards. The unauthorized use of a credit/debit card, or card number, to fraudulently obtain money or property is considered credit card fraud. Credit/debit card numbers can be stolen from unsecured websites, or can be obtained in an identity theft scheme" (Federal Bureau of Investigation Internet Crime Complaint Center 2017).

4. *Debt elimination*—"Debt elimination schemes generally involve websites advertising a legal way to dispose of mortgage loans and credit card debts. Most often, all that is required of the participant is to send $1,500 to $2,000 to the subject, along with all the particulars of the participant's loan information and a special power of attorney authorizing the subject to enter into transactions regarding the title of the participant's homes on their behalf. The subject then issues bonds and promissory notes to the lenders that purport to legally satisfy the debts of the participant. In exchange, the participant is

then required to pay a certain percentage of the value of the satisfied debts to the subject. The potential risk of identity theft related crimes associated with the debt elimination scheme is extremely high because the participants provide all of their personal information to the subject" (Federal Bureau of Investigation Internet Crime Complaint Center 2017).

5. *Parcel courier e-mail scheme*—"The Parcel Courier E-mail Scheme involves the supposed use of various National and International level parcel providers such as DHL, UPS, FedEx and the USPS. Often, the victim is directly e-mailed by the subject(s) following online bidding on auction sites. Most of the scams follow a general pattern which includes the following elements:

- The subject instructs the buyer to provide shipping information such as name and address.
- The subject informs the buyer that the item will be available at the selected parcel provider in the buyer's name and address, thereby identifying the intended receiver.
- The selected parcel provider checks the item and purchase documents to guarantee everything is in order.
- The selected parcel provider sends the buyer delivery notification verifying their receipt of the item.
- The buyer is instructed by the subject to go to an electronic funds transfer medium, such as Western Union, and make a funds transfer in the subject's name and in the amount of the purchase price.
- After the funds transfer, the buyer is instructed by the subject to forward the selected parcel provider the funds transfer identification number, as well as their name and address associated with the transaction.
- The subject informs the buyer the parcel provider will verify payment information and complete the delivery process.
- Upon completion of delivery and inspection of the item(s) by the receiver, the buyer provides the parcel provider funds transfer information, thus allowing the seller to receive his funds" (Federal Bureau of Investigation Internet Crime Complaint Center 2017).

6. *Employment/business opportunities*—"Employment/business opportunity schemes have surfaced wherein bogus foreign-based companies are recruiting citizens in the United States on several employment-search websites for work-at-home employment opportunities. These positions often involve reselling or reshipping merchandise to destinations outside the United States. Prospective employees are required to provide personal information, as well as copies of their identification, such as a driver's license, birth certificate, or social security card. Those employees that are 'hired' by these companies are then told that their salary will be paid by check from a United States company reported to be a creditor of the employer. This is done under the pretense that the employer does not have any banking set up in the United States. The amount of the check is significantly more than the employee is owed for salary and expenses, and the employee is instructed to deposit the check into their own account, and then wire the overpayment back to the employer's bank, usually located in Eastern Europe. The checks are later found to be fraudulent, often after the wire transfer has taken place. In a similar scam, some web-based international companies are advertising for affiliate opportunities, offering individuals the chance to sell high-end electronic items, such as plasma television sets and home theater systems, at significantly reduced prices. The affiliates are instructed to offer the merchandise on well-known Internet auction sites. The affiliates will accept the payments and pay the company, typically by means of wire transfer. The company is then supposed to drop-ship the merchandise directly to the buyer, thus eliminating the need for the affiliate to stock or warehouse merchandise. The merchandise never ships, which often prompts the buyers to take legal action against the affiliates, who in essence are victims themselves" (Federal Bureau of Investigation Internet Crime Complaint Center 2017).

7. *Escrow-services fraud*—"In an effort to persuade a wary Internet auction participant, the perpetrator will propose the use of a third-party escrow service to facilitate the exchange of money and merchandise. The victim is unaware the perpetrator has actually compromised a true escrow site and, in actuality, created one that closely resembles a legitimate escrow service. The victim sends payment to the phony escrow and receives nothing in return. Or, the victim sends

merchandise to the subject and waits for his/her payment through the escrow site which is never received because it is not a legitimate service" (Federal Bureau of Investigation Internet Crime Complaint Center 2017).

8. *Identity theft*—"Identity theft occurs when someone appropriates another's personal information without their knowledge to commit theft or fraud. Identity theft is a vehicle for perpetrating other types of fraud schemes. Typically, the victim is led to believe they are divulging sensitive personal information to a legitimate business, sometimes as a response to an e-mail solicitation to update billing or membership information, or as an application to a fraudulent Internet job posting" (Federal Bureau of Investigation Internet Crime Complaint Center 2017).

9. *Internet extortion*—"Internet extortion involves hacking into and controlling various industry databases, promising to release control back to the company if funds are received, or the subjects are given web administrator jobs. Similarly, the subject will threaten to compromise information about consumers in the industry database unless funds are received" (Federal Bureau of Investigation Internet Crime Complaint Center 2017).

10. *Investment fraud*—"Investment fraud is an offer using false or fraudulent claims to solicit investments or loans, or providing for the purchase, use, or trade of forged or counterfeit securities" (Federal Bureau of Investigation Internet Crime Complaint Center 2017).

11. *Lotteries*—"The lottery scheme deals with persons randomly contacting e-mail addresses advising them they have been selected as the winner of an International lottery. The Internet Crime Complaint Center has identified numerous lottery names being used in this scheme. The e-mail message usually reads similar to the following:

> 'This is to inform you of the release of money winnings to you. Your e-mail was randomly selected as the winner and therefore you have been approved for a lump sum payout of $500,000.00. To begin your lottery claim, please contact the processing company selected to process your winnings.' An agency name follows this body of text with

a point of contact, phone number, fax number, and an e-mail address. An initial fee ranging from $1,000 to $5,000 is often requested to initiate the process and additional fee requests follow after the process has begun. These e-mails may also list a United States point of contact and address while also indicating the point of contact at a foreign address" (Federal Bureau of Investigation Internet Crime Complaint Center 2017).

12. *Nigerian letters,* or *419 scams*—"Named for the violation of Section 419 of the Nigerian Criminal Code, the 419 scam combines the threat of impersonation fraud with a variation of an advance fee scheme in which a letter, e-mail, or fax is received by the potential victim. The communication from individuals representing themselves as Nigerian or foreign government officials offers the recipient the 'opportunity' to share in a percentage of millions of dollars, soliciting for help in placing large sums of money in overseas bank accounts. Payment of taxes, bribes to government officials, and legal fees are often described in great detail with the promise that all expenses will be reimbursed as soon as the funds are out of the country. The recipient is encouraged to send information to the author, such as blank letterhead stationery, bank name and account numbers, and other identifying information using a facsimile number provided in the letter. The scheme relies on convincing a willing victim to send money to the author of the letter in several installments of increasing amounts for a variety of reasons" (Federal Bureau of Investigation Internet Crime Complaint Center 2017).

13. *Phishing,* or *spoofing*—"Phishing and spoofing are somewhat synonymous in that they refer to forged or faked electronic documents. Spoofing generally refers to the dissemination of an e-mail which is forged to appear as though it was sent by someone other than the actual source. Phishing, often utilized in conjunction with a spoofed e-mail, is the act of sending an e-mail falsely claiming to be an established legitimate business in an attempt to dupe the unsuspecting recipient into divulging personal, sensitive information, such as passwords, credit card numbers, and bank account information after directing the user to visit a specified website. The website, however, is not genuine and was set up

only as an attempt to steal the user's information" (Federal Bureau of Investigation Internet Crime Complaint Center 2017).

14. *Ponzi* or *pyramid*—"Ponzi or pyramid schemes are investment scams in which investors are promised abnormally high profits on their investments. No investment is actually made. Early investors are paid returns with the investment money received from the later investors. The system usually collapses. The later investors do not receive dividends and lose their initial investment" (Federal Bureau of Investigation Internet Crime Complaint Center 2017).

15. *Reshipping*—"The 'reshipping' scheme requires individuals in the United States, who sometimes are coconspirators and other times are unwitting accomplices, to receive packages at their residence and subsequently repackage the merchandise for shipment, usually abroad. 'Reshippers' are being recruited in various ways, but the most prevalent are through employment offers and conversing, and later befriending, unsuspecting victims through Internet Relay Chat Rooms. Unknown subjects post help-wanted advertisements at popular Internet job search sites, and respondents quickly reply to the online advertisement. As part of the application process, the prospective employee is required to complete an employment application, wherein he/she divulges sensitive personal information, such as their date of birth and social security number which, unbeknownst to the victim employee, will be used to obtain credit in his/her name. The applicant is informed he/she has been hired and will be responsible for forwarding, or 'reshipping,' merchandise purchased in the United States to the company's overseas home office. The packages quickly begin to arrive and, as instructed, the employee dutifully forwards the packages to their overseas destination. Unbeknownst to the 'reshipper,' the recently received merchandise was purchased with fraudulent credit cards. The second means of recruitment involves the victim conversing with the unknown individual in various Internet Relay Chat Rooms. After establishing this new online 'friendship' or 'love' relationship, the unknown subject explains for various legal reasons his/her country will not allow direct business shipments into his/her country from the United States. He/she then asks for permission to send recently purchased items to the victim's United States address for subsequent shipments abroad for which the unknown subject explains he/she

will cover all shipping expenses. After the United States citizen agrees, the packages start to arrive at great speed. This fraudulent scheme lasts several weeks until the 'reshipper' is contacted. The victimized merchants explain to the 'reshipper' the recent shipments were purchased with fraudulent credit cards. Shortly thereafter, the strings of attachment are untangled and the boyfriend/girlfriend realizes their Cyber relationship was nothing more than an Internet scam to help facilitate the transfer of goods purchased online by fraudulent means" (Federal Bureau of Investigation Internet Crime Complaint Center 2017).

16. *Spam*—"With improved technology and worldwide Internet access, spam, or unsolicited bulk e-mail, is now a widely used medium for committing traditional white collar crimes including financial institution fraud, credit card fraud, and identity theft, among others. It is usually considered unsolicited because the recipients have not opted to receive the e-mail. Generally, this bulk e-mail refers to multiple identical messages sent simultaneously. Those sending this spam are violating the Controlling the Assault of Non-Solicited Pornography and Marketing (CAN-SPAM) Act, Title 18, US Code, Section 1037. Spam can also act as the vehicle for accessing computers and servers without authorization and transmitting viruses and botnets. The subjects masterminding this Spam often provide hosting services and sell open proxy information, credit card information, and e-mail lists illegally" (Federal Bureau of Investigation Internet Crime Complaint Center 2017).

17. *Third-party receiver of funds*—"A general trend has been noted by the Internet Crime Complaint Center regarding work-at-home schemes on websites. In several instances, the subjects, usually foreign, post work-at-home job offers on popular Internet employment sites, soliciting for assistance from United States citizens. The subjects allegedly are posting Internet auctions, but cannot receive the proceeds from these auctions directly because his/her location outside the United States makes receiving these funds difficult. The seller asks the United States citizen to act as a third party receiver of funds from victims who have purchased products from the subject via the Internet. The United States citizen, receiving the funds from the victims, then wires the money to the subject" (Federal Bureau of Investigation Internet Crime Complaint Center 2017).

Hacktivism

Hacktivism, as it relates to the cybercriminal element, is the unauthorized access into a computer or computer network by a cyber threat actor with a political or socially motivated goal.

Hacktivism is another cyber threat that can have a strategic impact on both the private and public sectors. Hacktivist groups such as Anonymous conduct cyberattacks on both sectors. During its peak, Anonymous conducted web defacements, denial-of-service attacks, and computer intrusions resulting in data breaches on numerous private- and public-sector entities.

It was numerous global law-enforcement actions conducted by the FBI and its international law-enforcement partners that resulted in the indictment and arrest of multiple Anonymous members in 2011 through 2013 (Federal Bureau of Investigation 2011).

Anonymous members Ryan "Kayla" Ackroyd, Jake "Topiary" Davis, Darren "Pwnsauce" Martyn, Donncha "Palladium" O'Cearrbhail, and Jeremy "Anarchaos" Hammond were all charged by the FBI on March 6, 2012, with computer hacking that affected over one million victims and victim companies, which included HB Gary Inc., Sony Pictures Entertainment, Fox Broadcasting Company, PBS, and Strategic Forecasting Inc. (Federal Bureau of Investigation 2012).

During 2015 and 2016, Anonymous continued to conduct cyberattacks against law-enforcement agencies in the United States that had officer-involved shootings that were caught on video and shared via social media. Some of these shootings raised questions, including the appropriate use of lethal force, and were the reason cited by Anonymous as to why the cyberattacks were conducted by Anonymous. During April 2015 (Federal Bureau of Investigation Internet Crime Complaint Center 2015) and November 2015 (Federal Bureau of Investigation Internet Crime Complaint Center 2015), the FBI IC3 issued two PSAs titled "Hacktivists Threaten to Target Law Enforcement Personnel and Public Officials" to warn the law-enforcement community about the targeting of law-enforcement personnel by hacktivists.

Business executives must treat hacktivist groups such as Anonymous with the same strategic level of concern as other cyber threat actors. These hacktivist groups have been very successful in conducting sophisticated cyberattacks by using various cyber-intrusion techniques against both private and public sectors.

Insider Threat

According to the Carnegie Mellon University Software Engineering Institute's CERT Insider Threat Center, an *insider threat* is a "current or former employee, contractor, or other business partner who has or had authorized access to an organization's network, system, or data and intentionally exceeded or misused that access in a manner that negatively affected the confidentiality, integrity, or availability of the organization's information or information system" (Carnegie Mellon University Software Engineering Institute CERT 2017).

Most business executives have heard of insider threats such as the FBI's Robert Hansen and the CIA's Aldrich Ames. Hansen, a twenty-five-year FBI agent employed as an FBI counterintelligence supervisor, spied for the Russians from 1979 until his arrest on February 18, 2001. Hansen compromised counterintelligence and military secrets, identities of dozens of human sources, and highly classified documents regarding US strategies in various areas (US Department of Justice Office of the Inspector General 2003). Hansen provided the Russians with US secrets, including the identities of three Russian agents who had been secretly recruited to spy for the United States, which was considered an extremely grave breach of national security (Johnston 2001).

Aldrich Ames, a thirty-one-year veteran CIA counterintelligence officer, spied for the Russians from 1985 until his arrest on February 21, 1994. During his debriefing by FBI agents after his guilty plea, Ames described his compromising the identities of both FBI and CIA human assets, which led to the execution of some of those human assets by Russian authorities (Federal Bureau of Investigation 2017).

The best example of the insider threat in today's digital landscape is Edward Snowden, the former US National Security Agency (NSA) contractor who leaked documents detailing US top-secret surveillance programs, and he acquired those documents while working at the NSA as a systems analyst. Snowden revealed himself as the leaker of those highly classified documents in a media interview on June 9, 2013. Subsequently, media outlets around the globe published details of the most-secret surveillance programs undertaken by the United States (Finn and Horwitz 2013).

During June 2013, the FBI charged Edward Snowden, via an unsealed complaint in the Eastern District of Virginia, with (1) theft of government property, (2) unauthorized communication of national-defense information, and (3) willful communication of classified communications intelligence information to an unauthorized person (Finn and Horwitz 2013). Edward Snowden currently resides in Russia as a fugitive from justice.

Another insider-threat example would be Jason Cornish, a former IT employee of Shionogi Inc., a US subsidiary of a Japanese pharmaceutical company that had operations in New Jersey. After Cornish resigned from Shionogi Inc. in September 2010, Shionogi Inc. announced it would have to implement layoffs, which directly impacted his former supervisor and close friend, identified only by B. N. in the press release provided by the US attorney's office in the District of New Jersey (Federal Bureau of Investigation 2011).

In February 2011, while connected to a McDonald's wireless network in Smyrna, Georgia, after making a purchase via his credit card, Cornish conducted a computer intrusion into Shionogi's computer networks. Cornish conducted the computer intrusion by accessing a Shionogi server via a Shionogi user account. While having this unauthorized network access, Cornish accessed software he had previously and secretly installed on this server several weeks earlier. Using this software, Cornish deleted the contents of fifteen virtual hosts (which are "subdivisions on a computer designed to make it function like several computers") of Shionogi's computer network. These fifteen virtual hosts housed the equivalent of eighty-eight different computer servers on Shionogi's computer network. The deleted servers included Shionogi's e-mail and BlackBerry servers, its financial-management software, and its order-tracking system. This cyberattack resulted in stopping Shionogi's operations for days and preventing Shionogi from writing checks, communicating by e-mail, and shipping its products, resulting in the loss of at least $300,000. In addition, Cornish had conducted computer intrusions of Shionogi's computer network from his home Internet connection by using administrative passwords that he had access to while employed by Shionogi. On July 1, 2011, Cornish was arrested by the FBI and charged via complaint with "knowingly transmitting computer code with the intent to damage computers in interstate commerce" (Federal Bureau of Investigation 2011).

On August 16, 2011, Cornish pleaded guilty and admitted to executing the cyber intrusion on Shionogi's computer networks (Federal Bureau of Investigation 2011). On December 9, 2011, Cornish was sentenced to forty-one months in federal prison and three years of supervised release, and he was ordered to make a restitution in the amount of $812,567 (US Attorney's Office for New Jersey 2011).

Robert Hansen and Aldrich Ames are great examples of the insider threat to the US intelligence community. Jason Cornish is a great example of today's IT professionals who become insider threats in the corporate world and can create strategic chaos to an organization by making a few key strokes from thousands of miles away. Edward Snowden is the best example of the insider threat in today's digital environment to both private- and public-sector entities because he damaged not only the United States and its national-security posture but also the reputations of the private-sector entities that employed Snowden as a contractor, as well as NSA and its employees.

International Cybercrime Cooperation

The Council of Europe Convention on Cybercrime (also known as the Budapest Convention) was signed on November 23, 2001. The Budapest Convention is "the first international treaty on crimes committed via the Internet and other computer networks, dealing particularly with infringements of copyright, computer-related fraud, child pornography and violations of network security. It also contains a series of powers and procedures such as the search of computer networks and interception" (Council of Europe 2017).

The Budapest Convention's main objective is to "pursue a common criminal policy aimed at the protection of society against cybercrime, especially adopting appropriate legislation and fostering international cooperation" (Council of Europe 2017).

The Budapest Convention's principal aims include (1) "harmonizing the domestic criminal substantive law elements of offences and connected provisions in the area of cyber-crime," (2) "providing for domestic criminal procedural law powers necessary for the investigation and prosecution of such offences as well as other offences committed by means of a computer system or evidence in relation to which is in electronic form," and (3) "setting up a fast and effective regime of international cooperation" (Council of Europe 2001).

The Budapest Convention contains four chapters: (1) "Use of Terms," (2) "Measures to Be Taken at a Domestic Level" (which include substantive law and procedural law), (3) "International Cooperation," and (4) "Final Clauses" (Council of Europe 2001).

As of July 15, 2017, fifty-five countries have ratified the convention, and four countries have signed but not ratified it. The United States signed the Budapest

Convention on November 23, 2001, and ratified the Budapest Convention on September 29, 2006 (Council of Europe 2017).

It should be noted that China and Russia, the two countries that are home to the greatest sources of cybercrime, have both refused to sign or ratify the Budapest Convention as of July 2017 (Drinkwater, "Estonia President Wants China and Russia to Help Fight Cyber-Crime" 2015).

International Cybercrime Investigations
GameOver Zeus Malware

Zeus, also known as Trojan Zbot, is a Trojan-horse malware that was discovered in January 2010 and impacts Windows operating systems. Zeus attempts to steal confidential information from a victim's compromised computer. It may also download updates from the Internet. This malware is distributed through spam campaigns and drive-by downloads. In addition, a potential victim may receive an e-mail message purporting to be from his or her bank or organizations, such as the FDIC, IRS, Facebook, or Microsoft, and the e-mail message usually warns a user of a problem with his or her financial information and suggests visiting a link provided in the e-mail. If the user visits the link, the computer will be compromised if it is not protected against this malware (Symantec 2016).

The FBI began investigating online account-takeover fraud related to Zeus in the summer of 2009. Starting in September 2011, the FBI began investigating a modified version of the Zeus Trojan, known as GameOver Zeus (GOZ). This malware was used to capture bank-account numbers, passwords, and personal-identification numbers used to log into online banking accounts. As of June 2014, it was believed that the GOZ malware had been responsible for infecting more than one million computers, resulting in an estimated $100 million in financial losses (US Department of Justice 2014).

In addition, the victims' infected computers also secretly became part of a global network of compromised computers known as a botnet. The GOZ botnet operated silently on the victims' computers by directing those computers to reach out to receive commands from other computers in the botnet and to funnel stolen banking credentials back to the criminals who were controlling the botnet (US Department of Justice 2014).

Evgeniy Mikhailovich Bogachev has been identified as the administrator of GOZ malware, along with others who were involved in this cybercriminal scheme to distribute spam and phishing e-mails that contained links to compromised websites. Computer users who visited these compromised websites became victims of the GOZ malware (US Department of Justice 2014).

On August 22, 2012, Evgeniy Mikhailovich Bogachev, also known by his online monikers "lucky12345" and "slavik," and eight others were indicted by a federal grand jury in the District of Nebraska on the following charges:

1. Conspiracy to participate in racketeering activity
2. Bank fraud
3. Conspiracy to violate the Computer Fraud and Abuse Act
4. Conspiracy to violate the Identity Theft and Assumption Deterrence Act
5. Aggravated identity theft (Federal Bureau of Investigation 2017)

On May 19, 2014, Bogachev was indicted in his true name by a federal grand jury in the Western District of Pennsylvania on the following charges:

1. Conspiracy
2. Computer fraud
3. Wire fraud
4. Bank fraud
5. Money laundering

On May 30, 2014, a criminal complaint was issued in the District of Nebraska that tied the previously indicted nickname lucky12345 to Bogachev and charged him with conspiracy to commit bank fraud.

Bogachev, last known to reside in Anapa, Russia, is currently on the FBI's most-wanted list for cyber criminals, and the US Department of State's Transnational Organized Crime Rewards Program is offering a reward of up to $3 million for information leading to Bogachev's arrest or conviction (Federal Bureau of Investigation 2017).

SpyEye

During April 2016, Aleksandr Andreevich Panin, also known as "Gribodemon," of Russia, and Hamza Bendelladj, also known as "Bx1," of Algeria, two international cyber threat actors who developed and distributed the malware known as SpyEye, were sentenced by a US federal judge to a combined sentence of over twenty-four years in federal prison. SpyEye caused hundreds of millions of dollars in losses to the financial industry around the world (US Attorney's Office Northern District of Georgia 2016).

SpyEye is a Trojan that captures key strokes and steals log-in credentials through a method known as "form grabbing." SpyEye sends captured data to a remote attacker, can download additional malicious components, and can use a rootkit component to hide malicious activity (Microsoft 2012).

SpyEye was the preeminent banking malware Trojan from 2010 through 2012 and was used by global cyber threat actors around the world to infect over fifty million computers, causing close to $1 billion in financial harm to both individuals and financial institutions around the world (US Attorney's Office Northern District of Georgia 2016).

SpyEye was designed to automate the theft of confidential financial information, such as banking usernames and passwords, credit-card information, and PINs. This malware allowed the cybercriminals to remotely control the victim computers via command and control servers. Once the target computers were infected with SpyEye, cyber threat actors remotely accessed the computers without authorization and stole the victims' financial information through web injects, keystroke loggers, and credit-card grabbers. The malware would then transmit this financial information to the command and control servers being controlled by the cyber threat actors. The cyber threat actors then used the stolen information to steal money from the victims' financial accounts (US Attorney's Office Northern District of Georgia 2016).

Aleksandr Panin, who operated from Russia from 2009 to 2011, was the primary developer and distributor of SpyEye. In November 2010, Evgeniy Mikhailovich Bogachev (the former administrator of the Zeus malware) provided the Zeus malware source code and rights to Panin, and Panin created SpyEye as a successor to Zeus. Panin created various versions of SpyEye and allowed cyber threat actors to customize their SpyEye malware, which targeted specific financial institutions and credit-card companies. SpyEye was marketed and sold on Russian online, invite-only criminal forums, such as Darkode.com (US Attorney's Office Northern District of Georgia 2016).

A *criminal forum* is an online forum that serves as a meeting place for those interested in buying, selling, and trading malware, botnets, stolen PII, credit-card information, hacked server credentials, and other pieces of data and software that facilitate complex cybercrimes all over the world (Federal Bureau of Investigation 2015).

Hamza Bendelladj from Algeria transmitted over one million spam e-mails containing the various versions of SpyEye, which resulted in hundreds of thousands of victims in the United States. Bendelladj also developed and sold malicious plug-ins, or add-ons, that were designed to surreptitiously automate the theft of funds from victim accounts and spread the malware. Bendelladj stole personally identifiable information from almost five hundred thousand victims, stole hundreds of thousands of credit-card and bank-account numbers, and caused millions of dollars in losses to victims around the globe (US Attorney's Office Northern District of Georgia 2016).

Panin was arrested on July 1, 2013, in Atlanta, Georgia, and on January 28, 2014, Panin pleaded guilty to conspiring to commit wire fraud and bank fraud. Panin was sentenced by US District Court Judge Amy Totenberg to nine years and six months in prison and then three years of supervised release (US Attorney's Office Northern District of Georgia 2016).

Bendelladj was apprehended in Bangkok, Thailand, on January 5, 2013, and extradited to the United States on May 2, 2013. On June 26, 2015, Bendelladj pleaded guilty to all twenty-three counts charged in an indictment returned against Panin and Bendelladj on December 20, 2011, in the Northern District of Georgia. On April 20, 2016, Bendelladj was sentenced by US District Court Judge Totenberg to fifteen years in prison followed by three years of supervised release (US Attorney's Office Northern District of Georgia 2016).

Business executives should note the dedicated and successful international investigative efforts that continue to be made by the FBI, US Secret Service, and international law-enforcement partners to prosecute cyber threat actors around the world. The Zeus and SpyEye investigations are great examples of the dedicated international law-enforcement effort of bringing to justice those cyber threat actors involved in development and distribution of malware that has caused hundreds of millions of dollars in losses due to unauthorized cyber intrusions around the globe.

The successful prosecutions of international cyber threat actors take time, international cooperation, financial resources, and both US and international prosecutorial assistance.

The investigation of the Zeus malware began in the summer of 2009, and federal indictments were returned in 2012 and 2014. Nine subjects were indicted, two were arrested, and a $3 million reward was posted for the creator of the malware. The downside to this success story is that this is only one malware family created and operated by one cybercrime group, and it took years and substantial resources to bring federal cyber-intrusion charges against the cyber threat actors using the Zeus malware. The SpyEye cybercrime subjects operated from 2009 through 2011, were arrested during 2013 and 2014, and sentenced to prison during 2015 and 2016.

In summary, business executives need to have a foundational understanding of the various tools used by cyber threat actors, who commit various types of cybercrime schemes, including business e-mail compromise and ransomware. As a business executive, one cannot wait the duration and cost of the dedicated cyber investigative efforts by US law enforcement and international law enforcement partners to stop these cybercrime actors. Business executives responsible for the security of their organization's data and information must do everything they can to strategically protect their organization's IT infrastructure from these global cyber threat actors from compromising their business organization's IT infrastructure, data and information.

9

CYBER UNDERGROUND

Business executives must always be vigilant about the organization's competitors and how their organization maintains its competitive advantage against the competition.

Imagine an environment where cybercriminals get together to assemble their cybercrime tools, cybercrime services, secure communications, IT infrastructures, money exchanges, and cybercriminal expertise to continue to improve their cybercrime efforts. This type of place does in fact exist and is known as the *cyber underground*.

A business organization must understand its competitors and gain all public intelligence regarding their competitor's business endeavors. The reverse is true as an organization must also protect its initiatives, processes, strategic planning, research and development and intellectual property from its competitors to maintain its competitive business advantage.

When it comes to the cyber threat, business executives need to understand that cybercriminal enterprises around the world are always evolving and constantly improving the sophistication of their trade, tools, tactics, and techniques. The cyber underground and its components could be described as an organization that is striving to be continually profitable by organizing cybercriminal expertise in an environment such as a cybercriminal forum, at which cybercriminals can purchase the latest sophisticated malware, purchase zero-day exploits, rent or lease a botnet, use a coder to create malicious software or applications, or use money exchangers to convert stolen funds into virtual currency, such as Bitcoin.

Business executives must properly prepare against its organization's competitors to continue as a profitable entity and maintain continued success amongst its competition. A business executive must also prepare and constantly evolve to defend their organization against the cyber underground threat.

The following are two examples of international law-enforcement actions against two cyber underground forums, the Dark Market forum (2008) and the Darkode forum, which were targeted by Operation Shrouded Horizon in 2015.

Dark Market Cyber Underground Forum Investigation (2008)

For two years, an FBI special agent worked undercover as Master Splynter, a spammer and hacker, whose dedicated efforts led to the dismantlement of the cyber underground forum Dark Market. The undercover agent, having a reputation as one of the world's top spammers, would eventually become the administrator of the Dark Market underground forum, running the server and hosting the entire forum's communications (Mills 2009).

Dark Market was a cyber underground forum for "carders"—that is, cyber threat actors who buy and sell stolen identities and credit-card information online. The members of the Dark Market forum committed cyber intrusions in which they stole and then sold credit card numbers. The Dark Market forum members also sold (1) counterfeit drivers' licenses, (2) manufactured fake credit cards, (3) stolen bank accounts and brokerage accounts, and (4) different types of malware, such as spyware and Trojan horses (Mills 2009).

At its peak, the Dark Market forum had over 2,500 registered members who all believed they were conducting their cybercriminal activities in a protected environment because they vetted all members and weeded out any individual who did not meet their vetting standards (Federal Bureau of Investigation 2008).

In October 2008, the undercover investigation of the Dark Market forum resulted in fifty-six arrests around the world and the prevention of $70 million in potential losses. This successful FBI criminal investigation of a cyber underground forum was the result of international law-enforcement cooperation from the UK Serious Organized Crime Agency, the Turkish National Police, and the German Federal Criminal Police (Federal Bureau of Investigation 2008).

Operation Shrouded Horizon (Darkode Forum Investigation 2015)

During July 2015, the FBI and international law-enforcement partners from twenty countries (Sweden, Finland, Latvia, Romania, Serbia, Macedonia,

Cyprus, Australia, Israel, Bosnia and Herzegovina, Nigeria, Croatia, Brazil, Colombia, Costa Rica, Germany, the United Kingdom, Canada, Denmark, and the United States) conducted the largest-ever coordinated global law-enforcement action against an online cyber underground criminal forum when they dismantled the forum known as Darkode (Federal Bureau of Investigation 2015).

The Darkode forum was a cyber underground, password-protected, online forum with members that developed, distributed, facilitated, and supported complex cybercrime schemes, such as buying, selling, and trading several things: botnets, malware, stolen PII, hacked server credentials, stolen credit-card information, and other malicious software and tools that facilitated global cybercrime (Federal Bureau of Investigation 2015).

Darkode had between 250 and 300 members whose detailed vetting process involved similar practices used by traditional organized crime, such as the Mafia. Darkode's vetting process was as follows: "A potential candidate for forum membership had to be sponsored by an existing member and sent a formal invitation to join. In response, the candidate had to post an online introduction—basically, a resume—highlighting the individual's past criminal activity, particular cyber skills, and potential contributions to the forum. The forum's active members decided whether to approve applications" (Federal Bureau of Investigation 2015).

This international law-enforcement action resulted in charges, arrests, and searches of seventy Darkode members around the world. In the United States, twelve subjects were indicted (including the Darkode administrator), several searches were conducted, and the FBI seized the Darkode forum's domain and servers (Federal Bureau of Investigation 2015).

Business executives need to understand the strategic threat that the cyber underground poses to private and public sectors around the world. As of 2015, there were estimated to be over eight hundred cyber underground forums operating in various languages around the world (US Department of Justice 2015). Just as business enterprises have become global in nature, so has the cyber underground. Business executives must treat the cyber underground as a global threat to their business organization's IT infrastructure, intellectual property, reputation, stock price, and strategic revenue growth.

In summary, business executives need to have a foundational understanding of the cyber underground and their various components and capabilities.

By understanding the constant evolution and sophisticated nature of the cyber underground, business executives will become better prepared to support the strategic, operational, and tactical requirements of their CIOs, CISOs, CSOs, or IT directors and IT personnel, and that support will help in defending against the cyber underground threat..

10

CYBER DEFENSE AND LIAISON WITH IT PERSONNEL

The concept of defense in depth has already been mentioned in previous chapters, but it will be explained in more detail in this chapter. Let's go back to information assurance and the ability to maintain the three primary pillars of information security: confidentiality, integrity, and availability. Business executives must understand how to balance these three pillars.

What does that mean? If a corporate organization conducts significant amounts of research and development and spends a disproportionate amount of revenue in these R&D endeavors, there is a probability that the organization will prioritize these three pillars of information security differently than other organizations not doing the same with their R&D functions. In this example, business executives must prioritize the confidentiality of the organization's intellectual property and the integrity of its IT infrastructure to protect, detect, and react against cyberattacks against its operations, personnel, and IT infrastructure. This could include the use of network-security managers, host- and network-based IDS/IPS, web proxies, full-packet capture of the various critical areas of the R&D network, investigative background checks of all R&D employees, the use of intrusion analysts to monitor all network activity, and other network-security implementations.

Now a different example would be an organization that earns most of its revenues through sales via the World Wide Web, such as an e-commerce business. An e-commerce organization would have different priorities regarding these three pillars of information security than the corporate organization attempting to protect its R&D, as mentioned in the previous example. The e-commerce organization's top priority would be to make its IT infrastructure available and secure. This e-commerce organization's executives would have to prioritize the availability of the organization's IT infrastructure so its clients could make any purchases of the organization's products online at any time of the day. Executives would have to ensure protection against cyberattacks that could impact its online availability, such as DDoS or DoS attacks against the organization's IT infrastructure, and be able to quickly reconstitute the organization's online services to its clients as a result of any disruption. This balance of confidentiality, integrity, and availability requires an investment in additional network IT infrastructure, such as load balancing, cloud services, additional network security, DDOS mitigation, penetration testing of websites and web servers, and cybersecurity training for the organization's webmasters and web designers. Executives would also need to prioritize the maintaining of the confidentiality of the organization's online clients' credit-card information and PII to ensure that this critical information is protected from all cyber threat actors. This would require the use of sophisticated encryption, additional network-security IT infrastructure, and the prioritization of the integrity of IT infrastructure to again protect, detect, react, and recover from cyberattacks.

A key component to the CIA triad is the integrity of the organization's IT infrastructure. What this means is ensuring that your organization's IT infrastructure is secure from all cyberattacks. As we have learned throughout this book, this is a very complex principle to implement at all levels. Business executives must understand that there are a multitude of cyber-intrusion vectors that can be used to exploit vulnerabilities in their organizations' IT infrastructures. These exploitable vulnerabilities can be found in hardware, software, wireless access, mobile access, remote access, web and web servers, and organizational personnel not trained in information security.

In defense in depth, an organization must focus on three elements to ensure the best cybersecurity posture for its organization: (1) the organization's personnel, (2) the organization's IT technology, and (3) the organization's operations (Citadel Information Group Inc. 2017).

People

As to business organizations' personnel, business executives must understand that an untrained workforce that does not properly understand strategic cyber threats is one of the greatest vulnerabilities that can be exploited at any time by cyber threat actors. The different intrusion vectors for an untrained workforce include social engineering, where a cyber threat actor obtains a password and username from an untrained help-desk employee, and that information provides the cyber threat actor valid credentials and thus instant access to the organization's IT infrastructure. Another very prominent intrusion vector in use today against non-cyber-savvy employees is phishing, in which non-cyber-savvy employees click on a link that contains malicious software (such as ransomware) and infect the organization's IT infrastructure.

Business executives must consider the implementation of annual or bi-annual information-security (InfoSec) training for all employees of their organizations, from the C-Suite down to the most junior associates who have any access to the organizations' IT infrastructures. In addition, to protect organizations from sophisticated and evolving cyber threat actors and their latest schemes, business executives should consider implementing a recurring strategic and enterprise-wide cyber threat briefing for all of their organizations' employees. An example of this cyber threat briefing would be to have the cyber-savvy IT staff obtain cyber intelligence from various public- and private-sector sources and create a monthly cyber threat bulletin encompassing all current cyber threats that can affect IT infrastructure, mobile devices, web, and personnel. A continual cyber threat briefing to all employees would allow an organization's personnel to maintain a more robust vigilance against the sophisticated, constantly evolving cyber threats and cyber threat actors.

As to organizations' IT personnel, business executives must understand that there must be a continual investment in cybersecurity training of organizations' IT personnel. If business executives do not understand the strategic importance of having a cybersecurity-trained IT staff to monitor, defend, secure, identify, contain, mitigate, and recover against cyberattacks, their organizations will suffer at the strategic level from tactical cybersecurity attacks. IT personnel must be trained in the most current cybersecurity methodologies to include the following:

- Cyber defense
- System administration
- Digital forensic investigations and media exploitation
- Penetration testing
- Incident response and threat hunting
- Management
- Secure software development
- Audit
- Intrusion analysis
- Legal
- Industrial control security (SANS Institute 2017)

Having non-cyber-savvy IT staff will result in the business organization's suffering from tactical events, such as a data breach caused by a non-cyber-savvy employee clicking on a phishing e-mail with a malicious attachment, which would infect the IT infrastructure with the latest sophisticated ransomware and thereby cause the organization to suffer negative strategic consequences. By compromising the IT infrastructure with the latest ransomware and access, the cyber threat actors infect the network topography, encrypt the organization's servers, and extort the organization for a payment to allegedly provide the key to decrypt the organization's servers. This tactical event has significant strategic consequences, as shown by the many organizations around the world that experienced with the WannaCry and Petya ransomware attacks during 2017. Some of these strategic consequences include corporate embarrassment with the public, the loss of customers, the loss of future revenue, the loss of corporate goodwill, the negative impact to the organization's stock price (if publicly traded), the overall incident response cost, legal costs, enterprise costs to upgrade IT infrastructure and its cybersecurity posture, costs of business downtime due to the cyber-attack, and the cost of credit monitoring of all potential victims whose PII or credit card information was compromised during this cyber-attack. This is a great example of why business executives must understand the strategic importance of having their IT staff trained in the best and most current cybersecurity methodologies to properly defend their organizations against the global cyber threat.

Technology

When it comes to a business organization's IT infrastructure, a business executive needs to understand that the cyber threat is constantly evolving and becoming more complex. Executives must understand that the costs of cybersecurity will also need to be increased to defend against the latest cyber threats.

What this means to a business organization's executives is to expect more requests for additional funding for cybersecurity resources in the forms of personnel and equipment. Business executives must understand this concept to support their CIOs, CISOs, CSOs, or IT directors in their funding requests, which may come at a faster pace than any other organizational funding requests. If you are a business executive who lacks an appreciation for the cyber threat and has a mind-set of trying to constantly save on organizational costs to be more efficient and effective, you are strategically endangering the organization. A cyber-savvy business executive understands that it takes a strategic commitment in resources to constantly secure and improve the cyber posture of an organization's IT infrastructure and personnel. A cyber-savvy business executive will ask questions regarding the differences in capabilities in proposed purchases of IT-infrastructure security components to obtain the best cybersecurity available at the best price for the organization. A non-cyber-savvy business executive will ask the CIO, CISO, CSO, or IT director to identify areas in his or her respective area of responsibility that can be cut to redirect a 10 percent "savings" to other expenses for the organization. Cyber-savvy business executives will include the projected annual costs of improving their cybersecurity posture in their annual budgets, alongside other projected costs, and will ensure this critical cybersecurity investment is not diverted and used for other nonstrategic expenses for their organizations.

Operations

Lastly, a business executive must understand the organization's operations and how the IT infrastructure supports those operations. Cyber-savvy business executives understand how the CIOs, CISOs, CSOs, or IT directors implement their strategic plans to secure their organizations' IT infrastructures. Cyber-savvy business executives understand the enterprise-network topography and its various networks that are interconnected throughout the dispersed geographic regions in the organization. A cyber-savvy business executive has a general understanding of the strategic requirement of continual hardware, software, certifying and accrediting changes to the IT infrastructure, security upgrades, enterprise-level penetration testing and vulnerability assessments. Cyber-savvy business executives also have a general understanding of enterprise-level network security to include an up-to-date system security policy, enterprise patch management, enterprise-level antivirus and antimalware protection, security incident and event management (SIEM) systems, network-security managers, web proxies, firewalls, DMZs, and other network devices, along with the appropriate cyber-trained personnel to monitor and conduct tactical and strategic analysis. Cyber-savvy business executives also understand the strategic importance of enterprise-level cyber-incident-response and recovery protocols and cyber-trained incident-response personnel to keep the best enterprise-level cybersecurity posture of the organization's IT infrastructure.

In summary, a business executive must understand and strategically assist in implementing an enterprise-level defense-in-depth strategy to ensure the best cybersecurity posture for his or her organization's personnel, IT technology, and operations. By understanding these IT infrastructure concepts, a cyber-savvy business executive understands that there are strategic-, operational-, and tactical-resource requirements associated with each of these various enterprise-cybersecurity components involved in securing the organization's cybersecurity posture against cyber threat actors. A cyber-savvy business executive who understands these strategic cybersecurity requirements will be an ally to the CIO, CISO, CSO, or IT director in supporting his or her funding requests to improve the overall cybersecurity posture of the organization.

11

INCIDENT RESPONSE AND DIGITAL FORENSICS

The May 2017 Harvey Nash / KPMG Chief Information Officer (CIO) Survey—the largest IT leadership survey in the world, which surveyed 4,498 CIOs and technology leaders across eighty-six countries—highlighted the following facts:

- Of these IT leaders, 32 percent reported that their organization had been subject to a major cyberattack in the past twenty-four months.
- Of these IT leaders, 21 percent reported that they were "very well" prepared for these cyberattacks.
- Of these IT leaders, 18 percent reported that their organization has "very effective" digital strategies (Harvey Nash KPMG 2017).

How does your business organization address and respond to cybersecurity incidents or cyberattacks? A business executive must understand the strategic importance of understanding the concept of incident response. Today's organizations are under the constant threat of attack by global cyber threat actors. As the previous chapters have noted, there is not a perfect "silver bullet" cybersecurity solution that can protect an organization's IT infrastructure, personnel, and operations from cyber threat actors, so organizations will experience cybersecurity incidents and cyberattacks.

A *cybersecurity incident* is a warning that there may be a threat to information or computer security. An example of a cybersecurity incident would be the misuse of confidential information, such as Social Security numbers or health records, which could include sensitive information, such as PII (Techopedia 2017).

A *cyberattack* is the "deliberate exploitation of computer systems, technology-dependent enterprises and networks" (Techopedia 2017).

Business executives need to understand how their organizations respond to cyber incidents and cyberattacks. As noted in previous chapters, there are many types of cyberattacks: malware attacks, denial-of-service attacks, cyber intrusions, unauthorized access to IT infrastructure, cross-site scripting attacks, SQL injections, insider attacks, and other cyberattacks.

A great public resource for any organization and its business executives is the US Department of Commerce National Institute of Standards and Technology (NIST) Special Publication 800–61 Revision 2, "Computer Security Incident Handling Guide" (National Institute of Standards and Technology 2012).

As noted in the "Purpose and Scope" section of this publication, "This document was created for computer security incident response teams (CSIRTs), system and network administrators, security staff, technical support staff, chief information security officers (CISOs), chief information officers (CIOs), computer security program managers and others who are responsible for preparing for, or responding to, security incidents" (National Institute of Standards and Technology 2012).

The table of contents of the NIST Computer Security Incident Handling Guide highlight some of the topic areas covered within the following sections:

1. Introduction
   1.1 Authority
   1.2 Purpose and Scope
   1.3 Audience
   1.4 Document Structure
2. Organizing a Computer Security Incident Response Capability
   2.1 Events and Incidents
   2.2 Need for Incident Response
   2.3 Incident Response Policy, Plan, and Procedure Creation
   2.4 Incident Response Team Structure
   2.5 Incident Response Team Services
   2.6 Recommendations

3. Handling an Incident
   3.1 Preparation
   3.2 Detecting and Analysis
   3.3 Containment, Eradication, and Recovery
   3.4 Post-Incident Activity
   3.5 Incident Handling Checklist
   3.6 Recommendations
4. Coordination and Information Sharing
   4.1 Coordination
   4.2 Information Sharing Techniques
   4.3 Granular Information Sharing
   4.4 Recommendations (National Institute of Standards and Technology 2012)

Business executives do not need to read the entire seventy-nine-page guide, but they must understand some incident-response concepts noted in this guide. Every business organization needs to have an incident-response plan to respond to cyber incidents and cyberattacks effectively and efficiently. A business organization's incident-response plan should address the following elements:

- Policy elements (senior-management commitment, purpose, objectives, etc.)
- Plan elements (mission, strategies, goals, organizational approach to incident response, etc.)
- Procedure elements (standard operating procedures)
- Sharing information with outside parties (law enforcement, media, Internet-service providers, other outside parties, etc.)
- Incident-response team structure
- Incident-response team services (National Institute of Standards and Technology 2012)

Senior business executives need to understand that they are part of their organizations' strategic incident-response plans and must be involved during exercises in testing those same incident-response plans. As with any threat, it is better to be properly prepared when faced by the threat (such as a cyberattack on an organization's IT infrastructure) than to be wholly unprepared and not know what to do as a business executive during the chaos after a business organization experiences a major cyberattack.

There are a number of issues that a business executive must understand in dealing with cybersecurity incidents. These issues include the strategic-communication aspect of dealing with the public as a result of a cyberattack, interacting with both outside and internal legal counsel to determine the best course of action in a post cyberattack environment, and understanding the procedures of the incident response. The latter may include having to take the network offline to address and mitigate an APT cyberattack, which could potentially cause enterprise-level disruptions. These elements can cause an organization to suffer negative strategic consequences if not handled properly, so the better prepared a business executive is, the better prepared that business executive will be in handling a major cyberattack on the organization's IT infrastructure.

Business executives need to understand the structure of their organizations' incident-response teams. Is the incident-response team one response team or multiple incident-response teams across the organization? Business executives must understand the staffing, equipment, cybersecurity, and digital forensic-training requirements for the incident-response team members. Another aspect is to understand whether this is an additional duty for the IT staff or if it will be a full-time duty for the incident-response team members. Business executives must understand that the incident-response teams must (1) prepare and train to prevent incidents; (2) understand the cyber threat actor's sophisticated tactics, techniques, and procedures (TTPs) and current cyberattack vectors; (3) detect and analyze the cyberattack to determine the extent of the incident; (4) be able to contain the incident and gather digital evidence via digital forensic procedures for potential legal purposes (such as a criminal prosecution); (5) mitigate the threat and stop its future impact on the IT infrastructure; (6) eradicate the threat; (7) recover from the cyberattack; and (8) conduct an after-action report with lessons learned to improve their capabilities.

Another great public resource for business organizations and their executives is the US Department of Commerce National Institute of Standards and Technology (NIST) Special Publication 800–184, "Guide for Cybersecurity Event Recovery" (National Institute of Standards and Technology 2016).

This guide was created because of the 2015 review of federal government agencies' cybersecurity capabilities by members of the US federal government that identified significant inconsistencies in event-response capabilities among the various federal agencies that had suffered cyberattacks. It was noted that although there were existing federal policies, standards, and guidelines on cyber-event handling, there was no guide that focused solely on cybersecurity recovery capabilities (National Institute of Standards and Technology 2016).

The NIST Guide for Cybersecurity Event Recovery provides guidance to assist organizations in planning and preparing for recovery from a cyberattack and in integrating the processes and procedures into organizations' enterprise risk-management plans. This guide supports organizations in improving their cybersecurity recovery plans, processes, and procedures, helping them to resume normal operations more quickly.

The NIST Guide for Cybersecurity Event Recovery is a fifty-three-page report, and it comprises the following seven sections:

- Section 1—Introduction
- Section 2—Planning for Cyber Event Recovery
- Section 3—Continuous Improvement
- Section 4—Recovery Metrics
- Section 5—Building the Playbook
- Section 6—An Example of a Data Breach Cyber Event Recovery Scenario
- Section 7—An Example of a Destructive Malware Event Recovery Scenario (National Institute of Standards and Technology 2016)

In summary, there are a lot of moving parts when it comes to the incident-response process and recovering from a cyberattack. Business executives must understand the foundational concepts of strategic incident-response protocols, have properly trained and equipped incident-response teams, and understand cybersecurity event recovery as described above, to be able to support their organizations' strategic cybersecurity-incident-response capability. Business executives have resources available to them to build this foundational knowledge, such as the NIST Computer Security Incident Handling Guide and NIST Guide for Cybersecurity Event Recovery. In addition, business executives must properly prepare for such cyberattacks and other cyber incidents by completing annual exercises in which organizations can practice their incident-response processes and cybersecurity recovery plans, from a simulated cyberattack.

12

CYBER TRAINING AND CYBER CERTIFICATIONS

Business executives need to understand the cybersecurity needs of their organizations. This is especially important when it comes to ensuring that their organizations have the best-trained IT staff to meet the cybersecurity needs of the organizations.

As a business executive, do you know where to recruit cyber-savvy employees? What cyber certifications does your onboard IT staff need? More important, as an executive, do you know what each of the various cyber certifications mean?

How does a business executive go about learning about the various cyber education opportunities that are available to all IT staff, from the CEO down to the computer-information-systems help-desk personnel?

This chapter focuses on the various entities that a business executive can use as strategic resources to understand and strategically provide and resource cybersecurity training opportunities for his or her organization's employees.

Cybersecurity-training programs available to organizations include the US National Institute of Standards and Technology's (NIST) National Initiative for Cybersecurity Education (NICE) program, the SANS Institute's Cyber Aces program, and cybersecurity training at academic institutions across the United States.

NIST's NICE program is a partnership between government, academia, and the private sector, and it focuses on cybersecurity education, training, and workforce development (National Initiative for Cybersecurity Education 2016).

The SANS's Cyber Aces program is the SANS initiative to help individuals discover and develop their cybersecurity skills. It donates free online courses in operating systems, networking, and systems administration. The program also organizes statewide competitions and connects Cyber Ace participants with potential employers (SANS Cyber Aces 2017).

US Community Colleges

Some of the best introductory cybersecurity programs in the country can be found at local community colleges. The author has selected the 2016–17 Northern Virginia (NOVA) Community College Information Technology associate of science degree and its six information-systems technology career certificates to provide business executives with an example of what is available for organizations and their employees at many US community colleges.

The 2016–17 NOVA Community College offers an associate of applied science degree program of study in information-systems technology, and the degree is designed for students seeking employment in the information-technology field. This two-year program requires twenty-one courses totaling sixty-seven credits for completion, and the program includes courses in computer applications and concepts, software design, multimedia software, telecommunications, web design, Unix, and network-security basics (Northern Virginia Commuity College 2017).

NOVA Community College also offers six different career-studies certificates in information-systems technology, which include (1) application programming, (2) database specialist, (3) IT technical support, (4) network administration, (5) network engineer (specialist), and (6) web design and development (Northern Virginia Community College 2017).

To provide the reader an example of what is required to obtain one of the NOVA Community College's six career-studies certificates in information-systems technology, the author has selected NOVA Community College's network-administration career-studies certificate. The network-administration career-studies certificate is designed to provide the student a broad background in networking technologies, administration, and support with a foundational knowledge covered in the CompTIA Network+ certification. The following are the seven required courses to obtain NOVA Community College's network-administration career-studies certificate:

First Semester

1. ITN 100 Introduction to Telecommunications—three credits
2. ITN 260 Network Security Basics—three credits
3. ITE 115 Introduction to Computer Applications and Concepts—three credits

Second Semester

4. ITN 101 Introduction to Network Concepts—three credits
5. ITN 200 Administration of Network Resources—three credits
6. ITN 208 Protocols and Communications—four credits
7. ITN 245 Network Troubleshooting—three credits

Completion of NOVA Community College's network-administration career-studies certificate requires twenty-two credits (Northern Virginia Community College 2017).

As noted above, many US community colleges offer organizations cybersecurity training opportunities and the potential recruitment pool of IT personnel, both of which can assist in strategically securing organizations' IT infrastructures.

National Security Agency (NSA) Centers of Academic Excellence in Cybersecurity

The US National Security Agency (NSA) sponsors the National Centers of Academic Excellence in Cybersecurity, whose goals include working jointly with DHS to reduce vulnerability in the US information infrastructure by promoting higher education and research in cyber defense and supporting the president's National Initiative for Cybersecurity Education (NICE), to create workers with cyber skills to support a cybersecure nation (National Security Agency 2017).

There are two programs in the NSA Centers of Academic Excellence in Cybersecurity: the national Centers of Academic Excellence in Cyber Defense (CAE-CD) program and the national Center of Academic Excellence (CAE) in Cyber Operations program.

The NSA and DHS jointly sponsor the national Centers of Academic Excellence in Cyber Defense (CAE-CD) program (National Security Agency 2017).

As noted on its website,

> The CAE-CD program comprises the following designations: Four-Year Baccalaureate/Graduate Education (CAE-CDE), Two-Year Education (CAE2Y) and Research (CAE-R). All regionally accredited two-year, four-year and graduate level institutions in the United States are eligible to apply. Prospective schools are designated after meeting stringent CAE criteria and mapping curricula to a core set of cyber defense knowledge units. Schools may also elect to map their curricula to specialized Focus Areas. CAE-CD institutions receive formal recognition from the US Government as well as opportunities for prestige and publicity for their role in securing our Nation's information systems...the initial National CAE in Information Assurance Education (CAE-IAE) program was started by NSA in 1998, with DHS joining as a partner in 2004. The CAE in IA Research component was added in 2008 to encourage universities and students to pursue higher-level doctoral research in cybersecurity. In 2010, the CAE2Y component was established to afford two-year institutions, technical schools, and government training centers the opportunity to receive such designation. (National Security Agency 2017)

As of May 2017, there are 224 NSA/DHS national CAE-designated institutions located in forty-four states and the District of Columbia and Puerto Rico. The current NSA/DHS national CAE-designated institutions can be found at https://www.iad.gov/nietp/reports/current_cae_designated_institutions.cfm.

NOVA Community College, the two-year community-college program noted above, is one of the NSA CAE-CDE two-year designated academic institutions (National Security Agency 2017).

The second program the NSA has established is the national Center of Academic Excellence in Cyber Operations Programs (National Security Agency 2017).

> The CAE-Cyber Operations program is intended to be a deeply technical, interdisciplinary, higher education program firmly grounded in the computer science (CS), computer engineering (CE), and/or electrical engineering (EE) disciplines, with extensive opportunities for hands-on applications via labs/exercises. The CAE-Cyber Operations program complements the existing Centers of Academic Excellence (CAE) in Cyber Defense (CAE-CD) programs, providing a particular emphasis on technologies and techniques related to specialized cyber operations (e.g., collection, exploitation, and response), to enhance the national security posture of our Nation. These technologies and techniques are critical to intelligence, military and law-enforcement organizations authorized to perform these specialized operations. (National Security Agency 2017)

As of May 2017, the following nineteen US academic institutions are designated as Centers of Academic Excellence in Cyber Operations. In addition, their academic years for the designation and level of study that met the criteria to be a current Center of Academic Excellence in Cyber Operations are noted:

1. Air Force Institute of Technology (Ohio), 2013–18 (graduate)
2. Auburn University (Alabama), 2013–18 (undergraduate and graduate)
3. Carnegie Mellon University (Pennsylvania), 2013–18 (graduate)
4. Dakota State University (South Dakota), 2012–17 (undergraduate)
5. Mississippi State University (Mississippi), 2013–18 (graduate)
6. Naval Postgraduate School (California), 2012–17 (graduate)
7. Northeastern University (Massachusetts), 2012–17 (undergraduate)
8. New York University Tandon School of Engineering (New York), 2014–19 (graduate)

9. Texas A&M University (Texas), 2017–22 (undergraduate)
10. Towson University (Maryland), 2014–19 (undergraduate)
11. United States Air Force Academy (Colorado), 2016–21 (undergraduate)
12. United States Military Academy at West Point (New York), 2014–19 (undergraduate)
13. University of Cincinnati (Ohio), 2014–19 (graduate)
14. University of Nebraska Omaha (Nebraska), 2017–22 (undergraduate)
15. University of New Orleans (Louisiana), 2014–19 (undergraduate and graduate)
16. University of Texas at Dallas (Texas), 2015–20 (graduate)
17. University of Texas at El Paso (Texas), 2016–21 (undergraduate)
18. University of Tulsa (Oklahoma), 2012–17 (undergraduate and graduate)
19. Virginia Polytechnic Institute and State University (Virginia), 2017–22 (National Security Agency 2017)

University Undergraduate and Graduate Programs

The author has selected George Mason University, located in northern Virginia, as an example of a university program that has both a computer science department and information sciences and technology Department. George Mason University's information sciences and technology department is also designated as an NSA CAE-CDE four-year designated academic institution. As of June 2017, George Mason University has thirty-four thousand students from all fifty states and 130 countries and ten schools and colleges (George Mason University 2017).

Below are some of the undergraduate and graduate programs offered by George Mason University's Computer Science and Information Sciences and Technology Departments.

George Mason University Department of Computer Science

The George Mason University Department of Computer Science offers two majors in its undergraduate computer-science program, a BS in computer science, and a BS in applied computer science. The BS in computer science

> provides students with essential background for studying the design and implementation of computer systems software, computer architecture, and computer software applications for science

and business. The program emphasizes both computer systems fundamentals and computer software applications. Required areas of study include data structures, analysis of algorithms, low-level programming, computer architecture and language translation, ethics and law for the computing professional, and software design and development. Evolving software technologies are a major concern. (George Mason University 2017)

The BS in applied computer science "has been created for those students who want and need the knowledge and expertise of computer science to work in one of the many disciplines that require advanced computing techniques. These fields do not merely *use* computing but create new and interesting problems for the computer scientist." The BS ACS has four concentrations—bioinformatics, computer-game design, geography, and software engineering (George Mason University 2017).

George Mason University's Department of Computer Science also offers two undergraduate minors in computer science and software engineering and an undergraduate certificate in computer science (George Mason University 2017).

George Mason University's Department of Computer Science also offers master's degree in (1) computer science, (2) information systems, (3) information security and assurance, and (4) software engineering, as well as three graduate certificates in (1) information security and assurance, (2) software engineering, and (3) web-based software engineering (George Mason University 2017).

George Mason University's Department of Information Sciences and Technology

George Mason University's Department of Information Sciences and Technology offers a bachelor of science in information technology. George Mason University's BS in information technology "prepares students to apply IT to support business processes" and "produces graduates with strong problem-solving, writing, and communication skills who successfully compete for technical employment and are prepared for advanced study" (George Mason University 2017).

George Mason University's Department of Information Sciences and Technology also offers a BS in information technology with a concentration in information security that makes students eligible to earn an NSA/DHS Center of Academic Excellence in Information Assurance/Cyber Defense Education Criteria Certificate. George Mason University's Department of Information Sciences and Technology also offers undergraduate certificates in information technology and information-technology entrepreneurship and a minor in information technology (George Mason University 2017).

George Mason University's Department of Information Sciences and Technology also offers BS or MS accelerated master's programs in (1) applied-information technology, (2) computer forensics, (3) information security and assurance, (4) information systems, (5) software engineering, and (6) telecommunications, as well as a bachelor of applied science for adult learners (George Mason University 2017).

As noted above, academic institutions across the United States have partnered with the NSA to provide an emphasis on cyber operations and with both the NSA and DHS to provide an emphasis on cyber defense. These NSA- and DHS-affiliated academic institutions offer organizations cybersecurity-training opportunities and the potential recruitment of IT personnel, both of which assist in strategically improving organizations' cybersecurity posture.

Computer-Programming Languages

As a business executive, do you know the most important computer programming languages that a business organization's cybersecurity and IT personnel must have to assist in securing that organization's IT infrastructure or to conduct successful cyber investigations?

Log analysis and cyber investigations require reviewing massive amounts of data to determine whether a malware infection is just that or the first stage of an APT actor's compromise of a victim organization's IT infrastructure. This data can range from gigabytes to terabytes of data and is obtained from various data storage devices, such as SIEMs, network-security managers, web proxies, storage servers, workstations, external drives, and USB drives. IT staff and cyber investigators need to use tools, such as computer-programming languages, to write lists of commands to automate computer processes, known as *scripts*

(Techopedia 2017), to assist them in parsing through this mountain of data to get to the nuggets of investigative relevance.

According to *IEEE Spectrum*, the magazine of the Institute of Electrical and Electronics Engineers, the top-ten computer-programming languages as of July 26, 2016, were the following:

1. C
2. Java
3. Python
4. C++
5. R
6. C#
7. PHP
8. JavaScript
9. Ruby
10. Go (Cass 2016)

Business executives do not need to know how these programming languages work but must understand that these computer-programming skills are a necessity for cybersecurity professionals. If the cybersecurity professionals have the adequate amount of skill, they can properly assist the executives in securing the relevant organizations' IT infrastructures and in conducting successful cyber investigations.

Cybersecurity Vendors and Certifications

Now that we have reviewed local community college, undergraduate, and graduate university cybersecurity programs and computer programming, let's discuss cybersecurity certifications and vendors.

In today's cybersecurity education market, there are numerous vendors with both in-person training and online training, which are afforded to organizations at different rates. As a business executive, do you know what all these acronyms for cybersecurity certifications mean? Does someone with a CompTIA A+ certification have the same training as a certified penetration tester, digital-forensics expert, network administrator, or Linux expert? This section will provide business executives with resources on the various cyber certifications from various private-sector cybersecurity vendors so that the executives will gain a better understanding of the meaning of the cybersecurity certifications, and it will explain what these certifications mean.

Business executives need to possess a foundational understanding of cyber certifications that are currently available in today's cybersecurity-education market. When individuals are hired to become an organization's IT director or IT staff, executives need to have a baseline understanding of what the new employees' educational and cybersecurity-training backgrounds are and what they mean. Executives need to understand what type of beginner, intermediate, and advanced cyber training is available for their organizations' employees, including the executives, the middle management, and the IT cybersecurity personnel. It should be noted that the author is not including information-security (InfoSec) training for all employees in this chapter.

There are cybersecurity certifications in many different areas of study. These cybersecurity certifications range from introductory courses in information security to advanced-level courses in network-penetration testing and specialty and expert classes in reverse-engineering malware and memory forensics.

A business executive needs to possess a foundational understanding of the various areas of certification in cybersecurity training. The following are some of the cybersecurity areas, and there are various levels (introductory, intermediate, advance, and expert):

1. Management
2. Cyber defense
3. System administration
4. Intrusion analysis
5. Digital forensic investigations and media exploitation
6. Penetration testing
7. Incident response and threat hunting
8. Secure software development
9. Audit
10. Industrial control systems
11. Legal (SANS Institute 2017)

To facilitate some of this foundational training for business executives, the author has identified seven major cybersecurity-training vendors currently available to provide cybersecurity training to business organizations' leadership and IT staff. The author has noted numerous cybersecurity courses and course descriptions to assist business executives to better understand these various vendor cybersecurity certifications.

The author notes that the selection of these seven private-sector vendors is based on the author's experience. There are other cybersecurity organizations that offer cybersecurity training, which the author has not listed in this book.

The following are the seven cybersecurity certification-training vendors that have been selected by the author:

1. (ISC)^2

    (ISC)^2 is an "international nonprofit membership association which focuses on inspiring a safe and secure cyber world." (ISC)^2 is best known for its acclaimed Certified Information Systems Security Professional (CISSP) certification ((ISC)^2 2017).

2. CompTIA

    The Computing Technology Industry Association (CompTIA) is a nonprofit trade association and the leading provider of vendor-neutral IT certifications in the world, with over two million IT certifications issued worldwide (CompTIA 2017).

3. ISACA

    Established in 1967, ISACA is an independent, nonprofit, global association that serves 140,000 professionals in 188 countries, with more than 215 chapters and offices worldwide, in Africa, Asia, Europe, Latin America, North America, and Oceania. ISACA engages in the development, adoption, and use of globally accepted, industry-leading knowledge and practices for information systems (ISACA 2017).

4. SANS Institute

    SANS Institute was established in 1989 as a cooperative research and education organization and currently serves more than 165,000 security professionals around the globe. SANS describes itself as the largest source of information-security training and security certification in the world (SANS Institute 2017).

5. Offensive Security

    Offensive Security describes itself as the industry-leading information-security-training and penetration-testing organization with the most realistic penetration-testing courses and real-world, performance-based information-security-training certifications (Offensive Security 2017).

6. EC-Council
   EC-Council was formed as a result of research conducted after the September 11, 2001, attacks on the World Trade Center. EC-Council operates in 145 countries, has certified over two hundred thousand information-security professionals, and is best known for its world-famous Certified Ethical Hacker certification (EC-Council 2017).

7. Cisco
   Cisco is the worldwide leader in IT and offers five levels of network certification (entry, associate, professional, expert, and architect) in the Cisco Career Certification program (CISCO 2017).

The author has provided a list of the certification courses, certificates, and undergraduate-and graduate-degree programs offered by these seven cybersecurity training vendors as a reference on cybersecurity certifications. The author has provided each vendor's cybersecurity certification, the vendor's own description of the cybersecurity certification, and the vendor's description of the areas covered by the cybersecurity certification.

(ISC)² Certifications

1. Certified Information Systems Security Professional (CISSP)
   CISSP is the most globally recognized certification in the information security market. CISSP validates an information security professional's deep technical and managerial knowledge and experience to effectively design, engineer, and manage the overall security posture of an organization. The broad spectrum of topics included in the CISSP Common Body of Knowledge (CBK) ensure its relevancy across all disciplines in the field of information security. Successful candidates are competent in the following eight domains: security and risk management, asset security, security engineering, communications and network security, identity and access management, security assessment and testing, security operations, and software development security. ((ISC)² 2017)

2. Systems Security Certified Practitioner (SSCP)

SSCP is the ideal certification for those with proven technical skills and practical, hands-on security knowledge in operational IT roles. It provides confirmation of a practitioner's ability to implement, monitor and administer IT infrastructure in accordance with information security policies and procedures that ensure data confidentiality, integrity and availability. The broad spectrum of topics included in the SSCP Common Body of Knowledge (CBK) ensure its relevancy across all disciplines in the field of information security. Successful candidates are competent in the following seven domains: Access Controls; Security Operations and Administration; Risk Identification, Monitoring, and Analysis; Incident Response and Recovery; Cryptography; Network and Communications Security; Systems and Application Security. $((ISC)^2$ 2017)

3. Certified Authorization Professional (CAP)

CAP is an information security practitioner who champions system security commensurate with an organization's mission and risk tolerance, while meeting legal and regulatory requirements. CAP confirms an individual's knowledge, skill, and experience required for authorizing and maintaining information systems within the Risk Management Framework as outlined in NIST SP 800-37 Rev 1. The broad spectrum of topics included in the CAP Common Body of Knowledge (CBK) ensure its relevancy across all disciplines in the field of information security. Successful candidates are competent in the following seven domains: Risk Management Framework (RMF); Categorization of Information Systems; Selection of Security Controls; Security Control Implementation; Security Control Assessment; Information System Authorization; Monitoring of Security Controls. $((ISC)^2$ 2017)

4. Certified Secure Software Lifecycle Professional (CSSLP)

CSSLP validates that software professionals have the expertise to incorporate security practices—authentication, authorization and auditing—into each phase of the software development lifecycle (SDLC), from software design and implementation to testing and deployment. The broad spectrum of topics included in the CSSLP Common Body of Knowledge (CBK) ensure its relevancy across all disciplines in the field of information security. Successful candidates are competent in the following eight domains: Secure Software Concepts; Secure Software Requirements; Secure Software Design; Secure Software Implementation/Programming; Secure Software Testing; Secure Lifecycle Management; Software Deployment, Operations, and Maintenance; Supply Chain and Software Acquisition. ((ISC)² 2017)

5. Certified Cyber Forensics Professional (CCFP)

The CCFP credential indicates expertise in forensics techniques and procedures, standards of practice, and legal and ethical principles to assure accurate, complete, and reliable digital evidence admissible in a court of law. It also indicates the ability to apply forensics to other information security disciplines, such as e-discovery, malware analysis, or incident response. In other words, the CCFP is an objective measure of excellence valued by courts and employers alike...for those who qualify, the CCFP exam will test their competence in the six CCFP domains of the (ISC)² CBK, which cover: Legal and Ethical Principles; Investigations; Forensic Science; Digital Forensics; Application Forensics; Hybrid and Emerging Technologies. ((ISC)² 2017)

6. Certified Cloud Security Professional (CCSP)

(ISC)² and the Cloud Security Alliance (CSA) developed the CCSP credential to ensure that cloud security professionals have the required knowledge, skills, and abilities in cloud security design, implementation, architecture, operations, controls, and compliance with regulatory frameworks. A CCSP applies information security expertise to a cloud computing environment and demonstrates competence in cloud security architecture, design, operations, and service orchestration. This professional competence is measured against a globally recognized body of knowledge. The CCSP is a standalone credential that complements and builds upon existing credentials and educational programs, including (ISC)²'s Certified Information Systems Security Professional (CISSP) and CSA's Certificate of Cloud Security Knowledge (CCSK). The topics included in the CCSP Common Body of Knowledge (CBK) ensure its relevancy across all disciplines in the field of cloud security. Successful candidates are competent in the following six domains: Architectural Concepts and Design Requirements; Cloud Data Security; Cloud Platform and Infrastructure Security; Cloud Application Security; Operations; Legal and Compliance. ((ISC)² 2017)

7. HealthCare Information Security and Privacy Practitioner (HCISPP) HCISPP is the ideal certification for those with the core knowledge and experience needed to implement, manage, or assess the appropriate security and privacy controls of a healthcare organization. HCISPP provides confirmation of a practitioner's knowledge of best practices and techniques to protect organizations and sensitive data against emerging threats and breaches. The broad spectrum of topics included in the HCISPP Common Body of Knowledge (CBK) ensures its relevancy across all disciplines in the field of information security. Successful candidates are competent in the following six domains: Healthcare Industry; Regulatory Environment; Privacy and Security in Healthcare; Information Governance and Risk Management; Information Risk Assessment; Third Party Risk Management. ((ISC)^2 2017)

CompTIA Certifications
Mastery Certifications

1. CompTIA Advanced Security Professional (CASP)—"CompTIA Advanced Security Practitioner (CASP) meets the growing demand for advanced IT security in the enterprise. Recommended for IT professionals with at least 5 years of experience, CASP certifies critical thinking and judgment across a broad spectrum of security disciplines and requires candidates to implement clear solutions in complex environments" (CompTIA 2017).

Specialty Certifications

2. The CompTIA Certified Document Imaging Architect+ (CDIA+)— "The CompTIA Certified Document Imaging Architect+ (CDIA+) certification allows IT professionals to validate their knowledge in document imaging and document management. The certification ensures IT professionals utilize best practices for planning, designing, implementing and maintaining a document imaging infrastructure" (CompTIA 2017).

3. CompTIA Cloud Essentials—"The CompTIA Cloud Essentials certification focuses on the real-world issues and practical solutions of cloud

computing in business and IT. It's the preferred cloud certification for business professionals and non-IT staff. While it isn't a technical-heavy certification, its coverage of cloud computing principles is anything but superficial" (CompTIA 2017).

4. CompTIA Certified Technical Trainer (CTT+)—"CompTIA Certified Technical Trainer (CTT+) certification is for instructors who want to verify they have attained a standard of excellence in the training field. CTT+ validates the knowledge and use of tools and techniques necessary for successfully teaching in today's learning environments" (CompTIA 2017).

Professional Certifications

5. CompTIA Security+ (Security+)—"CompTIA Security+ is the certification globally trusted to validate foundational, vendor-neutral IT security knowledge and skills. As a benchmark for best practices in IT security, this certification covers the essential principles for network security and risk management—making it an important stepping stone of an IT security career" (CompTIA 2017).

6. CompTIA A+ (A+)—"IT success stories start with CompTIA A+ certification. It validates understanding of the most common hardware and software technologies in business and certifies the skills necessary to support complex IT infrastructures. CompTIA A+ is a powerful credential that helps IT professionals worldwide ignite their IT career" (CompTIA 2017).

7. CompTIA Linux+ (Linux+)—"CompTIA Linux+ Powered by LPI certifies foundational skills and knowledge of Linux system administration. With Linux being the central operating system for much of the world's IT infrastructure, Linux+ is an essential credential for individuals working in IT" (CompTIA 2017).

8. CompTIA Network+ (Network+)—"CompTIA Network+ is a vendor neutral networking certification that is trusted around the world. It validates the essential knowledge and skills needed to confidently design, configure, manage and troubleshoot any wired and wireless networks. CompTIA Network+ certified individuals are in-demand worldwide" (CompTIA 2017).

9. CompTIA Cloud+ (Cloud+)—"The CompTIA Cloud+ certification validates the skills and expertise of IT practitioners in implementing and maintaining cloud technologies. Cloud+ accredits IT professionals with the constantly changing and advancing knowledge they need to be successful in today's cloud environment" (CompTIA 2017).

10. CompTIA Mobility+ (Mobility+)—"CompTIA Mobility+ has helped IT professionals stay ahead of the mobile-ready curve. It has validated expert knowledge in the latest mobility trends and the ability to work with an extensive variety of existing and emerging mobile technologies" (CompTIA 2017).

11. CompTIA Server+ (Server+)—"Today's IT environments demand planning, securing and maintaining a variety of server equipment. CompTIA Server+ certification validates IT professionals can do just that and more. As an industry-recognized credential, CompTIA Server+ helps boost the performance of IT professionals within businesses of all sizes" (CompTIA 2017).

12. CompTIA Cybersecurity Analyst (CSA+)—"CompTIA Cybersecurity Analyst (CSA+) is an international, vendor-neutral cybersecurity certification that applies behavioral analytics to improve the overall state of IT security. CSA+ validates critical knowledge and skills that are required to prevent, detect and combat cybersecurity threats" (CompTIA 2017).

13. CompTIA Project+ (Project+)—"CompTIA Project+ certifies the knowledge and skills of professionals in project management. Project+ validates the ability to initiate, manage and support a project or business initiative. And it's not just for IT technicians; Project+ is designed for any individual who wants to validate project management experience" (CompTIA 2017).

Foundational Certifications

14. CompTIA IT Fundamentals—"Prove that you know today's technologies with CompTIA IT Fundamentals. From networking and cybersecurity essentials to hardware and software basics, IT Fundamentals demonstrates your readiness for the digital workplace" (CompTIA 2017).

ISACA Certifications

1. Cybersecurity Nexus Practitioner (CSXP)—"The first performance-based cybersecurity certification, CSXP enables candidates to demonstrate the ability to be a first responder to cyber incidents, following established procedures and defined processes. CSXP indicates firewall, patching and antivirus experience, as well as the ability to implement common security controls and perform vulnerability scans and analysis" (ISACA 2017).

2. Certified Information Systems Auditor (CISA)—"The CISA certification is world-renowned as the standard of achievement for those who audit, control, monitor and assess an organization's information technology and business systems" (ISACA 2017).

3. Certified Information Security Manager (CISM)—"The uniquely management-focused CISM certification promotes international security practices and recognizes the individual who manages designs and oversees and assesses an enterprise's information security" (ISACA 2017).

4. Certified in the Governance of Enterprise IT (CGEIT)—"CGEIT recognizes a wide range of professionals for their knowledge and application of enterprise IT governance principles and practices. As a CGEIT certified professional, you demonstrate that you are capable of bringing IT governance into an organization—that you grasp the complex subject holistically, and therefore, enhance value to the enterprise" (ISACA 2017).

5. Certified in Risk and Information Systems Control (CRISC)—"CRISC is the only certification that prepares and enables IT professionals for the unique challenges of IT and enterprise risk management, and positions them to become strategic partners to the enterprise" (ISACA 2017).

6. Cybersecurity Nexus™ (CSX) is designed to provide cybersecurity training, credentials, events, and content for cybersecurity professionals at every level of their careers (ISACA 2017).

SANS Institute Global Information Assurance Certifications (GIAC)

1. GIAC Security Essentials Certification (GSEC)—"Security Professionals that want to demonstrate they are qualified for IT systems hands-on roles with respect to security tasks. Candidates are required to demonstrate

an understanding of information security beyond simple terminology and concepts" (SANS 2017).

2. GIAC Certified Incident Handler (GCIH)
    Incident handlers manage security incidents by understanding common attack techniques, vectors and tools as well as defending against and/or responding to such attacks when they occur. The GCIH certification focuses on detecting, responding, and resolving computer security incidents and covers the following security techniques: The steps of the incident handling process; Detecting malicious applications and network activity; Common attack techniques that compromise hosts; Detecting and analyzing system and network vulnerabilities; and continuous process improvement by discovering the root causes of incidents. (SANS 2017)

3. GIAC Certified Intrusion Analyst (GCIA)—"GIAC Certified Intrusion Analysts (GCIAs) have the knowledge, skills, and abilities to configure and monitor intrusion detection systems, and to read, interpret, and analyze network traffic and related log files" (SANS 2017).

4. GIAC Certified Pen Tester (GPEN)—"The GPEN certification is for security personnel whose job duties involve assessing target networks and systems to find security vulnerabilities. Certification objectives include penetration-testing methodologies, the legal issues surrounding penetration testing and how to properly conduct a penetration test as well as best practice technical and nontechnical techniques specific to conduct a penetration test" (SANS 2017).

5. GIAC Certified Web Application Pen Tester (GWAPT)
    Web applications are one of the most significant points of vulnerability in organizations today. Most organizations have them (both web applications and the vulnerabilities associated with them). Web app holes have resulted in the theft of millions of credit cards, major financial loss, and damaged reputations for hundreds of enterprises. The number of computers compromised by visiting websites altered by attackers is too high to count. This certification measures an individuals understanding of web application exploits and penetration testing methodology. Check your web applications for holes before the bad guys do. (SANS 2017)

6. GIAC Information Security Fundamentals (GISF)
   Proficient InfoSec administrators can network well on the eight layers of the ISO model (political), and the material contained in this track will help them to bridge the gap that often exists between managers and system administrators. GISF candidates will learn and be able to demonstrate key concepts of information security including the following: understanding the threats and risks to information and information resources, identifying best practices that can be used to protect them, and learning to diversify our protection strategy. (SANS 2017)

7. GIAC Certified Perimeter Protection Analyst (GPPA)—"GIAC Certified Perimeter Protection Analysts (GPPAs) have the knowledge, skills, and abilities to design, configure, and monitor routers, firewalls, and perimeter defense systems" (SANS 2017).

8. GIAC Certified Windows Security Administrator (GCWN)—"GIAC Certified Windows Security Administrators (GCWNs) have the knowledge, skills and abilities to secure Microsoft Windows clients and servers, including technologies such as PKI, IPSec, Group Policy, AppLocker, and PowerShell" (SANS 2017).

9. GIAC Certified Enterprise Defender (GCED)—"The GCED builds on the security skills measured by the GSEC (no overlap). It assesses more advanced, technical skills that are needed to defend the enterprise environment and protect an organization as a whole. Knowledge, skills and abilities assessed are taken from the areas of Defensive Network Infrastructure, Packet Analysis, Penetration Testing, Incident Handling, and Malware Removal" (SANS 2017).

10. GIAC Industrial Cyber Security Professional (GICSP)
    The GICSP bridges together IT, engineering and cyber security to achieve security for industrial control systems from design through retirement. This unique vendor-neutral, practitioner focused industrial control system certification is a collaborative effort between GIAC and representatives from a global industry consortium involving organizations that design, deploy, operate and/or maintain industrial automation and control system infrastructure. GICSP will assess a base level of knowledge and understanding across a diverse set of professionals who

engineer or support control systems and share responsibility for the security of these environments. (SANS 2017)

11. GIAC Assessing Wireless Networks (GAWN)—"The GAWN certification is designed for technologists who need to assess the security of wireless networks. The certification focuses on the different security mechanisms for wireless networks, the tools and techniques used to evaluate and exploit weaknesses, and techniques used to analyze wireless networks. Students will not only gain experience using tools to assess wireless networks, they will understand how the tools operate and the weaknesses in protocols that they evaluate" (SANS 2017).

12. GIAC Exploit Researcher and Advanced Penetration Tester (GXPN)—"Security personnel whose job duties involve assessing target networks, systems and applications to find vulnerabilities. The GXPN certifies that candidates have the knowledge, skills, and ability to conduct advanced penetration tests, how to model the abilities of an advanced attacker to find significant security flaws in systems, and demonstrate the business risk associated with these flaws" (SANS 2017).

13. GIAC Certified Unix Security Administrator (GCUX)—"GIAC Certified UNIX System Administrators (GCUXs) have the knowledge, skills and abilities to secure and audit UNIX and Linux systems" (SANS 2017).

14. GIAC Mobile Device Security Analyst (GMOB)—"Mobile phones and tablets continue to demonstrate their usefulness and importance in enterprises and government offices. With the amount of sensitive data that can be accessed on these devices and their lack of security, mobile devices are enticing targets for nefarious attackers. The GMOB ensures that the people charged with protecting systems and networks know how to properly secure the mobile devices accessing vital information" (SANS 2017).

15. GIAC Critical Controls Certification (GCCC)—"GIAC Critical Controls Certification (GCCC) is the only certification based on the Critical Security Controls, a prioritized, risk-based approach to security. This certification ensures that candidates have the knowledge and skills to implement and execute the Critical Security Controls recommended by the Council on Cybersecurity, and perform audits based on the standard" (SANS 2017).

16. GIAC Continuous Monitoring Certification (GMON)—"The GMON is targeted toward security architects, engineers, analysts, and managers

who want to demonstrate their ability to assess and implement defensible security architecture and continuous security monitoring. Successful GMON candidates will demonstrate the ability to securely architect a network resistant to breaches and that lends itself to monitoring. They will also demonstrate their ability to monitor, analyze detect threats and anomalies on the network" (SANS 2017).

17. GIAC Python Coder (GPYC)

A professional that can create and modify custom tools is a valuable member of any information security team. Code developers with information security skills can customize tools to their environment, create tools for the information security community, increase productivity by automating previously manual tasks, simulate advanced attacks, and more. The GPYC certification focuses on applying core programming concepts and techniques to the Python programming language. The certification has a special focus on skills and techniques that will assist an information security professional in penetration tests, daily work, and special projects. Certified individuals can create simple Python-based tools to interact with network traffic, create custom executables, test and interact with databases and websites, and parse logs or sets of data. (SANS 2017)

18. GIAC Certified Forensic Analyst (GCFA)

The GCFA certification is for professionals working in the information security, computer forensics, and incident response fields. The certification focuses on core skills required to collect and analyze data from Windows and Linux computer systems. The GCFA certifies that candidates have the knowledge, skills, and ability to conduct formal incident investigations and handle advanced incident handling scenarios, including internal and external data breach intrusions, advanced persistent threats, antiforensic techniques used by attackers, and complex digital forensic cases. (SANS 2017)

19. GIAC Certified Forensics Examiner (GCFE)

The GCFE certification is for professionals working or interested in the information-security, legal, and law-enforcement industries with a need to understand computer forensic analysis. The certification focuses on core skills required to collect and analyze data from Windows computer systems. The GCFE certifies that candidates have the knowledge, skills, and ability to conduct typical incident investigations including e-Discovery, forensic analysis and reporting, evidence acquisition, browser forensics and tracing user and application activities on Windows systems. (SANS 2017)

20. GIAC Reverse Engineering Malware (GREM)

The GIAC Reverse Engineering Malware (GREM) certification is designed for technologists who protect the organization from malicious code. GREM-certified technologists possess the knowledge and skills to reverse-engineer malicious software (malware) that targets common platforms, such as Microsoft Windows and web browsers. These individuals know how to examine inner-workings of malware in the context of forensic investigations, incident response, and Windows system administration. (SANS 2017)

21. GIAC Advanced Smartphone Forensics (GASF)—"The GASF certification is for professionals who want to demonstrate that they are qualified to perform forensic examinations on devices such as mobile phones and tablets. Candidates are required to demonstrate an understanding of the fundamentals of mobile forensics, device file system analysis, mobile application behavior, event artifact analysis and the identification and analysis of mobile device malware" (SANS 2017).

22. GIAC Security Leadership (GSLC)—"Security Professionals with managerial or supervisory responsibility for information security staff" (SANS 2017).

23. GIAC Information Security Professional (GISP)

Security Professionals that want to fill the gaps in their understanding of technical information security; System, Security, and Network Administrators that want to understand the pragmatic applications of the Common Body of Knowledge; managers that want to understand information security beyond simple terminology and concepts; anyone new to information security with some background in information systems and networking. Candidates may also wish to use this certification as an independent assessment of your mastery of the $(ISC)^2$ Common Body of Knowledge. (SANS 2017)

24. GIAC Certified Project Manager (GCPM)—"The GCPM certification is designed for security professionals and managers who participate in or lead project teams and wish to demonstrate an understanding of

technical project management methodology and implementation. This certification affirms the critical skill sets associated with making projects successful, including effective communication, time, cost, quality, procurement and risk management of IT projects and application development" (SANS 2017).

25. GIAC Systems and Network Auditor (GSNA)—"GIAC Systems and Network Auditors (GSNAs) have the knowledge, skills and abilities to apply basic risk analysis techniques and to conduct a technical audit of essential information systems" (SANS 2017).

26. GIAC Network Forensic Analyst (GNFA)—"The GNFA certification is for professionals who want to demonstrate that they qualified to perform examinations employing network forensic artifact analysis. Candidates are required to demonstrate an understanding of the fundamentals of network forensics, normal and abnormal conditions for common network protocols, the process and tools used to examine device and system logs, wireless communication and encrypted protocols" (SANS 2017).

27. GIAC Secure Software Programmer—Java (GSSP-JAVA)—"The GIAC Secure Software Programmers certification allows candidates to demonstrate mastery of the security knowledge and skills needed to deal with common programming errors that lead to most security problems. GIAC Certified secure software programmers (GSSP) have the knowledge, skills, and abilities to write secure code and recognize security shortcomings in existing code" (SANS 2017).

28. GIAC Certified Web Application Defender (GWEB)—"GIAC Certified Web Application Defenders (GWEB) have the knowledge, skills, and abilities to secure web applications and recognize and mitigate security weaknesses in existing web applications" (SANS 2017).

29. GIAC Law of Data Security & Investigation (GLEG)—"Security and IT Professionals, Lawyers, Paralegals, Auditors, Accountants, Technology Managers or Vendors. Anyone interested in the law of business, contracts, fraud, crime, IT security, IT liability and IT policy with a focus on electronically stored and transmitted records" (SANS 2017).

30. GIAC Secure Software Programmer—.NET (GSSP-.NET)—"GIAC Certified secure software programmers (GSSP) have the knowledge, skills, and abilities to write secure code and recognize security shortcomings in existing code" (SANS 2017).

31. GIAC Security Expert (GSE)—"The GSE certification is the most prestigious credential in the IT Security industry. The exam was developed by subject matter experts and top industry practitioners. The GSE's performance based, hands-on nature sets it apart from any other certifications in the IT security industry. The GSE will determine if a candidate has truly mastered the wide variety of skills required by top security consultants and individual practitioners" (SANS 2017).

32. GIAC Response and Industrial Defense (GRID)
The GRID certification is for professionals who want to demonstrate that they can perform Active Defense strategies specific to and appropriate for an Industrial Control System (ICS) network and systems. Candidates are required to demonstrate an understanding of the Active Defense approach, ICS-specific attacks and how these attacks inform mitigation strategies. Candidates must also show an understanding of the strategies and fundamental techniques specific to core subjects with an ICS-focus such as network-security monitoring (NSM), digital forensics and incident response (DFIR). (SANS 2017)

Masters Degrees—Information Security

33. SANS Masters of Science in Information Security Engineering (MSISE) Degree—"Prepare to lead. The MSISE program is a rigorous, challenging, and rewarding experience that provides you with the rare combination of an elite technical mastery and the leadership capability to mobilize people, organizations, and resources" (SANS 2017).

34. SANS Masters of Science in Information Security Management (MSISM) Degree—"The Master of Science in Information Security Management provides students with the executive skills needed to define and deliver organization-wide strategies, programs, and policies. It teaches many of the technical underpinnings of information security, but focuses information security personnel on auditing information systems, managing the legal implications of an incident, evaluating emerging solutions, and implementing organization-wide standards" (SANS 2017).

Graduate Certificates—Cyber Security

35. SANS Cybersecurity Engineering (Core)—"Spans from an introductory survey of fundamental information security tools and techniques to a more advanced study of the interrelationships between offensive (attack/penetration testing) and defensive (intrusion detection and incident response) information security best practices" (SANS 2017).
36. SANS Cyber Defense Operations—"Focuses on teaching the applied technologies used to defend and secure information assets and business systems at an organization" (SANS 2017).
37. SANS Penetration Testing and Ethical Hacking—"Focuses on developing the student's capability to discover, analyze, and understand the implications of information security vulnerabilities in systems/networks/applications in order to identify solutions before others exploit these flaws" (SANS 2017).
38. SANS Incident Response—"Focuses on developing the student's capability to manage both a computer and network-based forensics investigation as well as the appropriate incident responses" (SANS 2017).

Offensive Security

1. Offensive Security Certified Professional (OSCP)
   The OSCP is our accompanying information security certification to the Penetration Testing with Kali Linux course. The OSCP was the first security certification in the market that required a fully "hands on" performance-based approach, leaving no space for multiple choice questions. As the market leader in hands-on security training, the OSCP changed the landscape of the security certification marketplace. During the online security test, students are placed in a virtual lab network with several vulnerable machines. Points are then awarded if a successful compromise occurs. Students must demonstrate their depth of understanding by documenting both the steps they took to penetrate the box as well as captured flag files in a report at the conclusion of testing. (Offensive Security 2017)

2. Offensive Security Certified Expert (OSCE)

   The OSCE security certification is the challenge exam at the end of the Cracking the Perimeter (CTP) advanced penetration testing course. Going far beyond the material directly covered in the CTP online course, the OSCE exam validates the student's grasp of the concepts presented in the material and proves their ability to think laterally under pressure by devising creative methods to achieve the exam objectives. Due to the challenging nature of this exam, candidates are provided with 48 hours for completion. Widely regarded as one of the most respected and difficult to obtain technical information security certifications available, the OSCE is the industry premier advanced penetration testing certification. Holders of this certification are part of an elite group who have proven they have what it takes to be among the best and brightest in the field. (Offensive Security 2017)

3. Offensive Security Exploitation Expert (OSEE)

   The OSEE certification is the companion certification to the extremely demanding Advanced Windows Exploitation course. The OSEE certification thoroughly assesses the students' understanding of creating Windows based exploits in a manner that bypasses modern controls and antiexploitation technologies. In this extremely challenging exam, the student is provided with 72 hours in order to develop their exploits and fully document the steps taken. The OSEE is the most well known certification specifically focused on Windows based exploitation. Holders of this certification have proven they not only understand modern exploitation techniques, but additionally how to bypass complex antiexploitation controls and protections. (Offensive Security 2017)

4. Offensive Security Web Expert (OSWE)

   The OSWE certification is the accompanying certification to the Advanced Web Attacks and Exploitation course. In this 24-hour exam, students are placed in an unknown exam environment where they demonstrate their knowledge not only of the course material, but web application vulnerabilities in general. Exam candidates are required to analyze and exploit a selection of vulnerable targets and provide comprehensive documentation detailing their attacks. Holders of the OSWE certification have proven a deep understanding of web vulnerabilities and their associated impact leading to real-world compromises.

Certified individuals often are some of the most productive discoverers of zero-day web exploits in the work force. (Offensive Security 2017)

5. Offensive Security Wireless Professional (OSWP)

The OSWP security certification demonstrates that students of the Offensive Security Wireless Attacks (WiFu) course possess the knowledge and skills needed to successfully attack wireless networks in varying configurations and protections. In order to earn the OSWP certification, the student has to attack a series of wireless networks in a real-world configuration, requiring the student to be responsive to unexpected situations and demonstrate they know how to use the right Wi-Fi attack technique for any given scenario. The OSWP demonstrates proficiency in understanding Wi-Fi security issues surrounding wireless network deployments, and how to successfully compromise them in the real world. (Offensive Security 2017)

EC Council

1. EC-Council Certified Secure Computer User (CSCU)—"CSCU provides individuals with the necessary knowledge and skills to protect their information assets. This course covers fundamentals of various computer and network-security threats such as identity theft, credit card fraud, phishing, virus and backdoors, e-mail hoaxes, loss of confidential information, hacking attacks, and social engineering" (EC-Council 2017).

2. EC-Council Certified Network Defender (CND)—"CND is the world's most advanced network defense course that covers 14 of the most current network-security domains any individuals will ever want to know when they are planning to protect, detect, and respond to the network attacks. The course contains hands-on labs, based on major network-security tools and to provide network administrators real world expertise on current network-security technologies and operations" (EC-Council 2017).

3. EC-Council Certified Ethical Hacker (CEH)—"CEH is the world's most advanced certified ethical hacking course that covers 18 of the most current security domains any individual will ever want to know when they are planning to beef-up the information security posture of their organization. The accredited course provides the advanced hacking tools

and techniques used by hackers and information security professionals" (EC-Council 2017).

4. EC-Council Certified Security Analyst (ECSA)—"ECSA is a globally accepted hacking and penetration testing program that covers the testing of modern infrastructures, operating systems, and application environments while teaching the students how to document and write a penetration testing report. This program takes the tools and techniques covered in CEH to the next level by utilizing EC-Council's published penetration testing methodology" (EC-Council 2017).

5. EC-Council Certified Incident Handler (ECIH)
The ECIH program is designed to provide the fundamental skills to handle and respond to the computer security incidents in an information system. The course addresses various underlying principles and techniques for detecting and responding to current and emerging computer security threats. The comprehensive training program will make students proficient in handling as well as responding to various security incidents such as network-security incidents, malicious code incidents, and insider attack threats. (EC-Council 2017)

6. EC-Council Computer Hacking and Forensic Investigator (CHFI)—"CHFI is a comprehensive course covering major forensic investigation scenarios, enabling students to acquire hands-on experience. The program provides a strong baseline knowledge of key concepts and practices in the digital forensic domains relevant to today's organizations. Moreover, CHFI provides a firm grasp on the domains of digital forensics" (EC-Council 2017).

7. EC-Council Certified Secure Programmer (ECSP) Java—"The ECSP Java program is a comprehensive course that provides hands-on training covering Java security features, policies, strengths, and weaknesses. It helps developers understand how to write secure and robust Java applications, and provides advanced knowledge in various aspects of secure Java development that can effectively prevent hostile and buggy code" (EC-Council 2017).

8. EC-Council Certified Secure Programmer (ECSP). NET—"The ECSP. Net program covers identification of security flaws and implementation of security countermeasures throughout the software development lifecycle to improve the overall quality of products and applications. This

course is purposefully built with a number of labs with three days of training, offering participants critical hands-on time to fully grasp the new techniques and strategies in secure programming" (EC-Council 2017).

9. EC-Council Licensed Penetration Tester (LPT) Master—"The LPT (Master) credential is developed in collaboration with SMEs and practitioners around the world after a thorough job role, job task, and skills-gap analysis. The LPT (Master) practical exam is the capstone to EC-Council's entire information security track, right from the CEH to the ECSA Program. The LPT (Master) exam covers the skill-sets, technical analysis and report writing required to be a true professional penetration tester" (EC-Council 2017).

10. EC-Council CAST 611 Advanced Penetration Testing—"The CAST 611—Advanced Penetration Testing is a specialized training program covering key information security domains, at an advanced level. Students completing this course will gain in-depth knowledge about information gathering, scanning, enumeration, exploitation and post exploitation, data analysis and reporting, and a number of advanced techniques" (EC-Council 2017).

11. EC-Council CAST 612 Advanced Mobile Forensics and Security—"The CAST 612—Advanced Mobile Forensics and Security focuses on what today's mobile forensics practitioner requires. Some of the advanced areas this course covers are the intricacies of manual acquisition (physical vs. logical) and advanced analysis using reverse engineering, understanding how the popular Mobile OSs are hardened to defend against common attacks and exploits" (EC-Council 2017).

12. EC-Council CAST 613 Hacking and Hardening Corporate Web Apps—"The CAST 613—Hacking and Hardening Corporate Web Apps is a course designed with the average security unaware programmer in mind. The course is designed with more than 50 percent involving hands-on coding labs. The ideal participant should have a development background, coding, or architecting background either currently or previously" (EC-Council 2017).

13. EC-Council CAST 614 Advanced Network Defense—"The CAST 614—Advanced Network Defense will enable you to evaluate advanced hacking methods of defense fortification, bringing you closer to establishing

perfect security best practices and methodologies you can apply to secure environments. It will cover fundamental areas of fortifying your defenses by discovering methods of developing a secure baseline and hardening your enterprise architecture from the most advanced attacks" (EC-Council 2017).

14. EC-Council CAST 616 Securing Windows Infrastructure—"The CAST 616—Securing Windows Infrastructure focuses on the key aspects of Windows Infrastructure Security. It is designed with the single purpose of providing InfoSec professionals complete knowledge and practical skills necessary for ensuring the security of their network infrastructure, that is fast becoming, if already not, a top priority and a major challenge for most organizations" (EC-Council 2017).

15. EC-Council Disaster Recovery Professional (EDRP)
The EDRP course identifies vulnerabilities and takes appropriate countermeasures to prevent and mitigate failure risks for an organization. It also provides the networking professional a foundation in disaster recovery course principles, including preparation of a disaster recovery plan, assessment of risks in the enterprise, development of policies and procedures, an understanding of the roles and relationships of various members of an organization, implementation of a plan, and recovering from a disaster. (EC-Council 2017)

16. EC-Council Certified Chief Information Security Officer (C|CISO)
The C|CISO certification is an industry-leading program that recognizes the real-world experience necessary to succeed at the highest executive levels of information security. Bringing together all the components required for a C-Level position, the C|CISO program combines audit management, governance, IS controls, human capital management, strategic program development, and the financial expertise vital for leading a highly successful IS program. The C|CISO Training Program can be the key to a successful transition to the highest ranks of information security management. (EC-Council 2017)

17. EC-Council Bachelor of Science in Cyber Security (BSCS)—"The Bachelor of Science in Cyber Security (BSCS) prepares students the knowledge for careers in cyber security and assurance. The program consists of topical areas dealing with computer security management, incident response, and security threat assessment, etc." (EC-Council 2017).

18. EC-Council Graduate Certificate Programs

    EC-Council University's Graduate Certificate Program focuses on the competencies necessary for information assurance professionals to become managers, directors, and CIOs. Students will experience not only specialized technical training in a variety of IT security areas, but will also acquire an understanding of organizational structure and behavior, the skills to work within and across that organizational structure, and the ability to analyze and navigate its hierarchy successfully. Each certificate targets skills and understandings specific to particular roles in the IT security framework of an organization. The certificates can be taken singly or as a progressive set of five, each building on the one before it to move students from IT practitioner skill levels to IT executive skill levels. (EC-Council 2017)

19. EC-Council Master of Science in Cyber Security (MSS)

    The Master of Science in Cyber Security (MSS) Program prepares information technology professionals for careers in cyber security and assurance. The program consists of topical areas dealing with computer security management, incident response, and cyber security threat assessment, which require students to be the creators of knowledge and inventors of cyber security processes, not merely users of information. Additionally, students will receive instruction in leadership and management in preparation for becoming cyber security leaders, managers, and directors. (EC-Council 2017)

CISCO Career Certifications
Entry Certifications

1. Cisco Certified Entry Networking Technician (CCENT)—"This certification validates the ability to install, operate and troubleshoot a small enterprise branch network, including basic network security" (CISCO 2017).

2. Cisco Certified Technicians (CCT)—"Cisco Certified Technicians have the skills to diagnose, restore, repair, and replace critical Cisco networking and system devices at customer sites. Technicians work closely with the Cisco Technical Assistance Center (TAC) to quickly and efficiently resolve support incidents" (CISCO 2017).

3. Cisco Certified Technician Data Center (CCT Data Center)

   Cisco Certified Technician Data Center (CCT Data Center) certification focuses on the skills required for onsite support and maintenance of Cisco Unified Computing Systems and servers. Technicians in this area must be able to identify Cisco Unified Computing System components and servers, accessories, cabling and interfaces; understand the Cisco UCS and NX-OS operating modes and identify commonly found software; and be able to use the Cisco Graphical User Interface to connect and service product components. (Cisco 2017)

4. Cisco Certified Technician Routing and Switching (CCT Routing and Switching)

   Cisco Certified Technician Routing and Switching (CCT Routing and Switching) certification focuses on the skills required for onsite support and maintenance of Cisco routers, switches, and operating environments. Technicians in this area must be able to identify Cisco router and switch models, accessories, cabling, and interfaces; understand the Cisco IOS Software operating modes and identify commonly found software; and be able to use the Cisco Command Line Interface (CLI) to connect and service products. Achieving CCT Routing and Switching certification is considered the best foundation for supporting other Cisco devices and systems. (Cisco 2017)

Associate Certifications

5. Cisco Certified Design Associate (CCDA)

   Enterprise environments require networks designed for performance, availability, and scalability with the flexibility to meet rapidly evolving demands. To meet these challenges head on, skilled IT professionals are needed with up-to-date, fundamental network design skills. For network design engineers, system engineers, and sales engineers and individuals looking to build and validate Cisco network design fundamental knowledge, the Cisco CCDA certification program focuses on design methodologies and objectives, addressing and routing protocols, and network expansion considerations within basic campus, data center, security, voice, and wireless networks. (CISCO 2017)

6. Cisco Certified Network Associate (CCNA) Cloud—"The CCNA Cloud certification is a job role focused certification and training program that helps Cloud engineers, Cloud Administrators, and Network Engineers to develop, advance, and validate their cloud skill set, and enables them to help their IT organization meet changing business demands from technology transitions" (CISCO 2017).

7. Cisco Certified Network Associate (CCNA) Collaboration
    For network video engineers, collaboration engineers, IP telephony and IP network engineers who want to develop and advance their collaboration and video skills in line with the convergence of voice, video, data and mobile applications, the Cisco CCNA Collaboration certification is a job-role-focused training and certification program. It will allow you to maximize your investment in your education, and increase your professional value by giving you the skills to help your IT organization meet increased business demands resulting from these technology transitions. (CISCO 2017)

8. Cisco Certified Network Associate (CCNA) Cyber Ops—"The CCNA Cyber Ops certification prepares candidates to begin a career working with associate-level cybersecurity analysts within security operations centers" (CISCO 2017).

9. Cisco Certified Network Associate (CCNA) Data Center
    Agility is the hallmark of today's successful data center. Built for rapid application deployment and supported by a highly elastic infrastructure, the data center has become core to businesses competing in our digital era. CCNA Data Center certification provides the confidence and nimbleness you need to install, configure, and maintain data center technology. Gain grounding in data center infrastructure, data center networking concepts and technologies, storage networking, unified computing, network virtualization, data center automation and orchestration, and Cisco Application Centric Infrastructure (ACI). (CISCO 2017)

10. Cisco Certified Network Associate (CCNA Industrial)
    The Cisco Certified Network Associate Industrial (CCNA Industrial) certification is for plant administrators, control system engineers and traditional network engineers in the manufacturing, process control, and oil and gas industries, who will be involved with the convergence

of IT and Industrial networks. This certification provides candidates the necessary skills to successfully implement and troubleshoot the most common industry standard protocols while leveraging best practices needed for today's connected networks. (CISCO 2017)

11. Cisco Certified Network Associate (CCNA) Routing and Switching—"As Enterprises migrate toward controller based architectures, the role and skills required of a core network engineer are evolving and more vital than ever. To prepare for this network transition, the CCNA Routing and Switching certification will not only prepare you with the knowledge of foundational technologies, but ensure you stay relevant with skill sets needed for the adoption of next generation technologies" (CISCO 2017).

12. Cisco Certified Network Associate Security (CCNA Security)
Cisco Certified Network Associate Security (CCNA Security) validates associate-level knowledge and skills required to secure Cisco networks. With a CCNA Security certification, a network professional demonstrates the skills required to develop a security infrastructure, recognize threats and vulnerabilities to networks, and mitigate security threats. The CCNA Security curriculum emphasizes core security technologies, the installation, troubleshooting and monitoring of network devices to maintain integrity, confidentiality and availability of data and devices, and competency in the technologies that Cisco uses in its security structure. (CISCO 2017)

13. Cisco Certified Network Associate (CCNA) Service Provider—"Cisco Certified Network Associate Service Provider (CCNA SP) certification is for service provider network engineers, technicians and designers who focus on the latest in Service Provider industry core networking technologies and trends. With the ability to configure, implement, and troubleshoot baseline Cisco Service Provider Next-Generation networks, CCNA SP certified individuals deploy, maintain and improve carrier-grade network infrastructures" (CISCO 2017).

14. Cisco Certified Network Associate (CCNA) Wireless
Cisco Wireless technology growth places increased demands on networks and the professionals that support them. Ensuring this technology is optimally configured, monitored, and supported is paramount to achieving business outcomes and requires a workforce of skilled wireless professionals. Earn the CCNA Wireless certification and amplify your

basic Cisco Wireless LAN's configuration, monitoring, troubleshooting and support skills for optimal performance of Cisco Wireless networks. (CISCO 2017)

Cisco also offers professional-, expert-, and architect-level certifications in many of the above noted certifications. The *Cisco professional level* is an "advanced level of certification that shows more expertise with networking skills. Each certification covers a different technology to meet the needs of varying job roles... the *Cisco Certified Internetwork Expert* (CCIE) certification is accepted worldwide as the most prestigious networking certification in the industry." *Cisco's certified architect* is the "highest level of accreditation achievable and recognizes the architectural expertise of network designers who can support the increasingly complex networks of global organizations and effectively translate business strategies into evolutionary technical strategies"(CISCO 2017).

As noted above, there are many cybersecurity certifications, certificates, and undergraduate- and graduate-degree programs from these seven vendors. There are similarities in some of the cybersecurity training, and the costs vary from vendor to vendor. This list provides business executives with an informative resource on the varying types of cybersecurity certifications, certificates, and undergraduate and graduate degrees available for their executives, CIOs, CISOs, CSOs, IT directors, midlevel leaders, first-line leaders, IT cybersecurity personnel, and incident-response personnel.

In summary, business executives need to have a foundational understanding of the various cybersecurity-training and education resources being provided by government, academia, and private-sector cybersecurity vendors. An executive should investigate whether there is a NSA Centers of Academic Excellence in Cybersecurity designated educational institution in his or her local community because that institution can be a potential personnel resource for his or her organization's IT staff or cybersecurity team. Executives should have a foundational understanding of the top programming languages used by IT staff and cyber investigators because that knowledge can assist the executives in their current cybersecurity efforts. In addition, executives now have a resource of multiple cybersecurity vendors and their respective certificates of cybersecurity certifications and undergraduate- and graduate-degree programs—all of which can assist them in improving the cybersecurity-training posture and capabilities of their organizations' cybersecurity personnel.

13

PRIVATE- AND PUBLIC-SECTOR
AND CYBERSECURITY

Private- and Public-Sector Partnerships

Business executives need to know there are national organizations that are available to provide cybersecurity resources to their organizations. Organizations such as the National Cyber-Forensics & Training Alliance, InfraGard, the DHS Information Sharing and Analysis Centers (ISACs), and the Domestic Security Alliance Council are examples of these organizations which provide their members with cyber-threat intelligence and other cybersecurity information.

National Cyber-Forensics & Training Alliance (NCFTA)

The National Cyber-Forensics & Training Alliance (NCFTA) is a "nonprofit corporation founded in 2002, focused on identifying, mitigating, and neutralizing cybercrime threats globally. The NCFTA operates by conducting real time information sharing and analysis with Subject Matter Experts (SME) in the public, private, and academic sectors." The NCFTA proactively identifies cyber threats to help partners take preventive measures. The NCFTA has a proven track record and a global model for private and public partnerships. Today, the NCFTA model, best practices, and lessons learned are being emulated in countries around the world. The NCFTA membership is constantly growing both nationally and internationally across private industry, law enforcement, government, and academia (NCFTA 2017).

The NCFTA has collaborated with partners around the world, which has resulted in countless criminal and civil investigations. The NCFTA has provided intelligence that has aided in the successful prosecution of hundreds of cybercriminals worldwide and produced more than eight hundred cyber threat intelligence reports to support NCFTA's initiatives and partners (NCFTA 2017).

NCFTA has a trusted environment that provides (1) physical and remote forums to meet with all partners; (2) dedicated and trained staff who specialize in their respective NCFTA initiatives; (3) focused meetings and events for each NCFTA initiative; (4) intelligence feeds built and maintained by the NCFTA; (5) monthly NCFTA initiative calls that include updates on trends, law-enforcement efforts, and intelligence gaps; (6) contacts to help inform and encourage coordination with public- and private-sector partners; and (7) assessments and reports based on NCFTA intelligence (NCFTA 2017).

NCFTA specialty programs include the Cyber Financial Program (CyFin), the Brand and Consumer Protection Program (BCP), and the Malware and Cyber Threats Program.

The NCFTA Cyber Financial Program is "dedicated to the identification, mitigation and neutralization of cyber threats to the financial services industry" (NCFTA 2017).

The NCFTA Brand and Consumer Protection Program focuses on "the utilization of the Internet for the sale of retail goods, including fraud related to ecommerce transactions as well as the physical distribution of counterfeit merchandise" (NCFTA 2017).

The NCFTA Malware and Cyber Threats Program is "dedicated to researching, identifying, and providing timely alerts through data feeds and proactive intelligence on cyber threats under analysis" (NCFTA 2017).

InfraGard

InfraGard is a

> partnership between the FBI and the private sector. The InfraGard program provides a vehicle for seamless public-private collaboration with government that expedites the timely exchange of information and promotes mutual learning opportunities relevant to the protection of Critical Infrastructure. With thousands of vetted members nationally, InfraGard's membership includes business executives, entrepreneurs, military and government officials, computer professionals, academia and state and local law

enforcement; each dedicated to contributing industry specific insight and advancing national security. (InfraGard 2017)

InfraGard started in 1996 in Cleveland, Ohio, and currently has over eighty chapters with more than forty-three thousand members in the United States. Each InfraGard chapter is linked with one of the fifty-six domestic FBI field offices and is assigned an FBI special agent InfraGard coordinator. With the expertise and talents of the InfraGard network, information is shared to mitigate cyber threats to the US critical infrastructures and key resources. Over four hundred of the US Fortune 500 companies have a representative in InfraGard (InfraGard 2017).

Department of Homeland Security's (DHS) Information Sharing and Analysis Centers (ISACs)

DHS is the lead federal department for the protection of critical infrastructure. DHS has many cybersecurity information-sharing programs available for (1) the private sector, (2) state, local, tribal, and territorial governments, and (3) international partners.

The National Cybersecurity and Communications Integration Center (NCCIC) is DHS's twenty-four-seven cyber-situational-awareness, incident-response, and management center, which is a national nexus of cyber and communications integration for the US government, US intelligence community, and law enforcement. To build awareness of vulnerabilities, incidents, and mitigations, the NCCIC shares this information with both private-sector and public-sector partners (US Department of Homeland Security 2017).

Sector-specific information sharing and analysis centers (ISACs) are "nonprofit, member-driven organizations formed by critical infrastructure owners and operators to share information between government and industry. While the NCCIC works in close coordination with all of the ISACs, a few critical infrastructure sectors maintain a consistent presence within the NCCIC."

The Multi-State Information Sharing and Analysis Center (MS-ISAC) has been designated by DHS as the cybersecurity ISAC for state, local, tribal, and territorial (SLTT) governments. The MS-ISAC provides "services and information sharing that significantly enhances SLTT governments' ability to prevent, protect against, respond to and recover from cyberattacks and compromises. DHS maintains operational-level coordination with the MS-ISAC through the presence of MS-ISAC analysts in the NCCIC to coordinate directly with its own 24 x 7 operations center that connects with SLTT government stakeholders on cybersecurity threats and incidents." The Communications ISAC also maintains a presence at the NCCIC's National Coordinating Center for Communications (NCC), which includes having members from major US communications carriers on site. In addition to the MS-ISAC and Communications ISAC, the Financial Services Information Sharing and Analysis Center (FS-ISAC) and the Aviation Information Sharing and Analysis Center (A-ISAC) also maintain a presence at the NCCIC (US Department of Homeland Security 2017).

The Domestic Security Alliance Council (DSAC)
The Domestic Security Alliance Council (DSAC) is a

> strategic partnership between the US government and the US private industry that enhances communication and promotes the timely and effective exchange of security and intelligence information between the federal government and the private sector. Its goal is to advance the FBI's mission of detecting, preventing, and deterring criminal acts by facilitating strong, enduring relationships among its private sector member companies, FBI Headquarters, FBI field offices, Department of Homeland Security (DHS) Headquarters and Fusion Centers, and other federal government entities. DSAC also expands the US private sector's ability to protect its employees, assets, and information by providing ongoing access to security information and a network of security experts, as well as continuing education for corporate chief security officers (CSOs) and intelligence analysts. (Domestic Security Alliance Council 2017)

The DSAC program has more than 360 member companies representing almost every critical sector and over fifty unique business industries. DSAC member companies account for over 50 percent of the US gross domestic product and employ over twenty million people (Domestic Security Alliance Council 2017).

> DSAC increases coordination among FBI Headquarters divisions and FBI field offices to strengthen collaboration between the

federal government and the private sector. A significant element of this approach involves strategically assessing, realigning, and maximizing private sector points of contact to improve the value of both internal and external partnerships. Working with both member company Chief Security Officers (CSOs) and Special Agents in Charge of local FBI field offices, DSAC hosts regular executive-level meetings and encourages greater collaboration, understanding, and alignment of local, state, and national security priorities. (Domestic Security Alliance Council 2017)

DSAC offers the following benefits to members:

- Direct engagement with FBI and DHS leaders;
- Ongoing access to a network of diverse security experts at the highest levels of government and the private sector;
- Timely, customized intelligence products and security information from the FBI, DHS, and other federal agencies;
- Admittance to an exclusive, members-only web portal where private sector members and government officials collaborate, resolve problems, exchange best practices, and share intelligence and information with one another;
- Local, regional, and national training events, continuing education, and conferences; and
- The opportunity to acquire FBI-sponsored security clearances. (Domestic Security Alliance Council 2017)

In summary, private- and public-sector partnerships are a strategic and integral component of the success of an organization's overall cybersecurity program. Business executives should have a foundational understanding of the various benefits in working with and joining private-sector organizations, such as NCFTA, InfraGard, and DSAC. Business executives should also establish relationships with public-sector partners—such as DHS NCCIC and its sector-specific ISACs—as a cyber resource for their organizations.

Cybersecurity Breach Laws and Select US Regulators
Forty-eight states, including the District of Columbia, Puerto Rico, Guam, and the Virgin Islands have enacted legislation requiring both private- and

public-sector entities to notify individuals of data breaches which involve PII (National Conference of State Legislatures 2018).

New York State Department of Financial Services Cyber Regulation (NYSDFS)

On September 13, 2016, the New York State Department of Financial Services (NYSDFS) announced it would propose the first-in-the-nation cybersecurity regulation aimed at protecting New York from cyber threat actors. The proposed cybersecurity regulation would require banks, insurance companies and other financial services institutions regulated by the NYSDFS to establish and maintain a cybersecurity program designed to protect consumers and to ensure the safety and soundness of the New York State's financial services industry (New York State Department of Financial Services 2016).

This proposed regulation was designated the NYSDFS 23 NYCRR 500 -Cybersecurity Requirements for Financial Services Companies and became effective on March 1, 2017. This cybersecurity regulation has twenty-three sections which have serious cybersecurity requirements. These sections for covered entities include:

1. Definitions
2. Cybersecurity program with specific requirements
3. Cybersecurity policy with specific requirements
4. CISO designation
5. Penetration testing and vulnerability assessments
6. Audit trail
7. Access Privileges
8. Application security
9. Risk assessment
10. Cybersecurity personnel and intelligence
11. Third party service provider security policy
12. Multi-factor authentication
13. Limitations on data retention
14. Training and monitoring
15. Encryption of nonpublic information
16. Incident response plan
17. Notices to NYSDFS Superintendent

18. Confidentiality
19. Enforcement (New York State Department of Financial Services 2017).

This first of its kind cybersecurity regulation by the state of New York may spark a critical review and possible revision of the other forty-seven state breach laws.

There are two federal laws related to cybersecurity which are sector specific to a particular industry. These two laws, the Gramm-Leach-Bliley Act (GLBA) and the Health Insurance Portability and Accountability Act of 1996 (HIPAA), govern requirements for the financial sector and healthcare sector respectively (German 2015).

As of September 2017, there is no federal breach notification law. After the massive Yahoo data breach announced in 2016, there were calls for a federal breach notification law by both the Federal Trade Commission and officials from the US Department of Justice (The National Law Review 2016). Because of the Equifax data breach announced on September 8, 2017, US Congressman Jim Langevin reintroduced "The Personal Data Notification and Protection Act of 2017" legislation which would establish national standards to inform consumers when their data has been released via an unauthorized disclosure or data breach. This proposed legislation would require companies that use, store, or access sensitive or personally identifying information for more than 10,000 people per year to notify their customers within thirty days of discovering a breach. This legislation would also designate the Federal Trade Commission as the government's coordinating agency to ensure a company's customers are properly notified (Johnson 2017). Due to the constant reporting of massive data breaches, the author expects new legislation to be passed and new cybersecurity regulation to be enacted in the near future in order to address these enterprise level cybersecurity breaches.

Federal Trade Commission (FTC)
The US Federal Trade Commission (FTC) enforces federal consumer protection laws that prevent fraud, deception and unfair business practices. The FTC also administers a wide variety of laws and regulations, including the Gramm-Leach-Bliley Act (GLBA), Federal Trade Commission Act, Telemarketing Sale Rule, Identity Theft Act, Fair Credit Reporting Act, and Clayton Act (Federal Trade Commission 2018). Since 2000, the FTC has had over sixty data security settlements as a result of their enforcement actions against business entities

which have experienced data breaches. These data security settlements can include implementing a comprehensive privacy program and requiring third party assessments of this privacy program every two years for a period of twenty years (Federal Trade Commission 2018). The FTC provides business organizations with ten practical lessons learned from these data security settlements which can be found at https://www.ftc.gov/tips-advice/business-center/guidance/start-security-guide-business.

Department of Health and Human Services (HHS) Office of Civil Rights (OCR)

The US Department of Health and Human Services (HHS) Office for Civil Rights (OCR) enforces the Health Insurance Portability and Accountability Act (HIPAA) Privacy, Security, and Breach Notification Rules. HIPAA required HHS to adopt national standards for electronic health care transactions and code sets, unique health identifiers, and security (US Department of Health and Human Services 2018). HHS OCR can impose resolution agreements and civil money penalties on covered entities (general hospitals, health care providers, health plans, outpatient facilities, pharmacies, and private practices) who violate HIPAA privacy and security rules. Since 2008, HHS OCR has conducted many HIPAA enforcement actions which resulted in comprehensive correction action plans and civil money penalties, which in some cases resulted in settlement costs in the millions of dollars. HHS OCR enforcement actions can be found at https://www.hhs.gov/hipaa/for-professionals/compliance-enforcement/agreements/index.html (US Department of Health and Human Services 2018)

Securities and Exchange Commission (SEC)

The US Securities and Exchange Commission (SEC) mission is to protect investors, maintain fair, orderly and efficient markets, and facilitate capital formation (US Securities and Exchange Commission, 2016).

The SEC incorporates cybersecurity considerations in three areas: (1) in its disclosures and supervisory programs including in the context of the Commission's review of public company disclosures, (2) its oversight of critical market technology infrastructure, and (3) its oversight of other regulated entities, including broker -dealers, investment advisers and investment companies (US Securities and Exchange Commission 2017).

The SEC generally requires public companies to disclose material risk and events to shareholders and the markets. There is no existing disclosure requirement which explicitly refers to cybersecurity risks and cyber incidents. On October 13, 2011, the SEC Division of Corporation Finance (DCF) issued the Corporation Finance Disclosure Guidance Topic 2 on cybersecurity regarding disclosure requirements relating to cybersecurity risks and cyber incidents. The SEC DCF issued this guidance to provide public companies guidance on how to determine when cybersecurity risks and incidents are material and thus must be disclosed. This guidance attempts to balance the shareholder's need to know with the risk of the public company disclosing too much. It should be noted this SEC DCF represents the views of the DCF. This SEC DCF guidance is not a rule, regulation, or statement of the SEC (US Securities and Exchange Commission, 2011).

This guidance was prepared to assist public companies in assessing what, if any disclosures, should be provided about the cybersecurity matters in light of each public company's specific facts and circumstances. This determination can include factors such as (1) the frequency and severity of prior cybersecurity incidents, (2) measures of the magnitude of risks associated with cybersecurity, (3) the adequacy of the public company's protective measures in the context of the industry, and (4) the cybersecurity threats facing the public company (US Securities and Exchange Commission, 2011).

As of October 4, 2017, the SEC DCF has not had any enforcements as of yet against public companies for disclosure failures (Germaine 2017). This could change in the near future based on the position the SEC Chairman Jay Clayton is taking as noted in his testimony before the Senate Banking Committee on September 26, 2017. Chairman Clayton noted publicly traded companies need to do a better job of disclosing cyber risks they face in their filings with the SEC. Chairman Clayton also noted publicly traded companies should also be providing better disclosure about their risk profile and provide sooner disclosure about cyber intrusions if it may affect shareholder disclosure decisions (Chabrow 2017).

On September 20, 2017, the SEC reported it had suffered an unauthorized intrusion of its EDGAR test filing system which may have provided the basis for illicit gain through trading (US Securities and Exchange Commission, 2017).

On September 25, 2017, the SEC announced two new initiatives that will build on its Enforcement's Division ongoing efforts to address cyber-based threats and protect retail investors. These two initiatives include (1) the creation of a Cyber Unit and (2) the establishment of a retail strategy task force that will implement initiatives that directly affect retail investors. The Cyber Unit will focus on targeting cyber-related conduct such as (1) market manipulation schemes involving false information spread through electronic and social media, (2) hacking to obtain material nonpublic information, (3) violations involving distributed ledger technology and initial coin offerings, (4) misconduct perpetrated using the dark web, (5) intrusions into retail brokerage accounts, and (6) cyber-related threats to trading platforms and other critical market infrastructure (US Securities and Exchange Commission, 2017).

In summary, business executives must understand US and state cyber breach laws and understand US and state cybersecurity regulators are increasing their enforcement actions in today's business environment. These enforcement actions could include ordering an organization who has suffered a data breach to implement a comprehensive privacy program, require third party assessments of its privacy program for an extended period of time, implement a comprehensive correction action plan, and be fined substantial civil money penalties. These cybersecurity regulatory enforcement actions could have a negative strategic impact on an organization which suffers a data breach.

The CPA Profession and Cybersecurity

On Sept 7, 2017, Equifax, one of the largest U.S. credit bureaus, released a public statement acknowledging it had discovered a massive data breach of its company which may have affected 143 million Americans (Krebs 2017). This massive data breach was discovered by Equifax on July 29, 2017. A second breach was suffered by Equifax two months prior to the July 29, 2017 data breach which Equifax noted did not involve the same cyber threat actors (Weise 2017). On October 2, 2017 Equifax increased its initial estimate of impacted Americans who were affected by this massive data breach from 143 million to 145.5 million Americans (Cowley 2017). In addition to this massive data breach, the sales of $1.8 million worth of Equifax stock during August 2017 by three senior Equifax executives sparked a criminal investigation by the U.S. Department of Justice (DOJ). The DOJ and the FBI will conduct a criminal investigation to determine whether these three top Equifax officials violated insider trading laws when they sold company stock before the massive data breach was made public (McCoy 2017).

The strategic impact of this massive data breach has resulted in Equifax's CIO David Webb and CSO Susan Mauldin to retire on September 15, 2017 with criticism of CSO Mauldin for having studied music composition in college with no degree in security or related field (Popken 2017). On September 26, 2017, Equifax CEO Rick Smith announced his immediate retirement following this massive breach.

This massive data breach should serve as a strategic turning point for all publicly traded companies and business executives around the globe. Because of the two data breaches impacting 145.5 million Americans, senior Equifax cybersecurity executives lacking cybersecurity credentials, the sale of Equifax shares by senior Equifax executives prior to the data breach disclosure, and the two month delay in advising the public, these combined events will have a significant impact on the investor community. The totality of these combined events emanating from a single publicly traded company may cause investors to question the adequacy of the overall cybersecurity posture of publicly traded companies.

Business executives must understand cybersecurity of public companies will come under more scrutiny by investors, analysts and regulators. Investors will begin to ask what cybersecurity vulnerabilities exist in these publicly traded companies and search for unqualified opinions regarding the cybersecurity risk management practices by these publicly traded companies. Senior management, board of directors, audit committees, and auditors need to be aware of this strategic shift as they bear collective responsibility to ensure the best cybersecurity enterprise risk management practices are being implemented and continually assessed by the company. Business executives understand penetration testing, vulnerability testing, and other security assessments are an important requirement to continually monitor IT infrastructure for cybersecurity vulnerabilities. Business executives should also consider an independent and comprehensive periodic review of their enterprise level cybersecurity risk management program to verify their enterprise cybersecurity risk management program is operating as designed and effective in its controls to prevent cyber intrusions of its IT infrastructure, personnel, and operations.

During April 2017, the American Institute of Certified Public Accountants (AICPA) issued the *System and Organization Controls (SOC) for Cybersecurity*, a cybersecurity risk management reporting framework.

The American Institute of Certified Public Accountants (AICPA)is the world's largest member association representing the accounting profession with more than 418,000 members in 143 countries. The AICPA sets ethical standards for the accounting profession and US auditing standards for private companies, non-profit organizations, federal, state, and local governments. AICPA members represent many areas of practice to include consulting, public practice, education, government, business and industry. The AICPA also develops and grades the Uniform CPA examination and offers various specialty credentials for CPAs who concentrate on forensic accounting, information management and technology assurance, business valuation, and personal financial planning (AICPA 2017).

CPAs are known for being independent, objective and having a skeptical mindset. CPAs complete business and accounting courses in college, pass a rigorous CPA examination, and maintain and update their skills annually with their required continuing professional education as part of their commitment to their profession. CPAs have strong analytical skills, are experienced in measuring subject matters against criteria, and processes for testing and reporting the results. CPAs provide independent examinations using attestation standards such as providing an auditor opinion on the financial statements of an organization and provide an opinion on whether there are material misstatements in the financial statements. CPAs are considered the most trusted advisors in business who provide confidence, credibility and trust.

CPAs have been assisting organizations in addressing cybersecurity since 1974 when CPAs were required to consider the effects of information technology on financial statements during an audit of those statements. Today, four of the top ten cybersecurity consulting companies by revenue are all accounting firms. The top four cybersecurity consulting companies based on cybersecurity consulting sales are the accounting firms of Deloitte, Ernst & Young, PricewaterhouseCoopers, and KPMG, respectively. (Kuranda 2017).

Due to high-profile cybersecurity attacks which compromised critical data of major corporations, governments, not-for-profits and private companies, the AICPA has responded to this strategic crisis with a market-driven, flexible, and voluntary cybersecurity risk management framework. During April 2017, the AICPA issued the *System and Organization Controls (SOC) for Cybersecurity*, a cybersecurity risk management reporting framework. This market-driven, flexible and voluntary cybersecurity risk management reporting framework is designed to assist organizations to communicate pertinent information regarding the organization's cybersecurity risk management efforts and educate stakeholders, such as board of directors, senior management, investors, business partners, analysts and regulators, about the systems, processes and controls they have in place to detect, prevent and respond to cyber breaches. In addition, this voluntary cybersecurity risk management reporting framework enables a CPA to examine and report on the management-prepared cybersecurity information which increases the confidence that stakeholders may place on an organization's initiatives (AICPA 2017).

As noted before, data breaches caused by cyber threat actors have a strategic impact on an organization such as loss of intellectual property, damage to the organization's reputation, recovery and remediation costs, legal liability, and business disruption of the impacted organization.

The AICPA developed this voluntary cybersecurity framework as there is no widely accepted approach or professional standard for providing security assessments. There are numerous different cybersecurity frameworks (NIST Cybersecurity Framework, International Organization for Standardization (ISO) Information Security standards, etc.) which have caused confusion in the marketplace.

This AICPA cybersecurity risk management reporting framework is designed to:

1. Provide a common criterion for disclosure about an entity's cybersecurity risk management program
2. Provide a common criterion for assessing program effectiveness
3. Reduce communication and compliance burden on organizations
4. Provide useful information to a broad range of users, while minimizing the risk of creating vulnerabilities
5. Provide comparability
6. Permit management flexibility
7. Connect the dots on best practices
8. Be voluntary
9. Be scalable and flexible
10. Evolve to meet challenges (AICPA 2017).

There are three components to the entity-level cybersecurity reporting framework. The three components are:

1. "Management's description – The first component is a management-prepared narrative description of the entity's cybersecurity risk-management program. This description is designed to provide information

about how the entity identifies its sensitive information and systems, the ways in which the entity manages the cybersecurity risks that threaten it and the key security policies and processes implemented and operated to protect the information and systems against those risks. This provides the context needed to enable users to understand the conclusions management expressed in its assertion, and by the auditor in its opinion, about the effectiveness of the controls included in the entity's cybersecurity risk management program."

2. "Management's assertion — Management makes an assertion about whether the description is presented in accordance with the description criteria and whether the controls within the program were effective to achieve the entity's cybersecurity objectives based on the control criteria. Both sets of criteria are discussed in the next section."

3. "The practitioner's opinion — The final component in this approach is a CPA's opinion on the description and on the effectiveness of controls within that program to achieve the entity's cybersecurity objectives" (AICPA 2017).

The AICPA developed two sets of different but complementary criteria to use in a cybersecurity engagement:

1. *Description criteria* – which is the description criteria management uses when preparing a description of its cybersecurity risk management program and by the CPA when evaluating the presentation.

2. *Control criteria* – which is the control criteria management uses when assessing the effectiveness of controls within that program to achieve the entity's cybersecurity objectives (AICPA 2017).

By creating this SOC for cybersecurity entity level cybersecurity reporting framework, which is transparent, consistent across time, comparable between entities, reasonably complete, scalable and flexible, the AICPA believes that an entity, its board of directors, and all its stakeholders will be best served if a defined set of information intended to meet their common needs addresses cybersecurity concerns (AICPA 2017).

In summary, a cyber-savvy business executive now understands the various components of cybersecurity and its overall impact on an organization's

IT infrastructure, personnel, and operations. A cyber-savvy CEO and his or her senior leadership team needs to independently verify their implemented strategic cybersecurity risk management program is and continues to provide its organization with the best and most current cybersecurity posture to detect, prevent, respond, and recover against all cyber threats. A cyber-savvy business CEO and his or her senior leadership team should consider engaging a CPA firm to conduct a *System and Organization Controls (SOC) for Cybersecurity* attestation engagement of their organization's enterprise cybersecurity risk management program. This *System and Organization Controls (SOC) for Cybersecurity* attestation engagement will assist their organization to communicate pertinent information regarding their organization's cybersecurity risk management efforts and educate stakeholders about the systems, processes and controls they have in place to detect, prevent and respond to cyber breaches.

14

CYBER CHALLENGES FOR BUSINESS EXECUTIVES

Many strategic challenges face all business executives. We have reviewed the strategic impact the cyber threat can have on any business organization in the world today. Business executives with this
new foundational knowledge of the cyber threat landscape will now face even
more strategic challenges. The old saying "Ignorance is bliss" hits home as a
newly minted cyber-savvy business executive. As a newly minted cyber-savvy
business executive, you will now have a very different perspective regarding
the strategic cyber threat—a perspective that you probably did not have before
reading this book. Cyber-savvy business executives will have to incorporate the
strategic cyber element within their respective organizations' strategic, operational, and tactical planning and find creative solutions in addressing this strategic threat.

The first strategic reality to face is that there is no one "silver bullet" solution to the global cyber threat. Although there are international cybercrime
conventions, such as the Budapest Cybercrime Convention, cyberspace is the
Wild West of the twenty-first century, with limited global norms in addressing
the multitude of global cyber threat actors found in the cyber threat landscape.

Today's global cyber threat actors have the strategic advantage of being able
to exploit vulnerabilities of private- or public-sector organizations' IT infrastructures and of hiding their trail using various techniques. These techniques
include using servers from around the globe to conduct their cyberattacks;
using spam to send out phishing e-mails with malware (such as ransomware)
to millions of unsuspecting users globally; using encrypted virtual private

networks to hide their identities and communications; using bulletproof hosting to provide the necessary IT infrastructure to carry out their cyberattacks; using services (such as Tor) to hide their originating IP addresses; using virtual currencies (such as Bitcoin) to monetize their cybercriminal activities; using advanced malware (such as Stuxnet and Regin), along with sophisticated and stealthy techniques, tactics, and protocols (TTPs) to conduct devastating cyberattacks (such as the APT threat); exploiting industrial-control-system vulnerabilities and carrying out cyberattacks against critical infrastructures (such as the Ukraine civilian power grid); exploiting wireless, mobile-device, and web-server vulnerabilities with tools and malware to gain access to an organizations' IT infrastructures; and conducting cyberattacks against organizations because hacktivist groups disagree with the organizations' social or political stances.

Today's business executives are faced with a phenomenal strategic challenge in protecting their organizations' IT infrastructures from the multitude of different types of cyberattacks from global cyber threat actors. Today's business executives face this strategic challenge in addition to a number of internal challenges, such as having a cyber-trained, cyber-savvy executive-leadership team leading their organizations; having a strategically resourced and properly trained cybersecurity IT staff; having the most up-to-date enterprise-level network-security components (security incident and event-management systems, IDS/IPS, enterprise mobile-management systems, etc.) to secure the enterprises (network, mobile, web, wireless, etc.); conducting third party vendor risk assessments, conducting enterprise logging and monitoring of the enterprise activity for intrusions with cyber-trained personnel, web proxies, and network-security managers; conducting regularly scheduled penetration testing of the organizations' IT infrastructures to identify and mitigate vulnerabilities; providing regularly scheduled information-security (InfoSec) training and monthly cyber threat bulletins to all levels of employees (including midlevel and first-line leadership); having adequate cybersecurity policies to address today's cyber threat landscape; having an enterprise-wide incident-response and recovery plan and properly trained and resourced incident-response teams; having the appropriate private- and public-sector partnerships (InfraGard, DHS NCCIC, MS-ISAC, etc.) to receive the most current cyber threat intelligence to strategically protect the organizations' IT infrastructures; understanding US and state breach laws; and providing consideration in having an annual review of their strategic cybersecurity risk management program by a CPA firm.

Business executives also face the reality of law-enforcement limitations in addressing the cyber threat. Successful law-enforcement operations against global cyber threat actors require global law-enforcement cooperation and coordination. Each law-enforcement agency (state, local, tribal, territorial (SLTT), federal, and international partners) requires cybersecurity-trained investigators, prosecutors, and judges to successfully address these cyber threat actors in the criminal justice system. There are fifty-six FBI Cyber Task Forces and numerous US Secret Service Electronic Crimes Task Forces around the country, but it should be noted that not every SLTT law-enforcement agency has cybersecurity-trained investigators or cybercrime units dedicated to conducting cyber-intrusion investigations.

The US Department of Justice, the FBI, and its international and SLTT partners have been successful in conducting and prosecuting cybercrime investigations against nation-state actors (China, Iran, Syria, Russia, North Korea), cybercriminals (GameOver Zeus, SpyEye), cyber underground criminal forums (DarkMarket and Darkode), hacktivists (Anonymous), and many others over the last sixteen years, since the FBI Cyber Division was created in 2001. These long-term investigations require substantial resources to bring the cyber threat actors to justice. Just as the global private sector is strategically challenged in facing the cyber threat, the international law-enforcement community is also strategically challenged in facing and addressing this awesome strategic threat.

Successfully addressing the strategic threat will require strategic leadership in both private and public sectors. Cyber-savvy business and law-enforcement executives need to strategically implement strategic solutions to protect their organizations and their IT infrastructures from global cyber threat actors.

The Wild West of cyberspace will strategically begin to change into a more modern environment with international norms when the global private sector, global law-enforcement, and international governments come together to strategically address the global cyber threat. When cyber-savvy business and law-enforcement executive leaderships begin to strategically address the cyber threat and global cyber threat actors, a common ground will be created between the global private sector, public sector, and international governments. This common ground will allow for discussions, actions, policies, laws, and global cooperative efforts that will strategically raise the cost of conducting cybercrimes by the cyber threat actors and rogue nation-state actors. Cyber threat actors will find it harder to hide from international, national, state, and local law-enforcement efforts. There will be an exponential increase in the number of successful cybercrime prosecutions at all levels, which will force cyber threat actors to consider long-term prison sentences versus continuing their cyber-criminal activities. International governments will focus on the rogue nations conducting APT attacks and enforce diplomatic, information, military, or economic strategies to create international norms in cyberspace.

By collaborating strategically, the synergistic efforts of both the private and public sector will produce strategic and synergistic solutions that are not even being contemplated in today's environment.

Now, a challenge to each of you newly minted cyber-savvy business executives—you who are about to conclude the reading of this book—is the following: now that you have this foundational cyber knowledge, I challenge each of you to become an agent of strategic change within your organization and to make strategic changes in addressing the cyber threat at the strategic, operational, and tactical levels. Good luck, and God bless!

THE CYBER THREAT LANDSCAPE GLOSSARY

A.

Access Control—"Access control is way of limiting access to a system or to physical or virtual resources. In computing, access control is a process by which users are granted access and certain privileges to systems, resources, and information. In access control systems, users must present credentials before they can be granted access. In physical systems, these credentials may come in many forms, but credentials that can't be transferred provide the most security" (Techopedia 2017).

Advanced Persistent Threat (APT)

> An advanced persistent threat (APT) refers to a cyberattack launched by an attacker with substantial means, organization and motivation to carry out a sustained assault against a target. An APT is advanced in the sense that it employs stealth and multiple attack methods to compromise the target, which is often a high-value corporate or government resource. The attack is difficult to detect, remove, and attribute. Once the target is breached, backdoors are often created to provide the attacker with ongoing access to the compromised system. An APT is persistent because the attacker can spend months gathering intelligence about the target and use that intelligence to launch multiple attacks over an extended period of time. It is threatening because

perpetrators are often after highly sensitive information, such as the layout of nuclear power plants or codes to break into US defense contractors. (Techopedia 2017)

Adware—"Adware is free computer software that contains commercial advertisements. Adware programs include games, desktop toolbars, or utilities. Commonly, adware is web-based and collects web browser data to target advertisements, especially pop-ups. Adware is also known as freeware and pitchware" (Techopedia 2017).

Air Gap—"An air gap is a security measure implemented for computers, computer systems, or networks requiring airtight security without the risk of compromise or disaster. It ensures total isolation of a given system—electromagnetically, electronically and most importantly physically—from other networks, especially those that are not secure" (Technopedia 2017).

Antimalware—"Antimalware is any resource that protects the computers and systems against malware, including viruses, spyware and other harmful programs" (Techopedia 2017).

Antispyware—"Antispyware is a type of software that is designed to detect and remove unwanted spyware programs. Spyware is a type of malware that is installed on a computer without the user's knowledge in order to collect information about them. This can pose a security risk to the user, but more frequently spyware degrades system performance by taking up processing power, installing additional software, or redirecting users' browser activity" (Techopedia 2017).

Antivirus Software—"Antivirus software is a software utility that detects, prevents, and removes viruses, worms, and other malware from a computer. Most antivirus programs include an auto-update feature that permits the program to download profiles of new viruses, enabling the system to check for new threats. Antivirus programs are essential utilities for any computer but the choice of which one is very important. One AV program might find a certain virus or worm while another cannot, or vice-versa" (Techopedia 2017).

Application Software

Application software is a program or group of programs designed for end users. These programs are divided into two classes: system software and application software. While system software consists of low-level programs that interact with computers at a basic level, application software resides above system software and includes database programs, word processors, spreadsheets, etc. Application software may be grouped along with system software or published alone. Application software may simply be referred to as an application. (Techopedia 2017)

Authentication—"In the context of computer systems, authentication is a process that ensures and confirms a user's identity" (Techopedia 2017).

Availability—"In the context of a computer system, refers to the ability of a user to access information or resources in a specified location and in the correct format" (Techopedia 2017).

B.
Backdoor

A backdoor is a technique in which a system security mechanism is bypassed undetectably to access a computer or its data. The backdoor access method is sometimes written by the programmer who develops a program...a network administrator (NA) may intentionally create or install a backdoor program for troubleshooting or other official use. Hackers use backdoors to install malicious software (malware) files or programs, modify code or detect files and gain system and/or data access. Even backdoors installed by network administrators pose security risks because they provide a mechanism by which the system can by exploited if discovered. (Techopedia 2017)

Bluetooth—"Bluetooth is an open wireless technology standard for transmitting fixed and mobile electronic device data over short distances. Bluetooth was introduced in 1994 as a wireless substitute for RS-232 cables. Bluetooth communicates with a variety of electronic devices and creates personal networks operating within the unlicensed 2.4 GHz band. Operating range is based on device class. A variety of digital devices use Bluetooth, including MP3 players, mobile and peripheral devices and personal computers" (Techopedia 2017).

Botnet—"A botnet is a group of computers connected in a coordinated fashion for malicious purposes. Each computer in a botnet is called a bot. These bots form a network of compromised computers, which is controlled by a third party and used to transmit malware or spam, or to launch attacks" (Techopedia 2017).

Bridge

> A bridge is a type of computer network device that provides interconnection with other bridge networks that use the same protocol. Bridge devices work at the data link layer of the Open System Interconnect (OSI) Model, connecting two different networks together and providing communications between them. Bridges are similar to repeaters and hubs in that they broadcast data to every node. However, bridges maintain the media access control (MAC) address table as soon as they discover new segments, so subsequent transmission are sent to only the desired recipient. Bridges are also known as Layer 2 switches. (Techopedia 2017)

C.
Cascading Style Sheets (CSS)

> Cascading Style Sheets (CSS) is a standard (or language) that describes the formatting of markup language pages. CSS defines the formatting for the following document types: HyperText Markup Language (HTML); Extensible HyperText Markup Language (XHTML); Extensible Markup Language (XML); Scalable Vector Graphics (SVG); XML User Interface Language (XUL). CSS enables developers to separate content and visual elements for greater page control and flexibility. A CSS file is

normally attached to an HTML file by means of a link in the HTML file...HTML document formatting was tedious and complex before CSS because of built-in HTML style attributes. Specifically, styled tags required detailed and repetitious descriptions of the following elements: Font Colors, Background styles, Element alignments, Borders, and Sizes. CSS structurally defines elements for headings (h1), subheadings (h2), sub-subheadings (h3), etc. Element options are available for font, color, emphasis, size, etc." (Techopedia 2017).

Command Injection—"An attack in which the cyber threat actor's goal is to execute commands on the server's operating system via a vulnerable web application" (OWASP 2017).

Computer Network

A computer network is a group of computer systems and other computing hardware devices that are linked together through communication channels to facilitate communication and resource-sharing among a wide range of users. Networks are commonly categorized based on their characteristics...there are many types of networks, including: Local Area Networks (LAN); Personal Area Networks (PAN); Home Area Networks (HAN): Wide Area Networks (WAN); Campus Networks; Metropolitan Area Networks (MAN); Enterprise Private Networks; Internetworks; Backbone Networks (BBN); Global Area Networks (GAN); and the Internet. (Techopedia 2017)

Confidentiality—"In the context of computer systems, allows authorized users to access sensitive and protected data. Specific mechanisms ensure confidentiality and safeguard data from harmful intruders" (Techopedia 2017).

Configuration Management (CM)—"A configuration management (CM) system is used to keep track of an organization's hardware, software and related information. This includes software versions and updates installed on the organization's computer systems. CM also involves logging the network addresses belonging to the hardware devices used. Software is available for all of these tracking tasks" (Techopedia 2017).

Cookie—"A cookie is a text file that a web browser stores on a user's machine. Cookies are a way for web applications to maintain application state. They are used by websites for authentication, storing website information/preferences, other browsing information and anything else that can help the web browser while accessing web servers. HTTP cookies are known by many different names, including browser cookies, web cookies or HTTP cookies" (Techopedia 2017).

Criminal Forum—"An online forum which is a meeting place for those interested in buying, selling, and trading malware, botnets, stolen Personally Identifiable Information, credit card information, hacked server credentials and other pieces of data and software that facilitate complex cybercrimes all over the world" (Federal Bureau of Investigation 2015).

Cross-Site Request Forgery (CSRF)—"A type of website exploit carried out by issuing unauthorized commands from a trusted website user. CSRF exploits a website's trust for a particular user's browser, as opposed to cross-site scripting, which exploits the user's trust for a website. This term is also known as session riding or a one-click attack" (Techopedia 2017).

Cyberattack—"A cyberattack is deliberate exploitation of computer systems, technology-dependent enterprises and networks. Cyberattacks use malicious code to alter computer code, logic or data, resulting in disruptive consequences that can compromise data and lead to cybercrimes, such as information and identity theft. Cyberattack is also known as a computer network attack (CNA)" (Techopedia 2017).

D.
Data Forensics

> Data forensics, often used interchangeably with computer forensics, is essentially the study of digital data and how it is created and used for the purpose of an investigation. Data forensics is part of the great discipline of forensics, in which various types of evidence are

studied to investigate an alleged crime. Data forensics can involve many different tasks including data recovery or data tracking. Data forensics might focus on recovering information on the use of a mobile device, computer or other device. It might cover the tracking of phone calls, texts or e-mails through a network. Digital forensic investigators may also use various methodologies to pursue data forensics, such as decryption, advanced system searches, reverse engineering, or other high-level data analysis. (Techopedia 2017)

Demilitarized Zone (DMZ)—"A host or network that acts as a secure and intermediate network or path between an organization's internal network and the external, or nonpropriety, network. A DMZ serves as a frontline network that interacts directly with the external networks while logically separating it from the internal network. A demilitarized zone may also be known as a network perimeter or perimeter network" (Techopedia 2017).

Denial-of-Service (DoS) Attack

Any type of attack where the attackers (hackers) attempt to prevent legitimate users from accessing the service. In a DoS attack, the attacker usually sends excessive messages asking the network or server to authenticate requests that have invalid return addresses. The network or server will not be able to find the return address of the attacker when sending the authentication approval, causing the server to wait before closing the connection. When the server closes the connection the attacker sends more authentication messages with invalid return addresses. Hence, the process of authentication and server wait will begin again, keeping the network or server busy…a DoS attack can be done in several ways. The basic types of DoS attack include: (1) flooding the network to prevent legitimate network traffic; (2) disrupting the connections between two machines, thus preventing access to a service; (3) preventing a particular individual from accessing a service; (4) disrupting a service to a specific system or individual; and (5) disrupting the state of information, such as resetting of TCP sessions. (Techopedia 2017)

Distributed Control Systems (DCS)—"In a control system, refers to control achieved by intelligence that is distributed about the process to be controlled, rather than by a centrally located single unit" (National Institute of Standards and Technology Computer Security Division Computer Resource Center 2015).

Distributed Denial of Service (DDoS)

> A type of computer attack that uses a number of hosts to over-whelm a server, causing a website to experience a complete system crash. This type of denial-of-service attack is perpetrated by hackers to target large-scale, far-reaching and popular websites in an effort to disable them, either temporarily or permanently. This is often done by bombarding the targeted server with information requests, which disables the main system and prevents it from operating. This leaves the site's users unable to access the targeted website. DDoS differs from a denial-of-service (DoS) attack in that it uses several hosts to bombard a server, whereas in a DoS attack, a single host is used. (Techopedia 2017)

E.

Encryption—"Encryption is the process of using an algorithm to transform information to make it unreadable for unauthorized users. This cryptographic method protects sensitive data such as credit card numbers by encoding and transforming information into unreadable cipher text. This encoded data may only be decrypted or made readable with a key" (Techopedia 2017).

F.

Firewall—"A firewall is software used to maintain the security of a private network. Firewalls block unauthorized access to or from private networks and are often employed to prevent unauthorized web users or illicit software from gaining access to private networks connected to the Internet. A firewall may be implemented using hardware, software, or a combination of both. A firewall is recognized as the first line of defense in securing sensitive information. For better safety, the data can be encrypted" (Techopedia 2017).

G.

H.

Heuristic—"In computing, heuristic refers to a problem-solving method executed through learning-based techniques and experience. When exhaustive search methods are impractical, heuristic methods are used to find efficient solutions. Heuristic methods are designed for conceptual simplicity and enhanced computational performance—often at the cost of accuracy" (Techopedia 2017).

Heuristic Filtering

> Heuristic filtering refers to the use of various algorithms and resources to examine text or content in specific ways. The word *heuristic* describes a type of analysis that relies on experience or specific intuitive criteria, rather than simple technical metrics. The use of high-level algorithms allows for heuristic analysis of content, where humans can program computers to think in certain ways rather than just applying a purely quantitative analysis. Heuristic filtering is most widely used on the Internet to filter e-mail and web access" (Techopedia 2017).

Hub—"A hub, in the context of networking, is a hardware device that relays communication data. A hub sends data packets (frames) to all devices on a network, regardless of any MAC addresses contained in the data packet" (Techopedia 2017).

Human-Machine Interface (HMI)

> Software and hardware that allows human operators to monitor the state of a process under control, modify control settings to change the control objective, and manually override automatic control operations in the event of an emergency. The HMI also allows a control engineer or operator to configure set points or control algorithms and parameters in the controller. The HMI also displays process status information, historical information, reports, and other information to operators, administrators,

managers, business partners, and other authorized users. Operators and engineers use HMIs to monitor and configure set points, control algorithms, send commands, and adjust and establish parameters in the controller. The HMI also displays process status information and historical information. (National Institute of Standards and Technology Computer Security Division Computer Resource Center 2015)

Hypertext Markup Language (HTML)—"HyperText markup language (HTML) is the major markup language used to display web pages on the Internet. In other words, web pages are composed of HTML, which is used to display text, images or other resources through a web browser. All HTML is plaintext, meaning it is not compiled and may be a read by humans. The file extension for an HTML file is .htm or .html" (Techopedia 2017).

Hypertext Transfer Protocol (HTTP)

HyperText Transfer Protocol (HTTP) is an application-layer protocol used primarily on the World Wide Web. HTTP uses a client-server model where the web browser is the client and communicates with the webserver that hosts the website. The browser uses HTTP, which is carried over TCP/IP to communicate to the server and retrieve web content for the user. HTTP is a widely used protocol and has been rapidly adopted over the Internet because of its simplicity. It is a stateless and connectionless protocol. (Techopedia 2017)

Hypertext Transport Protocol Secure (HTTPS)—"Hypertext Transfer Protocol Secure (HTTPS) is a variant of the standard web transfer protocol (HTTP) that adds a layer of security on the data in transit through a secure socket layer (SSL) or transport layer security (TLS) protocol connection. HTTPS enables encrypted communication and a secure connection between a remote user and the primary web server" (Techopedia 2017).

I.

Industrial Control Systems (ICS)—"ICS is a general term that encompasses several types of control systems, including Supervisory Control and Data

Acquisition (SCADA) systems, Distributed Control Systems (DCS), and other control system configurations such as Programmable Logic Controllers (PLC) often found in the industrial sectors and critical infrastructures" (National Institute of Standards and Technology Computer Security Division Computer Resource Center 2015).

Information Assurance (IA)—"The steps involved in protecting information systems, like computer systems, and networks. There are commonly five terms associated with the definition of information assurance: Integrity; Availability; Authentication; Confidentiality; and Nonrepudiation" (Techopedia 2017).

Integrity—"In the context of computer systems, refers to methods of ensuring that data is real, accurate and safeguarded from unauthorized user modification" (Techopedia 2017).

IEEE 802.11

IEEE 802.11 refers to the set of standards that define communications for wireless LANs (wireless local area networks, or WLANs). The technology behind 802.11 is branded to consumers as Wi-Fi. As the name implies, IEEE 802.11 is overseen by the IEEE (Institute of Electrical and Electronics Engineers), specifically the IEEE LAN/MAN Standards Committee (IEEE 802). The current version of the standard is IEEE 802.11-2007... it's common to hear people refer to '802.11 standards' or the '802.11 family of standards.' However, to be more precise, there is only one standard (IEEE 802.11-2007) but many amendments. Commonly known amendments include 802.11a, 802.11b, 802.11g and 802.11n. (Techopedia 2017)

IEEE 802.1X

IEEE 802.1X is a standard component of the IEEE 802.11 network protocol group established by the Institute of Electrical and Electronics Engineers (IEEE). IEEE 802.1X adheres to IEEE 802.11 protocols to enhance wireless network security. IEEE

802.1X controls access to wireless or virtual local area networks (VLAN) and applies traffic policies based on user identity and credentials. IEEE 802.1X ensures a user authentication framework where network access is denied upon failed authentication. Built for wired networks, IEEE 802.1X requires very little processing power and is well-suited to wireless LAN applications. (Techopedia 2017)

Intrusion Detection System (IDS)

An intrusion detection system (IDS) is a type of security software designed to automatically alert administrators when someone or something is trying to compromise system information through malicious activities or through security policy violations. An IDS works by monitoring system activity through examining vulnerabilities in the system, the integrity of files and conducting an analysis of patterns based on already known attacks. It also automatically monitors the Internet to search for any of the latest threats which could result in a future attack. (Techopedia 2017)

Intrusion Prevention System (IPS)—"An intrusion prevention system (IPS) is a system that monitors a network for malicious activities such as security threats or policy violations. The main function of an IPS is to identify suspicious activity, and then log information, attempt to block the activity, and then finally report it. Intrusion prevention systems are also known as intrusion detection prevention systems (IDPS)" (Techopedia 2017).

J.
JavaScript (JS)

JavaScript (JS) is a scripting language primarily used on the web. It is used to enhance HTML pages and is commonly found embedded in HTML code. JavaScript is an interpreted language. Thus, it doesn't need to be compiled. JavaScript renders web pages in an interactive and dynamic fashion. This allowing the pages to react to events, exhibit special effects, accept variable text, validate data, create cookies, detect a user's browser, etc....HTML pages are fine for displaying static content, e.g., a simple image or text. However, most pages nowadays are rarely static. Many of today's pages have menus, forms, slideshows, and even images that provide user interaction. JavaScript is the language employed by web developers to provide such interaction. (Techopedia 2017)

K.

L.

Local Area Network (LAN)—"A local area network (LAN) is a computer network within a small geographical area such as a home, school, computer laboratory, office building or group of buildings. A LAN is composed of interconnected workstations and personal computers which are each capable of accessing and sharing data and devices, such as printers, scanners, and data storage devices, anywhere on the LAN. LANs are characterized by higher communication and data transfer rates and the lack of any need for leased communication lines" (Techopedia 2017).

Log Management

Log management is the general term for handling data from a defined continual source, or log, is used for a business process. A log may be digital or manual, and log management can help to classify and use the data within a number of different ways depending on what is useful to the organization. There are a number of different terms for the aggregation, organization and analysis of large data sets in IT. What log management services and systems do involves collecting and organizing this material, and might also in some cases involve analytical tools to help develop more useful results from the data that is presented. (Techopedia 2017)

M.

N.

Near Field Communication (NFC)—"Near field communication (NFC) is a wireless technology that allows a device to collect and interpret data from another closely located NFC device or tag. NFC employs inductive-coupling technology, in which power and data are shared through coupled inductive circuits over a very close proximity of a few centimeters. NFC is often employed through mobile phones or credit cards, where information may be read if it is passed very close to another such device or NFC tag" (Techopedia 2017).

Near Field Communication Tag (NFC Tag)

> A near field communication tag (NFC tag) is a sticker or wristband with small microchips that can be read by in range mobile devices. Information is stored in these microchips. A NFC tag has the ability to send data to other mobile phones with NFC capabilities. NFC tags also perform a variety of actions, such as changing handset settings or launching a website. Many of today's smartphones have built-in NFC capabilities, and smartphone users can purchase and acquire tags online. The amount of information stored on a NFC tag depends on the tag type, as tag memory capacity varies by tag. For example, a tag can store a phone number or URL. A modern example of a commonly used NFC tag function is mobile payment processing, where users swipe or flick a mobile phone on a NFC reader. Google's version of this system is Google Wallet. (Techopedia 2017)

Network Traffic Monitoring—"Network traffic monitoring is the process of reviewing, analyzing, and managing network traffic for any abnormality or process that can affect network performance, availability, and/or security… some of the technologies that incorporate network traffic monitoring include: Firewalls; Intrusion detection and prevention systems; Network monitoring, managing and performance software; and Antivirus/antimalware software" (Techopedia 2017).

Network Interface Card (NIC)—"A Network Interface Card (NIC) is a computer hardware component that allows a computer to connect to a network. NICs may be used for both wired and wireless connections. A NIC is also known as a network interface controller (NIC), network interface controller card, expansion card, computer circuit board, network card, LAN card, network adaptor or network adaptor card (NAC)" (Techopedia 2017).

Nonrepudiation—"Nonrepudiation is a method of guaranteeing message transmission between parties via digital signatures and/or encryption...nonrepudiation is often used for digital contracts, signatures, and e-mail messages" (Techopedia 2017).

O.
Open Systems Interconnection Model (OSI Model)

> The Open Systems Interconnection (OSI) Model is a conceptual and logical layout that defines network communication used by systems open to interconnection and communication with other systems. The model is broken into seven subcomponents, or layers, each of which represents a conceptual collection of services provided to the layers above and below it. The OSI Model also defines a logical network and effectively describes computer packet transfer by using different layer protocols...OSI's seven layers are divided into two portions: hot layers and media layers. The hot portion includes the application, presentation, session and transport layers; the media portion includes the network, data link and physical layers. (Techopedia 2017)

Operating System

> An operating system (OS), in its most general sense, is software that allows a user to run other applications on a computing device. While it is possible for a software application to interface directly with hardware, the vast majority of applications are written for an OS, which allows them to take advantage of common libraries and not worry about specific hardware details. The

operating system manages a computer's hardware resources including: Input devices such as a keyboard and mouse; Output devices such as display monitors, printers and scanners; Network devices such as modems, routers and network connections; and Storage devices such as internal and external drives. (Techopedia 2017)

P.

Patch—"A patch is a software update composed code inserted (or patched) into the code of an executable program. Typically, a patch is installed into an existing software program. Patches are often temporary fixes between full releases of a software package. Patches may do any of the following: Fix a software bug; Install new drivers; Address new security vulnerabilities; Address software stability issues; and Upgrade the software" (Techopedia 2017).

Patch Management—"Patch management is a strategy for managing patches or upgrades for software applications and technologies. A patch management plan can help a business or organization handle these changes efficiently. Software patches are often necessary in order to fix existing problems with software that are noticed after initial release. Many of these patches have to do with security. Others may have to do with specific functionality for programs" (Techopedia 2017).

Penetration Testing (Pen Testing)—"Penetration testing (pen testing or pentesting) is a method of testing, measuring and enhancing established security measures on information systems and support areas. Pen testing is also known as a security assessment" (Techopedia 2017).

Personally Identifiable Information (PII)—"Personal Identifiable Information (PII or pii) is a type of data that identifies the unique identity of an individual. It is one of the most basic forms of personal information and includes an individual's name, gender, address, telephone, e-mail address or basic biometric data information that is electronically stored within a device or application" (Techopedia 2017).

Programmable Logic Controller (PLC)

A PLC is a small industrial computer originally designed to perform the logic functions executed by electrical hardware (relays, switches, and mechanical timer/counters). PLCs have evolved into controllers with the capability of controlling complex processes, and they are used substantially in SCADA systems and DCS. PLCs are also used as the primary controller in smaller system configurations. PLCs are used extensively in almost all industrial processes. (National Institute of Standards and Technology Computer Security Division Computer Resource Center 2015)

Protocol—"A protocol is a set of rules and guidelines for communication data. Rules are defined for each step and process during communication between two or more computers. Networks have to follow these rules to successfully transmit data" (Techopedia 2017).

Q.

R.
Remote Terminal Unit (RTU)

A computer with radio interfacing used in remote situations where communications via wire is unavailable. Usually used to communicate with remote field equipment. PLCs with radio communication capabilities are also used in place of RTUs. Special purpose data acquisition and control unit designed to support DCS and SCADA remote stations. RTUs are field devices often equipped with network capabilities, which can include wired and wireless radio interfaces to communicate to the supervisory controller. Sometimes PLCs are implemented as field devices to serve as RTUs; in this case, the PLC is often referred to as an RTU. (National Institute of Standards and Technology Computer Security Division Computer Resource Center 2015)

Rootkit

A rootkit is software used by a hacker to gain constant administrator-level access to a computer or network. A rootkit is typically installed through a stolen password or by exploiting system vulnerabilities without the victim's consent or knowledge. Rootkits primarily aim at user-mode applications, but they also focus on a computer's hypervisor, the kernel, or even firmware. Rootkits can completely deactivate or destroy the antimalware software installed in an infected computer, thus making a rootkit attack difficult to track and eliminate. When done well, the intrusion can be carefully concealed so that even system administrators are unaware of it. (Techopedia 2017)

Router—"A router is a device that analyzes the contents of data packets transmitted within a network or to another network. Routers determine whether the source and destination are on the same network or whether data must be transferred from one network type to another, which requires encapsulating the data packet with routing protocol header information for the new network type" (Techopedia 2017).

S.

Scripts—"Scripts are lists of commands executed by certain programs or scripting engines. They are usually text documents with instructions written using a scripting language. They are used to generate web pages and to automate computer processes" (Techopedia 2017).

Security Incident—"A security incident is a warning that there may be a threat to information or computer security. The warning could also be that a threat has already occurred. Threats or violations can be identified by unauthorized access to a system. A computer security incident is a threat to policies that are related to computer security" (Techopedia 2017).

Security Incident and Event Management System (SIEM)

A Security incident and event management (SIEM) is the process of identifying, monitoring, recording, and analyzing security events or incidents within a real-time IT environment. It provides a comprehensive and centralized view of the security scenario of an IT infrastructure. There are, generally speaking, six main attributes of a SIEM system: Retention: Storing data for long periods so that decisions can be made off of more complete data sets; Dashboards: Used to analyze (and visualize) data in an attempt to recognize patterns or target activity or data that does not fit into a normal pattern; Correlation: Sorts data into packets that are meaningful, similar and share common traits. The goal is to turn data into useful information; Alerting: When data is gathered or identified that trigger certain responses—such as alerts or potential security problems—SIEM tools can activate certain protocols to alert users, like notifications sent to the dashboard, an automated e-mail or text message; Data Aggregation—Data can be gathered from any number of sites once SIEM is introduced, including servers, networks, databases, software and e-mail systems. The aggregator also serves a consolidating resource before data is sent to be correlated or retained; Compliance—Protocols in a SIEM can be established that automatically collect data necessary for compliance with company, organizational, or government policies. (Techopedia 2017)

Server

A server is a computer, a device or a program that is dedicated to managing network resources. Servers are often referred to as dedicated because they carry out hardly any other tasks apart from their server tasks. There are a number of categories of servers, including print servers, file servers, network servers and database servers...a server often has special characteristics and capabilities including: The ability to update hardware and software without a restart or reboot; Advanced backup capability for frequent backup of critical data; Advanced networking performance; Automatic (invisible to the user) data transfer between devices; and High security for resources, data and memory protection. (Techopedia 2017)

Service Set Identifier (SSID) "A service set identified (SSID) is a type of identifier that uniquely identifies a wireless local area network (WLAN). Service set identifiers differentiate wireless LANs by assigning each a unique, 32-bit alphanumeric character identifier. SSID is also referred to as network name" (Techopedia 2017).

Session

> In IT, the word 'session' is a reference to a certain time frame for communication between two devices, two systems or two parts of a system…in some cases, a session is user-initiated. For example, the time frame for an interaction between two personal computers used in online chatting or messaging is considered a session. The individual users initiate it, and end it when it is finished. Other kinds of sessions are initiated by technology. One of the most common is a client/server session between a server and a personal computer or other device or system accessing that server. Developers and others have developed session protocols for handling these interactions between systems. These cover all of the many interactions required for browsing the Internet, as well as sending and receiving e-mails through various e-mail clients. It is interesting to note that many of these sessions are actively hidden from end users; in other words, the common user does not recognize that these sessions are occurring, and does not know much about what happens during these sessions. Analysis of technology-initiated sessions is largely the province of network administrators, security experts and others with a close knowledge of an interactive network. (Techopedia 2017)

Software—"Software, in its most general sense, is a set of instructions or programs instructing a computer to do specific tasks. Software is a generic term used to describe computer programs. Scripts, applications, programs and a set of instructions are the terms used to describe software" (Techopedia 2017).

Spyware—"Spyware is infiltration software that secretly monitors unsuspecting users. It can enable a hacker to obtain sensitive information, such as passwords, from the user's computer. Spyware exploits user and application vulnerabilities and is often attached to free online software downloads or to links that are clicked by users" (Techopedia 2017).

SQL Injection Attack—"An SQL injection is a computer attack in which malicious code is embedded in a poorly designed application and then passed to the backend database. The malicious data then produces database-query results or actions that should never have been executed" (Techopedia 2017).

Static Web Page

> A static web page is a page that is built using HTML code and features the same presentation and content, regardless of user identity or other factors. Static web pages are easier to code and assemble than dynamic web pages, which may feature customizable content according to a user's identity or other factors. Static web pages are also known as static websites…another way to understand static web pages is to contrast them with dynamic web pages. The latter have controls and forms that are deep coded, so that the page displays differently to different users or in different situations. For example, a dynamic web page may access a database to find out about a user's identification and history, or to display custom items like the user's name or his/her collected preferences. In contrast, a static web page does not provide this kind of customization. (Techopedia 2017)

Structured Query Language (SQL)—"Structured Query Language (SQL) is a standard computer language for relational database management and data manipulation. SQL is used to query, insert, update and modify data. Most relational databases support SQL, which is an added benefit for database administrators (DBAs), as they are often required to support databases across several different platforms" (Techopedia 2017).

Supervisory Control and Data Acquisition (SCADA)

> A generic name for a computerized system that is capable of gathering and processing data and applying operational controls over long distances. Typical uses include power transmission

and distribution and pipeline systems. SCADA was designed for the unique communication challenges (e.g., delays, data integrity) posed by the various media that must be used, such as phone lines, microwave, and satellite. Usually shared rather than dedicated. (National Institute of Standards and Technology Computer Security Division Computer Resource Center 2015)

Switch—"A switch, in the context of networking, is a high-speed device that receives incoming data packets and redirects them to their destination on a local area network (LAN). A LAN switch operates at the data link layer (layer 2) or the network layer of the OSI Model and, as such, it can support all types of packet protocols" (Techopedia 2017).

T.
Trojan Horse

A Trojan horse is a seemingly benign program that when activated, causes harm to a computer system. The following are types of Trojan horses: Backdoor Trojan: Opens a back door for a user to access a victim's system at a later time; Downloader: This Trojan downloads malicious software and causes harm to the victim's computer system; Infostealer: This Trojan attempts to steal information from the victim's computer; Remote Access Trojan (RAT): This can be hidden in games or other programs of a smaller variety and give the attacker control of the victim's computer; Destructive Trojan: This destroys the victim's files; Proxy Trojan: As a proxy server, this allows the attacker to hijack a victim's computer and conduct illegal activities from the victim's computer. (Techopedia 2017)

U.

V.
Virtual Local Area Network (VLAN)

A virtual local area network (VLAN) is a logical group of workstations, servers and network devices that appear to be on the same

LAN despite their geographical distribution. A VLAN allows a network of computers and users to communicate in a simulated environment as if they exist in a single LAN and are sharing a single broadcast and multicast domain. VLANs are implemented to achieve scalability, security and ease of network management and can quickly adapt to change in network requirements and relocation of workstations and server nodes. Higher-end switches allow the functionality and implementation of VLANs. The purpose of implementing a VLAN is to improve the performance of a network or apply appropriate security features. (Techopedia 2017)

Virtual Machine—"A virtual machine (VM) is a software program or operating system that not only exhibits the behavior of a separate computer, but is also capable of performing tasks such as running applications and programs like a separate computer. A virtual machine, usually known as a guest, is created within another computing environment referred to as a 'host.' Multiple virtual machines can exist within a single host at one time" (Techopedia 2017).

Virtualization

Virtualization refers to the creation of a virtual resource such as a server, desktop, operating system, file, storage or network. The main goal of virtualization is to manage workloads by radically transforming traditional computing to make it more scalable. Virtualization has been a part of the IT landscape for decades now, and today it can be applied to a wide range of system layers, including operating system-level virtualization, hardware-level virtualization and server virtualization. The most common form of virtualization is the operating system-level virtualization. In operating system-level virtualization, it is possible to run multiple operating systems on a single piece of hardware. Virtualization technology involves separating the physical hardware and software by emulating hardware using software. When a different OS is operating on top of the primary OS by means of virtualization, it is referred to as a virtual machine. (Techopedia 2017)

Virus—"A virus is a type of malicious software (malware) comprised of small pieces of code attached to legitimate programs. When that program runs, the virus runs" (Techopedia 2017).

Vulnerability—"Vulnerability is a cybersecurity term that refers to a flaw in a system that can leave it open to attack. A vulnerability may also refer to any type of weakness in a computer system itself, in a set of procedures, or in anything that leaves information security exposed to a threat" (Techopedia 2017).

W.

Web-Based Application—"A web-based application is any program that is accessed over a network connection using HTTP, rather than existing within a device's memory. Web-based applications often run inside a web browser. However, web-based applications also may be client-based, where a small part of the program is downloaded to a user's desktop, but processing is done over the Internet on an external server. Web-based applications are also known as web apps" (Techopedia 2017).

Web Browser

> A web browser is a software program that allows users to locate, access, and display web pages. In common usage, a web browser is usually shortened to 'browser.' Browsers are used primarily for displaying and accessing websites on the Internet, as well as other content created using Hypertext Markup Language (HTML) and Extensible Markup Language (XML), etc. Browsers translate web pages and websites delivered using Hypertext Transfer Protocol (HTTP) into human readable content. They also have the ability to display other protocols and prefixes, such as secure HTTP (HTTPS), File Transfer Protocol (FTP), e-mail handling (mailto:), and files (file:). In addition, most browsers also support external plug-ins required to display active content, such as in-page video, audio and Flash content. A variety of web browsers are available with different features, look-and-feel, and designed to run on different operating systems. Common browsers

include Internet Explorer from Microsoft, Firefox from Mozilla, Google Chrome, Safari from Apple, and Opera. All major browsers have mobile versions that are lightweight versions for accessing the web on mobile devices. (Techopedia 2017)

Web Server—"A web server is a system that delivers content or services to end users over the Internet. A web server consists of a physical server, server operating system (OS) and software used to facilitate HTTP communication. A web server is also known as an Internet server" (Techopedia 2017).

Wi-Fi Protected Access (WPA)

Wi-Fi Protected Access (WPA) is a security standard to secure computers connected to a Wi-Fi network. Its purpose is to address serious weaknesses in the previous system, the Wired Equivalent Privacy (WEP) standard. Wi-Fi Protected Access (WPA) and WPA2 are concurrent security standards. WPA addressed the majority of the IEEE 802.11 standard, and the WPA2 certification achieved full compliance. However, WPA2 will not work with some older network cards, thus the need for concurrent security standards. (Techopedia 2017).

Wi-Fi Protected Access II (WPA2)—"Wi-Fi Protected Access II (WPA2) is a security standard to secure computers connected to a Wi-Fi network. Its purpose is to achieve complete compliance with IEEE 802.11i standard, only partially achieved with WPA, and to address the security flaw in the 128-bit 'temporary key integrity protocol' (TKIP) in WPA by replacing it with Counter Mode/CBC-MAC Protocol (CCMP)" (Techopedia 2017).

Wired Equivalent Privacy (WEP)—"Wired Equivalent Privacy (WEP) was first released as a portion of the IEEE 802.11 standard in 1999. Its security was deemed to be the equivalent of any wired medium, hence its name. As the years passed, WEP was deemed broken, and it has since been replaced by two other iterations of wireless security protocols, Wi-Fi Protected Access (WPA) and WPA2" (Techopedia 2017).

Wireless Access Point (WAP)—"A wireless access point (WAP) is a hardware device or configured node on a local area network (LAN) that allows wireless capable devices and wired networks to connect through a wireless standard, including Wi-Fi or Bluetooth. WAPs feature radio transmitters and antennae, which facilitate connectivity between devices and the Internet or a network. A WAP is also known as a hotspot" (Techopedia 2017).

Wireless Fidelity (Wi-Fi)

Wi-Fi is a type of wireless network technology used for connecting to the Internet. The frequencies Wi-Fi works at are 2.4 Ghz or 5 Ghz, ensure no interference with cellphones, broadcast radio, TV antenna and two-way radios are encountered during transmission. To simplify, Wi-Fi is basically just radio waves broadcast from a Wi-Fi router, a device detecting and deciphering the waves, and then sending them back to the router. It works very similar to an AM/FM radio but it is a two-way communication channel. Wi-Fi works over longer distances than Bluetooth or infrared and is also a low power unobtrusive technology, making it suitable for portable devices such as laptops and palmtops. Wi-Fi is governed by the Wi-Fi Alliance, an association of manufacturers and regulators defining standards and certifying products as Wi-Fi compatible. (Techopedia 2017)

Wireless Local Area Network (WLAN)—"A wireless local area network (WLAN) is a wireless distribution method for two or more devices that use high-frequency radio waves and often include access points to the Internet. A WLAN allows users to move around the coverage area, often a home or small office, while maintaining a network connection. A WLAN is sometimes called a local area wireless network (LAWN)" (Techopedia 2017).

Workstation

A workstation is a computer dedicated to a user or group of users engaged in business or professional work. It includes one or more high resolution displays and a faster processer than a personal computer (PC). A workstation also has greater multitasking capability because of additional random access memory (RAM), drives and drive capacity. A workstation may also have higher-speed graphics adapters and more connected peripherals. The term workstation also has been used to reference PC or mainframe terminal on a local area network (LAN). These workstations may share network resources with one or more large client computers and network servers. (Techopedia 2017)

World Wide Web (WWW)

The World Wide Web (WWW) is a network of online content that is formatted in Hypertext Markup Language (HTML) and accessed via Hypertext Transfer Protocol (HTTP). The term refers to all the interlinked HTML pages that can be accessed over the Internet. The World Wide Web was originally designed in 1991 by Tim Berners-Lee while he was a contractor at CERN. The World Wide Web is what most people think of as the Internet. It is all the web pages, pictures, videos and other online content that can be accessed via a web browser. The Internet, in contrast, is the underlying network connection that allows us to send e-mail and access the World Wide Web. (Techopedia 2017)

Worms—"A worm is a type of malicious software (malware) that replicates while moving across computers, leaving copies of itself in the memory of each computer in its path" (Techopedia 2017).

X.

Y.

Z.

REFERENCES

2017. "A List of Wireless Network Attacks." July 9. Accessed July 9, 2017. http://searchsecurity.techtarget.com/feature/A-list-of-wireless-network-attacks.

2017. "Security Concerns with NFC Technology." July 9. Accessed July 9, 2017. http://nearfieldcommunication.org/nfc-security.html.

2016. "USENIX Enigma 2016—NSA TAO Chief on Disrupting Nation State Hackers." January 28. Accessed July 3, 2017. https://www.youtube.com/watch?v=bDJb8WOJYdA.

(ISC)². 2017. "About (ISC)²." June 29. Accessed June 29, 2017. https://www.isc2.org/aboutus/default.aspx.

(ISC)². 2017. "CAP—Certified Authorization Professional." June 28. Accessed June 28, 2017. https://www.isc2.org/cap/default.aspx.

———. 2017. "CCFP—Certified Cyber Forensics Professional." June 28. Accessed June 28, 2017. https://www.isc2.org/ccfp/default.aspx.

———. 2017. "CCSP—Certified Cloud Security Professional." June 28. Accessed June 28, 2017. https://www.isc2.org/ccsp/default.aspx.

———. 2017. "CISSP®—Certified Information Systems Security Professional." June 28. Accessed June 28, 2017. https://www.isc2.org/cissp/default. aspx.

———. 2017. "CSSLP—Certified Secure Software Lifecycle Professional." June 28. Accessed June 28, 2017. https://www.isc2.org/csslp/default.aspx.

———. 2017. "HCISPP—HealthCare Information Security and Privacy Practitioner." June 28. Accessed June 28, 2017. https://www.isc2.org/ hcispp/default.aspx.

———. 2017. "SSCP®—Systems Security Certified Practitioner." June 28. Accessed June 28, 2017. https://www.isc2.org/sscp/default.aspx.

———. 2017. "CAP—Certified Authorization Professional." June 28. https:// www.isc2.org/cap/default.aspx.

———. 2017. "CCFP—Certified Cyber Forensics Professional." June 28. https:// www.isc2.org/ccfp/default.aspx.

———. 2017. "CCSP—Certified Cloud Security Professional" June 28. https:// www.isc2.org/ccsp/default.aspx.

———. 2017. "CISSP®—Certified Information Systems Security Professional." June 28. https://www.isc2.org/cissp/default.aspx.

———. 2017. "CSSLP—Certified Secure Software Lifecycle Professional." June 28. https://www.isc2.org/csslp/default.aspx.

———. 2017. "HCISPP—HealthCare Information Security and Privacy Practitioner." June 28. https://www.isc2.org/hcispp/default.aspx.

———. 2017. "SSCP®—Systems Security Certified Practitioner." June 28. https://www.isc2.org/sscp/default.aspx.

AICPA, 2017. "About the AICPA." September 3. Accessed September 3, 2017. http://www.aicpa.org/ABOUT/Pages/default.aspx.

AICPA. 2017. "SOC for Cybersecurity." April. Accessed February 11, 2018. https://www.aicpa.org/InterestAreas/FRC/AssuranceAdvisoryServices/DownloadableDocuments/SOC-for-Cybersecurity-Backgrounder.pdf.

Amadeo, Ron. 2015. "First-Ever Monthly Android Security Updates Start to Roll Out." September 10. Accessed July 9, 2017. https://arstechnica.com/gadgets/2015/09/first-ever-monthly-android-security-updates-start-to-roll-out/.

Android. 2017. "Dashboards Platform Versions." July 9. Accessed July 9, 2017. https://developer.android.com/about/dashboards/index.html#Platform.

2017. *Android, The World's Most Popular Mobile Platform.* July 9. https://developer.android.com/about/index.html.

Atkinson, Claire. 2016. "Verizon Wants $1B Discount on Yahoo Deal after Reports of Hacking, Spying." October 6. Accessed January 25, 2017. http://nypost.com/2016/10/06/verizon-wants-1b-discount-on-yahoo-deal-after-hacking-reports/.

AV-Test. 2017. "AV Test the Independent IT-Security Institute." July 2. Accessed July 2, 2017. https://www.av-test.org/en/statistics/malware/.

———. 2017. "Security Report 2015/16." July 3. Accessed July 3, 2017. https://www.av-test.org/fileadmin/pdf/security_report/AV-TEST_Security_Report_2015-2016.pdf.

Bapna, Subham. 2017. "Here's What to Note about Android Nougat's Security Features." March 11. Accessed July 9, 2017. https://www.droidmen.com/android-nougat-security-features/.

Carnegive Mellon University Software Engineering Institute CERT. 2017. "CERT Insider Threat Center." July 12. Accessed July 12, 2017. https://www.cert.org/insider-threat/cert-insider-threat-center.cfm.

———. 2016. *CERT Insider Threat Center.* October 30. https://www.cert.org/insider-threat/cert-insider-threat-center.cfm.

Cass, Stephen. 2016. "The 2016 Top Programming Languages." July 26. Accessed July 13, 2017. http://spectrum.ieee.org/computing/software/the-2016-top-programming-languages.

Chabrow, Eric. 2017. "SEC Chair Wants More Cyber Risk Disclosure From Public Firms." September 26. Accessed October 4, 2017. https://www.bankinfosecurity.com/sec-chair-more-cyber-risk-disclosure-from-public-firms-a-10336.

CISCO. 2017. "CCDA." June 29. Accessed June 29, 2017. http://www.cisco.com/c/en/us/training-events/training-certifications/certifications/associate/ccda.html.

———. 2017. "CCENT." June 29. Accessed June 29, 2017. http://www.cisco.com/c/en/us/training-events/training-certifications/certifications/entry/ccent.html.

———. 2017. "CCNA Cloud." June 29. Accessed June 29, 2017. http://www.cisco.com/c/en/us/training-events/training-certifications/certifications/associate/ccna-cloud.html.

———. 2017. "CCNA Collaboration." June 29. Accessed June 29, 2017. http://www.cisco.com/c/en/us/training-events/training-certifications/certifications/associate/ccna-collaboration.html.

———. 2017. "CCNA Cyber Ops." June 29. Accessed June 29, 2017. http://www.cisco.com/c/en/us/training-events/training-certifications/certifications/associate/ccna-cyber-ops.html.

———. 2017. "CCNA Data Center." June 29. Accessed June 29, 2017. http://www.cisco.com/c/en/us/training-events/training-certifications/certifications/associate/ccna-data-center.html.

———. 2017. "CCNA Industrial." June 29. Accessed June 29, 2017. http://www.cisco.com/c/en/us/training-events/training-certifications/certifications/associate/ccna-industrial.html.

———. 2017. "CCNA Routing and Switching." June 29. Accessed June 29, 2017. http://www.cisco.com/c/en/us/training-events/training-certifications/certifications/associate/ccna-routing-switching.html.

———. 2017. "CCNA Security." June 29. Accessed June 29, 2017. http://www.cisco.com/c/en/us/training-events/training-certifications/certifications/associate/ccna-security.html.

———. 2017. "CCNA Service Provider." June 29. Accessed June 29, 2017. http://www.cisco.com/c/en/us/training-events/training-certifications/certifications/associate/ccna-service-provider.html.

———. 2017. "CCNA Wireless." June 29. Accessed June 29, 2017. http://www.cisco.com/c/en/us/training-events/training-certifications/certifications/associate/ccna-wireless.html.

———. 2017. "CCT Data Center." June 29. Accessed June 29, 2017. http://www.cisco.com/c/en/us/training-events/training-certifications/certifications/entry/technician-cct/data-center.htmlhttp://www.cisco.com/c/en/us/training-events/training-certifications/certifications/entry/technician-cct/data-center.html.

———. 2017. "CCT Routing & Switching." June 29. Accessed June 29, 2017. http://www.cisco.com/c/en/us/training-events/training-certifications/certifications/entry/technician-cct/routing-switching.html.

———. 2017. "Technician (CCT)." June 28. Accessed June 28, 2017. http://www.cisco.com/c/en/us/training-events/training-certifications/certifications/entry/technician-cct.html.

———. 2017. "Training & Certifications." June 29. Accessed June 29, 2017. http://www.cisco.com/c/en/us/training-events/training-certifications/certifications.html#~Cert.

———. 2017. "Training & Certifications." June 29. Accessed June 29, 2017. http://www.cisco.com/c/en/us/training-events/training-certifications/certifications.html.

———. 2017. *CT Routing & Switching.* June 29. http://www.cisco.com/c/en/us/ training-events/training-certifications/certifications/entry/technician-cct/routing-switching.html.

Citadel Information Group Inc. 2017. "Securing the IT Network (NSA Defense in Depth)." July 2. Accessed July 2, 2017. https://citadel-information. com/wp-content/uploads/2010/12/nsa-defense-in-depth.pdf.

CompTIA. 2017. "About CompTIA." June 29. Accessed June 29, 2017. https:// certification.comptia.org/about-us.

———. 2017. "CompTIA A+." June 29. Accessed June 29, 2017. https:// certification.comptia.org/certifications/a.

———. 2017. "CompTIA Advanced Security Practitioner." June 29. Accessed June 29, 2017. https://certification.comptia.org/certifications/comptia-advanced-security-practitioner.

———. 2017. "CompTIA CSA+." June 29. Accessed June 29, 2017. https:// certification.comptia.org/certifications/cybersecurity-analyst.

———. 2017. "CompTIA Cloud Essentials." June 29. Accessed June 29, 2017. https://certification.comptia.org/certifications/cloud-essentials.

———. 2017. "CompTIA Cloud+." June 29. Accessed June 29, 2017. https:// certification.comptia.org/certifications/cloud.

———. 2017. "CompTIA CTT+." June 29. Accessed June 29, 2017. https:// certification.comptia.org/certifications/ctt.

———. 2017. "CompTIA IT Fundamentals." June 29. Accessed June 29, 2017. https://certification.comptia.org/certifications/it-fundamentals.

———. 2017. "CompTIA Linux+." June 29. Accessed June 29, 2017. https:// certification.comptia.org/certifications/linux.

———. 2017. "CompTIA Mobility+." June 29. Accessed June 29, 2017. https://certification.comptia.org/certifications/mobility.

———. 2017. "CompTIA Network+." June 29. Accessed June 29, 2017. https://certification.comptia.org/certifications/network.

———. 2017. "COMPTIA SECURITY+." June 29. Accessed June 29, 2017. https://certification.comptia.org/certifications/security.

———. 2017. "CompTIA Server+." June 29. Accessed June 29, 2017. https://certification.comptia.org/certifications/server.

———. 2017. "CompTIIA Project+." June 29. Accessed June 29, 2017. https://certification.comptia.org/certifications/project.

———. 2017. *CompTIA CDIA+*. June 29. https://certification.comptia.org/certifications/cdia.

———. 2016. *CompTIA Healthcare IT Technician*. November 2. https://certification.comptia.org/certifications/healthcare-it-technician.

———. 2016. *CompTIA Social Media Security Professional*. November 2. https://certification.comptia.org/certifications/social-media-security.

Council of Europe. 2017. "Chart of Signatures and Ratifications of Treaty 185 Convention on Cybercrime." July 12. Accessed July 12, 2017. https://www.coe.int/en/web/conventions/full-list/-/conventions/treaty/185/signatures.

———. 2017. "Details of Treaty No.185 Convention on Cybercrime." July 12. Accessed July 12, 2017. https://www.coe.int/en/web/conventions/full-list/-/conventions/treaty/185.

———. 2001. *Explanatory Report*. Budapest: Council of Europe. Accessed July 12, 2017. https://rm.coe.int/16800cce5b.

———. 2016. "Chart of Signatures and Ratifications of Treaty 185 Convention on Cybercrime." October 30. https://www.coe.int/en/web/conventions/full-list/-/conventions/treaty/185/signatures.

———. 2016. *Details of Treaty No.185 Convention on Cybercrime.* October 30. https://www.coe.int/en/web/conventions/full-list/-/conventions/treaty/185.

———. 2001. *Explanatory Report.* Budapest: Council of Europe.

Cowley, Stacy. 2017. "2.5 Million More People Potentially Exposed in Equifax Breach." October 2. Accessed October 3, 2017. https://www.nytimes.com/2017/10/02/business/equifax-breach.html.

Das, Krishna N., and Jonathan Spicer. 2016. "The SWIFT Hack: How the New York Fed Fumbled over the Bangladesh Bank Cyber-Heist." July 21. Accessed July 3, 2017. http://www.reuters.com/investigates/special-report/cyber-heist-federal/.

DHS and ODNI. 2016. "Joint Statement from the Department Of Homeland Security and Office of the Director of National Intelligence on Election Security." October 7. Accessed July 3, 2017. https://www.dhs.gov/news/2016/10/07/joint-statement-department-homeland-security-and-office-director-national.

Domestic Security Alliance Council. 2017. "About DSAC." July 16. Accessed July 16, 2017. https://www.dsac.gov/about.

———. 2017. "DSAC Member Benefits." July 16. Accessed July 16, 2017. https://www.dsac.gov/about/dsac-member-benefits.

Drinkwater, Doug. 2015. "Estonia President Wants China and Russia to Help Fight Cyber-Crime." January 26. Accessed July 12, 2017. http://www.scmagazineuk.com/estonia-president-wants-china-and-russia-to-help-fight-cyber-crime/article/394366/.

Dunn, John E. 2017. "The 12 Worst Types of Ransomware—We Name the Internet's Nastiest Extortion Malware." June 27. Accessed July 27, 2017. http://www.

computerworlduk.com/galleries/security/worst-ransomware-attacks-we-name-internets-nastiest-extortion-malware-3641916/.

Dwoskin, Elizabeth, and Karla Adam. 2017. "More Than 150 Countries Affected by Massive Cyberattack, Europol Says." May 14. Accessed July 2, 2017. https://www.washingtonpost.com/business/economy/more-than-150-countries-affected-by-massive-cyberattack-europol-says/2017/05/14/5091465e-3899-11e7-9e48-c4f199710b69_story.html?utm_term=.aa7237abbfe9.

EC-Council. 2017. "Cyber Security Programs Download Our Certification Track." June 29. Accessed June 29, 2017. https://www.eccouncil.org/programs/.

———. 2017. "History of the Company." June 29. Accessed June 29, 2017. https://www.eccouncil.org/about/.

———. 2016. *CCISO Certification Navigation.* November 2. https://ciso.eccouncil.org/cciso-certification/cciso-domain-details/.

———. 2017. *Certified Ethical Hacking Certification.* June 29. https://www.eccouncil.org/programs/certified-ethical-hacker-ceh/.

———. 2017. *CERTIFIED NETWORK DEFENDER PROGRAM.* June 29. https://www.eccouncil.org/programs/certified-network-defender-cnd/.

———. 2017. *CERTIFIED NETWORK DEFENDER PROGRAM.* June 29. https://www.eccouncil.org/programs/certified-network-defender-cnd/.

———. 2017. *Computer Hacking Forensic Investigator Certification.* June 29. https://www.eccouncil.org/programs/computer-hacking-forensic-investigator-chfi/.

———. 2016. *EC-Council Certified Encryption Specialist (ECES).* November 2. https://www.eccouncil.org/programs/ec-council-certified-encryption-specialist-eces/.

———. 2016. *EC-COUNCIL CERTIFIED INCIDENT HANDLER PROGRAM.* November 2. https://www.eccouncil.org/programs/ec-council-certified-incident-handler-ecih/.

———. 2017. *EC-COUNCIL CERTIFIED SECURITY ANALYST (ECSA)*. June 29. https://www.eccouncil.org/programs/certified-security-analyst-ecsa/.

———. 2016. *The EC-Council Licensed Penetration Tester (Master) Credential.* November 2. https://www.eccouncil.org/programs/licensed-penetration-tester-lpt-master/.

Eilperin, Juliet, and Adam Entous. 2016. "Russian Operation Hacked a Vermont Utility, Showing Risk to US Electrical Grid Security, Officials Say." December 31. Accessed July 3, 2017. https://www.washingtonpost.com/world/national-security/russian-hackers-penetrated-us-electricity-grid-through-a-utility-in-vermont/2016/12/30/8fc90cc4-ceec-11e6-b8a2-8c2a61b0436f_story.html?utm_term=.73efee7304c4.

Elkind, Peter. 2015. "Inside the Hack of the Century." June 25. Accessed July 3, 2017. http://fortune.com/sony-hack-part-1/.

FBI and DHS. 2016. "GRIZZLY STEPPE—Russian Malicious Cyber Activity." December 29. Accessed July 3, 2017. https://www.us-cert.gov/sites/default/files/publications/JAR_16-20296A_GRIZZLY%20STEPPE-2016-1229.pdf.

Federal Bureau of Investigation. 2008. "'Dark Market' Takedown." October 20. Accessed July 13, 2017. https://archives.fbi.gov/archives/news/stories/2008/october/darkmarket_102008.

———. 2015. "Cyber Criminal Forum Taken Down Members Arrested in 20 Countries." July 15. Accessed July 13, 2017. https://www.fbi.gov/news/stories/cyber-criminal-forum-taken-down.

———. 2017. "Famous Cases & Criminals." July 12. Accessed July 12, 2017. https://www.fbi.gov/history/famous-cases/aldrich-ames.

———. 2011. "Former Shionogi Employee Arrested, Charged with Hack Attack on Company Servers." July 1. Accessed July 12, 2017. https://archives.fbi.gov/archives/newark/press-releases/2011/

former-shionogi-employee-arrested-charged-with-hack-attack-on-company-servers.

———. 2016. "Incidents of Ransomware on the Rise: Protect Yourself and Your Organization." April 29. Accessed July 3, 2017. https://www.fbi.gov/news/stories/incidents-of-ransomware-on-the-rise.

———. 2016. "Incidents of Ransomware on the Rise." April 29. Accessed July 13, 2017. https://www.fbi.gov/news/stories/incidents-of-ransomware-on-the-rise.

———. 2016. "Iranian DDos Attacks." October 23. Accessed July 3, 2017. https://www.fbi.gov/wanted/cyber/iranian-ddos-attacks.

———. 2017. "'Most Wanted Evgeniy Mikhailovich Bogachev.'" www.fbi.gov. July 13. Accessed July 13, 2017. https://www.fbi.gov/wanted/cyber/evgeniy-mikhailovich-bogachev.

———. 2012. "Six Hackers in the United States and Abroad Charged for Crimes Affecting over One Million Victims." March 6. Accessed July 13, 2017. https://archives.fbi.gov/archives/newyork/press-releases/2012/six-hackers-in-the-united-states-and-abroad-charged-for-crimes-affecting-over-one-million-victims.

———. 2011. "Sixteen Individuals Arrested in the United States for Alleged Roles in Cyber Attacks." July 19. Accessed July 13, 2017. https://archives.fbi.gov/archives/news/pressrel/press-releases/sixteen-individuals-arrested-in-the-united-states-for-alleged-roles-in-cyber-attacks.

———. 2016. "Syrian Cyber Hackers Charged." March 22. Accessed July 3, 2017. https://www.fbi.gov/news/stories/two-from-syrian-electronic-army-added-to-cybers-most-wanted/two-from-syrian-electronic-army-added-to-cybers-most-wanted.

———. 2014. "US Charges Five Chinese Military Hackers with Cyber Espionage against US Corporations and a Labor Organization for Commercial Advantage." May 19. Accessed July 3, 2017. https://www.

fbi.gov/contact-us/field-offices/pittsburgh/news/press-releases/u.s.-charges-five-chinese-military-hackers-with-cyber-espionage-against-u.s.-corporations-and-a-labor-organization-for-commercial-advantage.

———. 2014. "Update on Sony Investigation." December 19. Accessed July 3, 2017. https://www.fbi.gov/news/pressrel/press-releases/update-on-sony-investigation.

———. 2016. *Famous Cases & Criminals.* October 30. https://www.fbi.gov/history/famous-cases/aldrich-ames.

———. 2011. *Former Shionogi Employee Admits to Hack Attack on Company Servers.* August 16. https://ucr.fbi.gov/newark/press-releases/2011/former-shionogi-employee-admits-to-hack-attack-on-company-servers.

Federal Bureau of Investigation Internet Crime Complaint Center. 2017. "Business E-Mail Compromise: The 3.1 Billion Dollar Scam." July 12. Accessed July 12, 2017. https://www.ic3.gov/media/2017/170504.aspx.

———. 2016. "Business E-Mail Compromise: The 3.1 Billion Dollar Scam." June 14. https://www.ic3.gov/media/2016/160614.aspx.

———. 2015. "Criminals Continue to Defraud and Extort Funds from Victims Using Cryptowall Ransomware Schemes." June 23. Accessed July 13, 2017. https://www.ic3.gov/media/2015/150623.aspx.

———. 2017. "Internet Crime Schemes." July 12. Accessed July 12, 2017. https://www.ic3.gov/crimeschemes.aspx#item-12.

———. 2017. "Internet Crime Schemes." July 15. Accessed July 15, 2017. https://www.ic3.gov/crimeschemes.aspx#item-12.

———. 2016. "Criminal Continue to Defraud and Extort Funds from Victims Using Cryptowall Ransomware Schemes." June 23. https://www.ic3.gov/media/2015/150623.aspx.

————. 2015. "Hacktivists Threaten to Target Law Enforcement Personnel and Public Officials." April 21. Accessed July 13, 2017. https://www.ic3.gov/media/2015/150421.aspx.

————. 2015. "Hacktivists Threaten to Target Law Enforcement Personnel and Public Officials." November 18. Accessed July 13, 2017. https://www.ic3.gov/media/2015/151118.aspx.

————. 2016. "Internet Crime Schemes." October 30. https://www.ic3.gov/crimeschemes.aspx#item-12.

Federal Bureau of Investigation. 2016. "Most Wanted Evgeniy Mikhailovich Bogachev." October 30. https://www.fbi.gov/wanted/cyber/evgeniy-mikhailovich-bogachev.

————. 2017. "Most Wanted Evgeniy Mikhailovich Bogachev." July 13. https://www.fbi.gov/wanted/cyber/evgeniy-mikhailovich-bogachev.

————. 2016. "WANTED BY THE FBI EVGENIY MIKHAILOVICH BOGACHEV." *WANTED BY THE FBI.* October 30. https://www.fbi.gov/wanted/cyber/evgeniy-mikhailovich-bogachev/download.pdf.

Fiegerman, Seth. 2017. "Verizon Cuts Yahoo Deal Price by $350 Million." February 21. Accessed June 25, 2017. http://money.cnn.com/2017/02/21/technology/yahoo-verizon-deal.

————. 2016. "Yahoo Says Data Stolen from 1 Billion Accounts." December 15. Accessed January 25, 2017. http://money.cnn.com/2016/12/14/technology/yahoo-breach-billion-users/?iid=EL.

Finn, Peter, and Sari Horwitz. 2013. "US Charges Snowden with Espionage." June 21. Accessed July 12, 2017. https://www.washingtonpost.com/world/national-security/us-charges-snowden-with-espionage/2013/06/21/507497d8-dab1-11e2-a016-92547bf094cc_story.html.

Gartner. 2017. "Magic Quadrant for Enterprise Mobility Management Suites." June 6. Accessed June 6, 2017. https://www.gartner.com/doc/3740018/magic-quadrant-enterprise-mobility-management.

George Mason University. 2017. "About Mason." June 30. Accessed June 30, 2017. https://www2.gmu.edu/about-mason.

———. 2017. "BS in Applied Computer Science." June 30. Accessed June 30, 2017. http://cs.gmu.edu/prospective-students/undergraduate-programs/bs-in-applied-computer-science/.

———. 2017. "Department of Computer Science BS in Computer Science." June 30. Accessed June 30, 2017. http://cs.gmu.edu/prospective-students/undergraduate-programs/bs-in-computer-science/.

———. 2017. "Department of Computer Science Masters Programs." June 30. Accessed June 30, 2017. http://cs.gmu.edu/prospective-students/ms-programs/.

———. 2017. "Department of Computer Science Undergraduate Programs." June 30. Accessed June 30, 2017. http://cs.gmu.edu/prospective-students/undergraduate-programs/.

———. 2017. "Department of Information Sciences and Technology Information Technology with NSA/DHS Center of Academic Excellence in Information Assurance/Cyber Defense Education Criteria Certificate." June 30. Accessed June 30, 2017. http://ist.gmu.edu/programs/undergraduate-programs/bsit-nsa-dhs-certificate/.

———. 2017. "Department of Information Sciences and Technology." June 30. Accessed June 30, 2017. http://ist.gmu.edu/programs/undergraduate-programs/.

———. 2016. "BS in Applied Computer Science." November 1. http://cs.gmu.edu/prospective-students/undergraduate-programs/bs-in-applied-computer-science/.

———. 2016. "Department of Computer Science BS in Computer Science" November 1. http://cs.gmu.edu/prospective-students/undergraduate-programs/bs-in-computer-science/.

———. 2016. "Department of Computer Science Masters Programs." November 1. http://cs.gmu.edu/prospective-students/ms-programs/.

———. 2016. "Department of Computer Science Undergraduate Programs." November 1. http://cs.gmu.edu/prospective-students/undergraduate-programs/.

———. 2016. "Department of Information Sciences and Technology." November 1. http://ist.gmu.edu/programs/undergraduate-programs/.

———. 2016. "Department of Information Sciences and Technology BS, Information Technology." November 1. http://ist.gmu.edu/programs/undergraduate-programs/bsit/.

———. 2017. "Department of Information Sciences and Technology BS, Information Technology." June 30. Accessed June 30, 2017. http://ist.gmu.edu/programs/undergraduate-programs/bsit/.

———. 2016. "Department of Information Sciences and Technology Information Technology with NSA/DHS Center of Academic Excellence in Information Assurance/Cyber Defense Education Criteria Certificate." November 1. http://ist.gmu.edu/programs/undergraduate-programs/bsit-nsa-dhs-certificate/.

Germaine, Carmen. 2017. "SEC Poised To Turn Cybersecurity Focus Into Enforcement." Accessed October 4, 2017. https://www.law360.com/articles/937197/sec-poised-to-turn-cybersecurity-focus-into-enforcement.

German, Rachel. 2015. "What Are the Chances for a Federal Breach Notification Law?" April 14. Accessed September 17, 2017. https://identity.utexas.edu/id-experts-blog/what-are-the-chances-for-a-federal-breach-notification-law.

Goodin, Dan. 2015. "950 Million Android Phones Can Be Hijacked by Malicious Text Messages." July 27. Accessed July 9, 2017. http://arstechnica.com/security/2015/07/950-million-android-phones-can-be-hijacked-by-malicious-text-messages/.

Greenberg, Andy. 2017. "How a Bug in an Obscure Chip Exposed a Billion Smartphones to Hackers." July 27. Accessed July 27, 2017. https://www.wired.com/story/broadpwn-wi-fi-vulnerability-ios-android.

Harris, Shon, and Fernando Maymi. 2016. *All-in-One CISSP Exam Guide, Seventh Edition.* New York: McGraw-Hill Education.

Harrison, Virginia, and Jose Pagliery. 2015. "Nearly 1 Million New Malware Threats Released Every Day." April 14. Accessed July 2, 2017. http://money.cnn.com/2015/04/14/technology/security/cyber-attack-hacks-security/.

Harvey Nash KPMG. 2017. "The Harvey Nash/KPMG CIO Survey 2016 Press Release." May 23. Accessed July 15, 2017. http://www.hnkpmgciosurvey.com/press-release/.

Hildenbrand, Jerry. 2016. "Inside the Different Android Versions." March 9. Accessed July 9, 2017. http://www.androidcentral.com/android-versions.

Horwitz, Peter Finn and Sari. 2013. "US Charges Snowden with Espionage." June 21. https://www.washingtonpost.com/world/national-security/us-charges-snowden-with-espionage/2013/06/21/507497d8-dab1-11e2-a016-92547bf094cc_story.html.

IACP. 2017. "FBI Cyber Shield Alliance." July 15. Accessed July 15, 2017. http://www.iacpcybercenter.org/resource-center/fbi-cyber-shield-alliance/.

IBM. 2016. "2016 Cost of Data Breach Study: Global Study." June 1. Accessed July 25, 2017. http://www-01.ibm.com/common/ssi/cgi-bin/ssialias?htmlfid=SEL03094WWEN.

———. 2017. "IBM & Ponemon Institute Study: Data Breach Costs Rising, Now $4 Million Per Incident." July 1. Accessed July 25, 2017. https://www-03. ibm.com/press/us/en/pressrelease/49926.wss.

———. 2015. "Ponemon Institute's 2015 Global Cost of Data Breach Study Reveals Average Cost of Data Breach Reaches Record Levels." May 27. Accessed July 25, 2017. http://www-03.ibm.com/press/us/en/pressrelease/47022.wss.

InfraGard. 2017. "About InfraGard." July 15. Accessed July 15, 2017. https:// www.infragard.org/.

International Association of Chiefs of Police Law Enforcement Cyber Center. 2017. *FBI Cyber Shield Alliance.* July 16. http://www.iacpcybercenter.org/ resource-center/fbi-cyber-shield-alliance/.

Investopedia. 2017. "Chief Financial Officer - CFO." July 2. Accessed July 2, 2017. http://www.investopedia.com/terms/c/cfo.asp.

———. 2017. "Chief Information Officer - CIO." July 2. Accessed July 2, 2017. http://www.investopedia.com/terms/c/cio.asp.

———. 2017. "Chief Executive Officer - CEO." July 2. http://www.investopedia. com/terms/c/ceo.asp.

ISACA. 2017. "About ISACA." June 28. Accessed June 28, 2017. http://www. isaca.org/about-isaca/Pages/default.aspx.

———. 2017. "Certified in Risk and Information Systems Control (CRISC)." June 28. Accessed June 28, 2017. http://www.isaca.org/Certification/ CRISC-Certified-in-Risk-and-Information-Systems-Control/Pages/ default.aspx.

———. 2017. "Certified in the Governance of Enterprise IT (CGEIT)." June 28. Accessed June 28, 2017. http://www.isaca.org/Certification/ CGEIT-Certified-in-the-Governance-of-Enterprise-IT/Pages/default. aspx.

———. 2017. "Certified Information Security Manager (CISM)." June 28. Accessed June 28, 2017. http://www.isaca.org/Certification/CISM-Certified-Information-Security-Manager/Pages/default.aspx.

———. 2017. "CSX Practictioner Certification." July 7. Accessed July 7, 2017. https://cybersecurity.isaca.org/csx-certifications/csx-practitioner-certification.

———. 2017. "Cybersecurity Nexus (CSX)." July 7. Accessed July 7, 2017. https://cybersecurity.isaca.org/csx-nexus.

———. 2017. "ISACA Certification: IT Audit, Security, Governance and Risk." June 28. Accessed June 28, 2017. http://www.isaca.org/CERTIFICATION/Pages/default.aspx.

Johnson, Derek B. 2017. "House Dem Revives Data Breach Bill After Equifax Hack." September 18. Accessed October 3, 2017. https://fcw.com/articles/2017/09/18/langevin-equifax-breach-bill.aspx.

Johnston, David. 2001. "FBI Agent Charged as Spy Who Aided Russia 15 Years." February 21. Accessed July 12, 2017. http://www.nytimes.com/2001/02/21/us/fbi-agent-charged-as-spy-who-aided-russia-15-years.html?pagewanted=all.

Kaspersky. 2017. "Kaspersky Security Bulletin Overall Statistics for 2016." July 2. Accessed July 2, 2017. https://go.kaspersky.com/Global_Security_Bulletin_2016_Stats_SOC_2016.html.

Kaspersky Lab. 2017. "Mobile Malware Evolution 2016." February 28. Accessed July 9, 2017. https://securelist.com/mobile-malware-evolution-2016/77681/.

Kaspersky Lab Securelist. 2016. *IT Threat Evolution in Q2 2016. Statistics.* August 11. https://securelist.com/analysis/quarterly-malware-reports/75640/it-threat-evolution-in-q2-2016-statistics/.

Kaspersky Labs Securelist. 2015. "Equation: The Death Star of Malware Galaxy." February 16. Accessed July 3, 2017. https://securelist.com/blog/research/68750/equation-the-death-star-of-malware-galaxy/.

Kuranda, Sarah. 2017. "Gartner: 10 Biggest Cybersecurity Consulting Companies by Revenue." August 9. Assessed September 3, 2017. http://www.crn.com/slide-shows/security/300090181/gartner-10-biggest-cybersecurity-consulting-companies-by-revenue.htm.

Krebs, Brian. 2016. "KrebsOnSecurity Hit with Record DDoS." September 16. Accessed November 2, 2016. https://krebsonsecurity.com/2016/09/krebsonsecurity-hit-with-record-ddos/.

Krebs, Brian. 2017. "Breach at Equifax May Impact 143M Americans." September 17. Accessed October 3, 2017. https://krebsonsecurity.com/2017/09/breach-at-equifax-may-impact-143m-americans/.

Maymi, Shon Harris, and Fernando. 2016. "Malware Components." In *All-in-One CISSP Exam Guide, Seventh Edition*, by Shon Harris and Fernando Maymi, 1,182. New York: McGraw-Hill Education.

McAfee. 2017. "McAfee Labs Threats Report." April 1. Accessed July 2, 2017. https://www.mcafee.com/us/resources/reports/rp-quarterly-threats-mar-2017.pdf.

McCoy, Kevin. 2017. "Feds Reportedly Investigate Equifax Executives' Stock Sales." September 18. Accessed October 3, 2017. https://www.usatoday.com/story/money/2017/09/18/feds-reportedly-investigate-equifax-executives-stock-sales/677003001/.

McMillan, Robert. 2016. "Yahoo Says Information on at Least 500 Million User Accounts Was Stolen." September 22. Accessed January 25, 2017. http://www.wsj.com/articles/yahoo-says-information-on-at-least-500-million-user-accounts-is-stolen-1474569637.

Microsoft. 2017. "Customer Guidance for WannaCrypt Attacks." May 12. Accessed July 2, 2017. https://blogs.technet.microsoft.com/msrc/2017/05/12/customer-guidance-for-wannacrypt-attacks/.

———. 2012. "Malware Protection Center Trojan: Win32/EyeStye." October 1. Accessed July 13, 2017. https://www.microsoft.com/security/portal/threat/encyclopedia/entry.aspx?Name=%0A%09%09%09%09Trojan:Win32/EyeStye%0A%09%09%09%09.

———. 2014. "What Is End of Support?" April 8. Accessed July 2, 2017. https://www.microsoft.com/en-us/windowsforbusiness/end-of-xp-support.

Mills, Elinor. 2009. "Q&A: FBI Agent Looks Back on Time Posing as a Cybercriminal." June 29. Accessed July 13, 2017. https://www.cnet.com/news/q-a-fbi-agent-looks-back-on-time-posing-as-a-cybercriminal/.

Mitre. 2017. "Common Vulnerabilities and Exposures." July 2. Accessed July 2, 2017. https://cve.mitre.org/about/.

———. 2017. "Common Vulnerabilities and Exposures." July 1. Accessed July 1, 2017. https://cve.mitre.org/.

Mlot, Stephanie. 2014. "HVAC Vendor Confirms Link to Target Data Breach." February 7. Accessed September 13, 2017. https://www.pcmag.com/article2/0,2817,2430505,00.asp.

Nakashima, Ellen. 2017. "US Officials Say Russian Government Hackers Have Penetrated Energy and Nuclear Company Business Networks." July 8. Accessed August 22, 2017. https://www.washingtonpost.com/world/national-security/us-officials-say-russian-government-hackers-have-penetrated-energy-and-nuclear-company-business-networks/2017/07/08/bbfde9a2-638b-11e7-8adc-fea80e32bf47_story.html?utm_term=.a4ba6ba96608.

National Conference of State Legislatures. 2018. "Security Breach Notification Laws." February 6. Accessed February 11, 2018. http://www.ncsl.org/

research/telecommunications-and-information-technology/security-breach-notification-laws.aspx.

National Initiative for Cybersecurity Education. 2016. "About NICE." October 30. Accessed July 13, 2017. http://csrc.nist.gov/nice/about/index.html.

National Institute of Standards and Technology. 2015. "Computer Security Division Computer Security Resource Center NIST Special Publications." May. Accessed July 3, 2017. http://nvlpubs.nist.gov/nistpubs/SpecialPublications/NIST.SP.800-82r2.pdf.

———. 2012. "Computer Security Incident Handling Guide." Gaithersburg, MD: National Institute of Standards and Technology. Accessed July 15, 2017. http://nvlpubs.nist.gov/nistpubs/SpecialPublications/NIST.SP.800-61r2.pdf.

———. 2016. "Guide for Cybersecurity Event Recovery." Gaithersburg, MD: NIST, 53. Accessed 15 2017, July. https://www.nist.gov/news-events/news/2016/12/nist-guide-provides-way-tackle-cybersecurity-incidents-recovery-plan.

National Institute of Standards and Technology Computer Security Division Computer Resource Center. 2015. "Guide to Industrial Control Systems (ICS) Security." May. Accessed July 3, 2017. http://nvlpubs.nist.gov/nistpubs/SpecialPublications/NIST.SP.800-82r2.pdf.

National Security Agency. 2017. "Centers of Academic Excellence in Cybersecurity." June 30. Accessed June 30, 2017. https://www.nsa.gov/resources/educators/centers-academic-excellence/.

———. 2017. "National Centers of Academic Excellence in Cyber Defense." June 30. Accessed June 30, 2017. https://www.nsa.gov/resources/educators/centers-academic-excellence/cyber-defense/.

———. 2017. "National Centers of Academic Excellence in Cyber Operations List of Centers of Academic Excellence for Cyber Operations." June

18. Accessed June 18, 2017. https://www.nsa.gov/resources/educators/centers-academic-excellence/cyber-operations/centers.shtml.

———. 2017. "National Centers of Academic Excellence in Cyber Operations." June 30. Accessed June 30, 2017. https://www.nsa.gov/resources/educators/centers-academic-excellence/cyber-operations/.

———. 2017. "NSA/DHS Current National CAE Designated Institutions." May 18. Accessed May 18, 2017. https://www.iad.gov/nietp/reports/current_cae_designated_institutions.cfm.

National Vulnerability Database. 2017. "CVE-2017-0194 Detail." July 2. Accessed July 2, 2017. https://nvd.nist.gov/vuln/detail/CVE-2017-0194#vulnDescriptionTitle.

———. 2017. "CVE-2017-0204 Detail." July 2. Accessed July 2, 2017. https://nvd.nist.gov/vuln/detail/CVE-2017-0204.

———. 2017. "CVE-2017-0265 Detail." July 2. Accessed July 2, 2017. https://nvd.nist.gov/vuln/detail/CVE-2017-0265.

———. 2017. "CVE-2017-0266 Detail." July 2. Accessed July 2, 2017. https://nvd.nist.gov/vuln/detail/CVE-2017-0266#vulnDescriptionTitle).

———. 2017. "CVE-2017-0281 Detail." July 2. Accessed July 2, 2017. https://nvd.nist.gov/vuln/detail/CVE-2017-0281.

———. 2017. "CVE-2017-2530 Detail." July 2. Accessed July 2, 2017. https://nvd.nist.gov/vuln/detail/CVE-2017-2530#vulnDescriptionTitle.

———. 2017. "CVE-2017-2546 Detail." July 2. Accessed July 2, 2017. https://nvd.nist.gov/vuln/detail/CVE-2017-2546#vulnDescriptionTitle.

———. 2017. "CVE-2017-3065 Detail." July 2. Accessed July 2, 2017. https://nvd.nist.gov/vuln/detail/CVE-2017-3065.

———. 2017. "CVE-2017-3066 Detail." July 2. Accessed July 2, 2017. https://nvd. nist.gov/vuln/detail/CVE-2017-3066#vulnDescriptionTitle.

———. 2017. "CVE-2017-3067 Detail." July 2. Accessed July 2, 2017. https://nvd. nist.gov/vuln/detail/CVE-2017-3067#vulnDescriptionTitle.

———. 2017. "CVE-2017-3071 Detail." July 2. Accessed July 2, 2017. https://nvd. nist.gov/vuln/detail/CVE-2017-3071#vulnDescriptionTitle.

———. 2017. "CVE-2017-3074 Detail." July 2. Accessed July 2, 2017. https://nvd. nist.gov/vuln/detail/CVE-2017-3074#vulnDescriptionTitle.

———. 2017. "CVE-2017-6978 Detail." July 2. Accessed July 2, 2017. https://nvd. nist.gov/vuln/detail/CVE-2017-6978.

———. 2017. "CVE-2017-6981 Detail." July 2. Accessed July 2, 2017. https://nvd. nist.gov/vuln/detail/CVE-2017-6981#vulnDescriptionTitle.

———. 2017. "CVE-2017-6984 Detail." July 2. Accessed July 2, 2017. https://nvd. nist.gov/vuln/detail/CVE-2017-6984#vulnDescriptionTitle.

———. 2017. "CVE-2017-3074 Detail." July 2. https://nvd.nist.gov/vuln/detail/ CVE-2017-3074#vulnDescriptionTitle.

———. 2017. "CVE-2017-6517 Detail." July 2. https://nvd.nist.gov/vuln/detail/ CVE-2017-6517#vulnDescriptionTitle.

NCFTA. 2017. "National Cyber-Forensics & Training Alliance." July 15. Accessed July 15, 2017. https://www.ncfta.net/.

Northern Virginia Commuity College. 2017. "College Catalog 2016–2017 Information Systems Technology Assocate of Applied Science Degree." June 30. Accessed June 30, 2017. http://www.nvcc.edu/ catalog/cat2016/academics/programs/programdetail.aspx?prog_ id=2900&subprog_id=0&level=1.

———. 2016. *Information Systems Technology Network Engineering (Specialist)*. October 30. http://www.nvcc.edu/catalog/cat2016/academics/programs/programdetail.aspx?prog_id=2900&subprog_id=5&level=2.

———. 2017. "College Catalog 2016-2017." June 30. Accessed June 30, 2017. http://www.nvcc.edu/catalog/cat2016/academics/programs/default.aspx.

———. 2017. "Information Systems Technology Network Administration." June 30. Accessed June 30, 2017. http://www.nvcc.edu/catalog/cat2016/academics/programs/programdetail.aspx?prog_id=2900&subprog_id=4&level=2.

———. 2016. *College Catalog 2016-2017*. October 30. http://www.nvcc.edu/catalog/cat2016/academics/programs/default.aspx.

———. 2016. *Information Systems Technology*. October 30. http://www.nvcc.edu/catalog/cat2016/academics/programs/programdetail.aspx?prog_id=2900&subprog_id=2&level=2.

———. 2016. *Information Systems Technology Application Programming*. October 30. http://www.nvcc.edu/catalog/cat2016/academics/programs/programdetail.aspx?prog_id=2900&subprog_id=1&level=2.

———. 2016. *Information Systems Technology IT Technical Support*. October 30. http://www.nvcc.edu/catalog/cat2016/academics/programs/programdetail.aspx?prog_id=2900&subprog_id=3&level=2.

———. 2016. *Information Systems Technology Network Administration*. October 30. http://www.nvcc.edu/catalog/cat2016/academics/programs/programdetail.aspx?prog_id=2900&subprog_id=4&level=2.

———. 2016. *Information Systems Technology Web Design and Development*. October 30. http://www.nvcc.edu/catalog/cat2016/academics/programs/programdetail.aspx?prog_id=2900&subprog_id=7&level=2.

New York State Department of Financial Services. 2016. "Governor Cuomo Announces Proposal of First-In-The-Nation Cybersecurity Regulation to

Protect Consumers and Financial Institutions." September 13. Accessed October 3, 2017. http://www.dfs.ny.gov/about/press/pr1609131.htm.

New York State Department of Financial Services. 2017. "Cybersecurity Requirements for Financial Services Companies." September 27. Accessed October 4, 2017. https://www.governor.ny.gov/sites/governor. ny.gov/files/atoms/files/Cybersecurity_Requirements_Financial_ Services_23NYCRR500.pdf.

Offensive Security. 2017. "Offensive Security Certified Expert—OSCE Certification." June 28. Accessed June 28, 2017. https://www.offensive-security.com/information-security-certifications/#sign-up.

———. 2017. "Offensive Security Certified Professional—OSCP Certification." June 28. Accessed June 28, 20147. https://www.offensive-security.com/ information-security-certifications/#sign-up.

———. 2017. "Offensive Security Exploitation Expert—OSEE Certification." June 28. Accessed June 28, 2017. https://www.offensive-security.com/ information-security-certifications/#sign-up.

———. 2017. "Offensive Security Training, Certifications and Services." June 29. Accessed June 29, 2017. https://www.offensive-security.com/.

———. 2017. "Offensive Security Web Expert—OSWE Certification." June 28. Accessed June 28, 2017. https://www.offensive-security.com/ information-security-certifications/#sign-up.

———. 2017. "Offensive Security Wireless Professional—OSWP Certification." June 28. Accessed June 28, 2017. https://www.offensive-security.com/ information-security-certifications/#sign-up.

Olson, Parmy. 2016. "Apple Is Breaking Down Its Walled Garden to Keep Selling iPhones." June 13. Accessed July 9, 2017. http://www.forbes.com/sites/ parmyolson/2016/06/13/apple-is-breaking-down-its-walled-garden-to-keep-selling-iphones/#26adf2862cec.

OWASP. 2017. "Command Injection." July 11. Accessed July 11, 2017. https://www.owasp.org/index.php/Command_Injection.

———. 2017. "Mobile Top 10 2016-Top 10." July 9. Accessed July 9, 2017. https://www.owasp.org/index.php/Mobile_Top_10_2016-Top_10.

———. 2017. "OWASP Mobile Checklist Final 2016." July 9. Accessed July 9, 2017. https://drive.google.com/file/d/0BxOPagp1jPHWYmg3Y3BfLVhMcmc/view.

———. 2017. "OWASP Mobile Security Project." July 9. Accessed July 9, 2017. https://www.owasp.org/index.php/OWASP_Mobile_Security_Project.

———. 2017. "OWASP Testing Guide v4 Table of Contents." July 10. Accessed July 10, 2017. https://www.owasp.org/index.php/OWASP_Testing_Guide_v4_Table_of_Contents.

———. 2017. "OWASP Zed Attack Proxy Project." July 11. Accessed July 11, 2017. https://www.owasp.org/index.php/OWASP_Zed_Attack_Proxy_Project.

———. 2017. "Testing for Input Validation." July 10. Accessed July 10, 2017. https://www.owasp.org/index.php/Testing_for_Input_Validation.

———. 2017. "Testing: Introduction and Objectives." July 10. Accessed July 10, 2017. https://www.owasp.org/index.php/Testing:_Introduction_and_objectives.

———. 2017. "Welcome to OWASP." July 10. Accessed July 10, 2017. https://www.owasp.org/index.php/Main_Page.

Popken, Ben. 2017. "Equifax Execs Resign; Security Head, Mauldin, Was Music Major." September 15. Accessed October 3, 2017. https://www.nbcnews.com/business/consumer/equifax-executives-step-down-scrutiny-intensifies-credit-bureaus-n801706.

Popper, Ben. 2017. "Google Announces over 2 Billion Monthly Active Devices on Android." May 17. Accessed July 9, 2017. https://www.theverge.com/2017/5/17/15654454/android-reaches-2-billion-monthly-active-users.

Portswigger Web Security. 2017. "Burp Suite." July 11. Accessed July 11, 2017. https://portswigger.net/burp/.

PwC. 2017. "Uncovering a New Sustained Global Cyber Espionage Campaign." April. Accessed July 3, 2017. https://www.pwc.co.uk/issues/cyber-security-data-privacy/insights/operation-cloud-hopper.html.

Rashid, Fahmida Y. 2015. "Inside the Aftermath of the Saudi Aramco Breach." August 8. Accessed August 22, 2017. http://www.darkreading.com/attacks-breaches/inside-the-aftermath-of-the-saudi-aramco-breach/d/d-id/1321676.

Ramakrishnan, Sruthi and Nandita Bose. 2017. "Target in $18.5 million multi-state settlement over data breach." May 23. Accessed September 13, 2017. https://www.reuters.com/article/us-target-cyber-settlement/target-in-18-5-million-multi-state-settlement-over-data-breach-idUSKBN18J2GH.

Reisinger, Don. 2016. *Tom's Guide*. November 11. https://www.tomsguide.com/us/android-nougat-market-share, news-23837.html.

Robert, Jeff John. 2017. "Home Depot to Pay Banks $25 Million in Data Breach Settlement." May 17. Accessed September 13, 2017. http://fortune.com/2017/03/09/home-depot-data-breach-banks/.

Roth, Andrew, and Ellen Nakashima. 2017. *Massive Cyberattack Hits Europe with Widespread Ransom Demands*. June 27. Accessed July 27, 2017. https://www.washingtonpost.com/world/europe/ukraines-government-key-infrastructure-hit-in-massive-cyberattack/2017/06/27/7d22c7dc-5b40-11e7-9fc6-c7ef4bc58d13_story.html?utm_term=.2139b3586c88.

SANS. 2017. "GIAC Advanced Smartphone Forensics (GASF)." June 29. Accessed June 29, 2017. http://www.giac.org/certification/advanced-smartphone-forensics-gasf.

———. 2017. "GIAC Assessing and Auditing Wireless Networks (GAWN)." June 28. Accessed June 28, 2017. http://www.giac.org/certification/ assessing-auditing-wireless-networks-gawn.

———. 2017. "GIAC Certified Enterprise Defender (GCED)." June 28. Accessed June 28, 2017. http://www.giac.org/certification/ certified-enterprise-defender-gced.

———. 2017. "GIAC Certified Forensic Analyst (GCFA)." June 28. Accessed June 28, 2017. http://www.giac.org/certification/ certified-forensic-analyst-gcfa.

———. 2017. "GIAC Certified Forensic Examiner (GCFE)." June 28. Accessed June 28, 2017. http://www.giac.org/certification/certified- forensic-examiner-gcfe.

———. 2017. "GIAC Certified Incident Handler (GCIH)." June 28. Accessed June 28, 2017. http://www.giac.org/certification/certified- incident-handler-gcih.

———. 2017. "GIAC Certified Intrusion Analyst (GCIA)." June 28. Accessed June 28, 2017. http://www.giac.org/certification/certified- intrusion-analyst-gcia.

———. 2017. "GIAC Certified Perimeter Protection Analyst (GPPA)." June 28. Accessed June 28, 2017. http://www.giac.org/certification/ certified-perimeter-protection-analyst-gppa.

———. 2017. "GIAC Certified Project Manager (GCPM)." June 29. Accessed June 29, 2017. http://www.giac.org/certification/certified- project-manager-gcpm.

———. 2017. "GIAC Certified UNIX Security Administrator (GCUX)." June 29. Accessed June 29, 2017. http://www.giac.org/certification/ certified-unix-security-administrator-gcux.

———. 2017. "GIAC Certified Web Application Defender (GWEB)." June 29. Accessed June 29, 2017. https://www.giac.org/certification/certified-web-application-defender-gweb.

———. 2017. "GIAC Certified Windows Security Administrator (GCWN)." June 28. Accessed June 28, 2017. http://www.giac.org/certification/certified-windows-security-administrator-gcwn.

———. 2017. "GIAC Continuous Monitoring Certification (GMON)." June 29. Accessed June 29, 2017. http://www.giac.org/certification/continuous-monitoring-certification-gmon.

———. 2017. "GIAC Critical Controls Certification (GCCC)." June 29. Accessed June 29, 2017. http://www.giac.org/certification/critical-controls-certification-gccc.

———. 2017. "GIAC Exploit Researcher and Advanced Penetration Tester (GXPN)." June 28. Accessed June 28, 2017. http://www.giac.org/certification/exploit-researcher-advanced-penetration-tester-gxpn.

———. 2017. "GIAC Information Security Fundamentals (GISF)." June 28. Accessed June 28, 2017. http://www.giac.org/certification/information-security-fundamentals-gisf.

———. 2017. "GIAC Information Security Professional (GISP)." June 28. Accessed June 28, 2017. http://www.giac.org/certification/information-security-professional-gisp.

———. 2017. "GIAC Law of Data Security & Investigations (GLEG)." June 29. Accessed June 29, 2017. https://www.giac.org/certification/law-data-security-investigations-gleg.

———. 2017. "GIAC Mobile Device Security Analyst (GMOB)." June 29. Accessed June 29, 2017. http://www.giac.org/certification/mobile-device-security-analyst-gmob.

———. 2017. "GIAC Network Forensic Analyst (GNFA)." June 29. Accessed June 29, 2017. https://www.giac.org/certification/ network-forensic-analyst-gnfa.

———. 2017. "GIAC Penetration Tester (GPEN)." June 28. Accessed June 28, 2017. http://www.giac.org/certification/penetration-tester-gpen.

———. 2017. "GIAC Python Coder (GPYC)." June 29. Accessed June 29, 2017. http://www.giac.org/certification/python-coder-gpyc.

———. 2017. "GIAC Response and Industrial Defense (GRID)." June 29. Accessed June 29, 2017. https://www.giac.org/certification/response -industrial-defense-grid.

———. 2017. "GIAC Reverse Engineering Malware (GREM)." June 28. Accessed June 28, 2017. http://www.giac.org/certification/ reverse-engineering-malware-grem.

———. 2017. "GIAC Secure Software Programmer - .NET (GSSP-.NET)." June 29. Accessed June 29, 2017. https://www.giac.org/certification/ secure-software-programmer-net-gssp-net.

———. 2017. "GIAC Secure Software Programmer-Java (GSSP-JAVA)." June 29. Accessed June 29, 2017. https://www.giac.org/certification/ secure-software-programmer-java-gssp-java.

———. 2017. "GIAC Security Essentials (GSEC)." June 28. Accessed June 28, 2017. http://www.giac.org/certification/security-essentials-gsec.

———. 2017. "GIAC Security Expert (GSE) Certification." June 29. Accessed June 29, 2017. https://www.giac.org/certification/ security-expert-gse.

———. 2017. "GIAC Security Leadership (GSLC)." June 28. Accessed June 28, 2017. http://www.giac.org/certification/security-leadership-gslc.

———. 2017. "GIAC Systems and Network Auditor (GSNA)." June 28. Accessed June 28, 2017. http://www.giac.org/certification/systems-network-auditor-gsna.

———. 2017. "GIAC Web Application Penetration Tester (GWAPT)." June 28. Accessed June 28, 2017. http://www.giac.org/certification/web-application-penetration-tester-gwapt.

———. 2017. "Global Industrial Cyber Security Professional (GICSP)." June 28. Accessed June 28, 2017. http://www.giac.org/certification/global-industrial-cyber-security-professional-gicsp.

———. 2017. "Graduate Certificates - Cyber Security." June 29. Accessed June 29, 2017. https://www.sans.edu/academics/certificates.

———. 2017. "Masters Degrees - Information Security." June 29. Accessed June 29, 2017. https://www.sans.edu/academics/degrees/msise.

SANS Cyber Aces. 2017. "About Us." June 30. Accessed June 30, 2017. http://www.cyberaces.org/about.

SANS. 2017. *GIAC Certified Forensic Analyst (GCFA).* June 29. http://www.giac.org/certification/certified-forensic-analyst-gcfa.

SANS Institute. 2017. "About SANS." June 29. Accessed June 29, 2017. https://www.sans.org/about/.

———. 2017. "Curricula." July 15. Accessed July 15, 2017. https://www.sans.org/curricula/.

———. 2017. "Curricula." June 30. Accessed June 30, 2017. https://www.sans.org/curricula/.

Seals, Tara. 2016. "90% of Android Phones Are Running Outdated OS." January 19. Accessed July 9, 2017. http://www.infosecurity-magazine.com/news/90-of-android-phones-are-running/.

Smith, Chris. 2015. "Google's Greed Is to Blame for Android's Major Security Mess." November 6. Accessed July 9, 2017. http://bgr.com/2015/11/06/google-android-security-issues-fix/.

Soha Systems, 2016. "Soha Systems' Survey Reveals Only Two Percent of IT Experts Consider Third-Party Secure Access a Top Priority, Despite the Growing Number of Security Threats Linked to Supplier and Contractor Access." May 17. Accessed September 17, 2017. http://www.marketwired.com/press-release/soha-systems-survey-reveals-only-two-percent-it-experts-consider-third-party-secure-2125559.htm.

StatCounter GlobalStats. 2017. "Desktop Operating System Market Share Worldwide." July 2. Accessed July 2, 2017. http://gs.statcounter.com/os-market-share/desktop/worldwide.

SWIFT. 2017. "About Us." July 3. Accessed July 3, 2017. https://www.swift.com/about-us.

Symantec. 2016. "Internet Security Threat Report." April 21. Accessed July 9, 2017. https://www.symantec.com/content/dam/symantec/docs/reports/istr-21-2016-en.pdf.

———. 2017. "Internet Security Threat Report." April. Accessed July 9, 2017. https://s1.q4cdn.com/585930769/files/doc_downloads/lifelock/ISTR22_Main-FINAL-APR24.pdf.

———. 2014. "Regin: Top-Tier Espionage Tool Enables Stealthy Surveillance." November 23. Accessed July 3, 2017. https://www.symantec.com/connect/blogs/regin-top-tier-espionage-tool-enables-stealthy-surveillance.

———. 2012. "The Shamoon Attacks." August 16. Accessed July 3, 2017. https://www.symantec.com/connect/blogs/shamoon-attacks.

———. 2016. "Trojan.Zbot." August 16. Accessed July 13, 2017. https://www.symantec.com/security_response/writeup.jsp?docid=2010-011016-3514-99.

———. 2015. *Adobe Flash Player CVE-2015-7645 Remote Code Execution Vulnerability*. October 13. https://www.symantec.com/security_response/vulnerability. jsp?bid=77081.

———. 2016. "Adware.Getprivate." May 16. https://www.symantec.com/ security_response/writeup.jsp?docid=2016-051613-0047-99.

———. 2016. "Adware.Savepathdeals." April 19. https://www.symantec.com/ security_response/writeup.jsp?docid=2016-041913-2758-99.

———. 2016. "Downloader.Picgoo." June 29. https://www.symantec.com/ security_response/writeup.jsp?docid=2016-062921-0532-99.

———. 2016. "JS.Retefe." June 28. https://www.symantec.com/security_ response/writeup.jsp?docid=2016-062820-3631-99.

———. 2016. *Microsoft Internet Explorer CVE-2016-3211 Remote Memory Corruption Vulnerability*. June 14. https://www.symantec.com/security_response/ vulnerability.jsp?bid=91103.

———. 2016. *Microsoft Office CVE-2016-0025 Memory Corruption Vulnerability*. June 14. https://www.symantec.com/security_response/vulnerability. jsp?bid=91089.

———. 2016. *Microsoft Windows PDF Library CVE-2016-3203 Remote Code Execution Vulnerability*. June 14. https://www.symantec.com/security_response/ vulnerability.jsp?bid=91086.

———. 2015. *Oracle Java SE CVE-2015-2590 Remote Security Vulnerability*. July 14. https://www.symantec.com/security_response/vulnerability.jsp?bid=75818.

———. 2016. *PUA.DexonAgent*. June 23. https://www.symantec.com/security_ response/writeup.jsp?docid=2016-062206-3651-99.

———. 2016. *PUA.Drivereasy*. April 20. https://www.symantec.com/security_ response/writeup.jsp?docid=2016-042006-5924-99.

———. 2016. *PUA.Gyplyraminer.* June 24. https://www.symantec.com/security_response/writeup.jsp?docid=2016-062412-0035-99.

———. 2016. *Ransom.Apocalypse.* June 30. https://www.symantec.com/security_response/writeup.jsp?docid=2016-063013-2557-99.

———. 2016. *Security Response.* October 18. https://www.symantec.com/security_response/landing/threats.jsp.

———. 2016. *Security Response/Risks.* October 18. https://www.symantec.com/security_response/landing/risks/.

———. 2016. *Security Response/Threats.* October 18. https://www.symantec.com/security_response/landing/threats.jsp.

———. 2016. *Security Response/Vunerabilities.* October 18. https://www.symantec.com/security_response/landing/vulnerabilities.jsp.

———. 2016. *Trojan.Fakeransomdel.* June 28. https://www.symantec.com/security_response/writeup.jsp?docid=2016-062819-0945-99.

Symantec.com. 2016. *Android.Vibleaker.* June 21. https://www.symantec.com/security_response/writeup.jsp?docid=2016-062312-4850-99.

Technopedia. 2017. "Air Gap." August 22. Accessed August 22, 2017. https://www.techopedia.com/definition/17037/air-gap.

———. 2017. "Wi-Fi Protected Access (WPA)." July 9. Accessed July 9, 2017. https://www.techopedia.com/definition/4166/wi-fi-protected-access-wpa.

———. 2017. "Access Control." August 22. Accessed August 22, 2017. https://www.techopedia.com/definition/5831/access-control.

———. 2017. "Advanced Persistent Threat (APT)." July 3. Accessed July 3, 2017. https://www.techopedia.com/definition/28118/advanced-persistent-threat-apt.

———. 2017. "Adware." July 2. Accessed July 2, 2017. https://www.techopedia.com/definition/4215/adware.

———. 2017. "Anti-Malware." August 22. Accessed August 22, 2017. https://www.techopedia.com/definition/25873/anti-malware.

———. 2017. "Anti-Spyware." August 22. Accessed August 22, 2017. https://www.techopedia.com/definition/23142/anti-spyware.

———. 2017. "Anti-Virus Software." July 2. Accessed July 2, 2017. https://www.techopedia.com/definition/5416/anti-virus-software.

———. 2017. "Application Software." August 22. Accessed August 22, 2017. https://www.techopedia.com/definition/4224/application-software.

———. 2017. "Authentication." July 2. Accessed July 2, 2017. https://www.techopedia.com/definition/342/authentication.

———. 2017. "Availability." June 2. Accessed July 2, 2017. https://www.techopedia.com/definition/990/availability.

———. 2017. "Backdoor." August 22. Accessed August 22, 2017. https://www.techopedia.com/definition/3743/backdoor.

———. 2017. "Blacklist." July 2. Accessed July 2, 2017. https://www.techopedia.com/definition/1638/blacklist.

———. 2017. "Bluetooth." August 22. Accessed August 22, 2017. https://www.techopedia.com/definition/26198/bluetooth.

———. 2017. "Botnet." June 2. Accessed June 2, 2017. https://www.techopedia.com/definition/384/botnet.

———. 2017. "Bridge." August 22. Accessed August 22, 2017. https://www.techopedia.com/definition/3160/bridge.

———. 2017. "Cascading Style Sheet (CSS)." July 10. Accessed July 10, 2017. https://www.techopedia.com/definition/26268/cascading-style-sheet-css.

———. 2017. "Computer Network." August 22. Accessed August 22, 2017. https://www.techopedia.com/definition/25597/computer-network.

———. 2017. "Confidentiality." June 2. Accessed June 2, 2017. https://www.techopedia.com/definition/10254/confidentiality.

———. 2017. "Configuration Management (CM)." August 22. Accessed August 22, 2017. https://www.techopedia.com/definition/24822/configuration-controlconfiguration-management-cm.

———. 2017. "Cookie." July 10. Accessed July 10, 2017. https://www.techopedia.com/definition/7624/cookie.

———. 2017. "Cross Site Scripting (XSS)." July 10. Accessed July 10, 2017. https://www.techopedia.com/definition/24435/cross-site-scripting-xss.

———. 2017. "Cross-Site Request Forgery (CSRF)." July 11. Accessed July 11, 2017. https://www.techopedia.com/definition/172/cross-site-request-forgery-csrf.

———. 2017. "Cyberattack." July 15. Accessed July 15, 2017. https://www.techopedia.com/definition/24748/cyberattack.

———. 2017. "Data Forensics." August 22. Accessed August 22, 2017. https://www.techopedia.com/definition/28036/data-forensics.

———. 2017. "Data Validation." July 10. Accessed July 10, 2017. https://www.techopedia.com/definition/10283/data-validation.

———. 2017. "Demilitarized Zone (DMZ)." August 22. Accessed August 22, 2017. https://www.techopedia.com/definition/10266/demilitarized-zone-dmz.

———.2017. "Denial-of-Service Attack (DoS)." June 2. Accessed June 2, 2017. https://www.techopedia.com/definition/24841/denial-of-service-attack-dos.

———. 2017. "Distributed Denial of Service (DDoS)." July 2. Accessed July 2, 2017. https://www.techopedia.com/definition/10261/distributed-denial-of-service-ddos.

———. 2017. "Encryption." August 22. Accessed August 22, 2017. https://www.techopedia.com/definition/5507/encryption.

———. 2017. "Firewall." July 2. Accessed July 2, 2017. https://www.techopedia.com/definition/5355/firewall.

———. 2017. "Heuristic Filtering." August 22. Accessed August 22, 2017. https://www.techopedia.com/definition/28881/heuristic-filtering.

———. 2017. "Heuristic." August 22. Accessed August 22, 2017. https://www.techopedia.com/definition/5436/heuristic.

———. 2017. "Hub (Networking)." August 22. Accessed August 22, 2017. https://www.techopedia.com/definition/26350/hub-networking.

———. 2017. "Hypertext Markup Language (HTML)." July 10. Accessed July 10, 2017. https://www.techopedia.com/definition/1892/hypertext-markup-language-html.

———. 2017. "Hypertext Transfer Protocol (HTTP)." July 10. Accessed July 10, 2017. https://www.techopedia.com/definition/2336/hypertext-transfer-protocol-http.

———. 2017. "Hypertext Transport Protocol Secure (HTTPS)." July 10. Accessed July 10, 2017. https://www.techopedia.com/definition/5361/hypertext-transport-protocol-secure-https.

———. 2017. "IEEE 802.11." July 6. Accessed July 6, 2017. https://www.techopedia.com/definition/24967/ieee-80211.

———. 2017. "IEEE 802.1X." July 9. Accessed July 9, 2017. https://www.techopedia.com/definition/509/ieee-8021x.

———. 2017. "Information Assurance (IA)." July 2. Accessed July 2, 2017. https://www.techopedia.com/definition/5/information-assurance-ia.

———. 2017. "Instrusion Prevention System (IPS)." July 2. Accessed July 2, 2017. https://www.techopedia.com/definition/15998/intrusion-prevention-system-ips.

———. 2017. "Integrity." June 2. Accessed June 2, 2017. https://www.techopedia.com/definition/10284/integrity.

———. 2017. "Intrusion Detection System (IDS)." July 2. Accessed Jully 2, 2017. https://www.techopedia.com/definition/3988/intrusion-detection-system-ids.

———. 2017. "JavaScript (JS)." July 10. Accessed July 10, 2017. https://www.techopedia.com/definition/3929/javascript-js.

———. 2017. "Local Area Network (LAN)." July 6. Accessed July 6, 2017. https://www.techopedia.com/definition/5526/local-area-network-lan.

———. 2017. "Malicous Software (Malware)." June 2. Accessed June 2, 2017. https://www.techopedia.com/definition/4015/malicious-software-malware.

———. 2017. "Master Boot Record (MBR)." July 3. Accessed July 3, 2017. https://www.techopedia.com/definition/3386/master-boot-record-mbr.

———. 2017. "Near Field Communication (NFC)." July 9. Accessed July 9, 2017. https://www.techopedia.com/definition/27583/near-field-communication-nfc.

———. 2017. "Near Field Communication Tag (NFC Tag)." August 22. Accessed August 22, 2017. https://www.techopedia.com/definition/28812/near-field-communication-tag-nfc-tag.

———. 2017. "Network Interface Card (NIC)." August 22. Accessed August 22, 2017. https://www.techopedia.com/definition/5306/network-interface-card-nic.

———. 2017. "Network Traffic Monitoring." August 22. Accessed August 22, 2017. https://www.techopedia.com/definition/29977/network-traffic-monitoring.

———. 2017. "Nonrepudiation." July 2. Accessed July 2, 2017. https://www.techopedia.com/definition/4031/nonrepudiation.

———. 2017. "Open Systems Interconnection Model (OSI Model)." August 22. Accessed August 22, 2017. https://www.techopedia.com/definition/24205/open-systems-interconnection-model-osi-model.

———. 2017. "Operating System (OS)." August 22. Accessed August 22, 2017. https://www.techopedia.com/definition/3515/operating-system-os.

———. 2017. "Patch Management." August 22. Accessed August 22, 2017. https://www.techopedia.com/definition/13835/patch-management.

———. 2017. "Patch." August 22. Accessed August 22, 2017. https://www.techopedia.com/definition/24537/patch.

———. 2017. "Penetration Testing (Pen-Testing)." July 2. Accessed July 2, 2017. https://www.techopedia.com/definition/16130/penetration-testing-pen-testing.

———. 2017. "Personally Identifiable Information (PII)." August 22. Accessed August 22, 2017. https://www.techopedia.com/definition/4046/personally-identifiable-information-pii.

———. 2017. "Protocol." July 10. Accessed July 10, 2017. https://www.techopedia.com/definition/4528/protocol.

———. 2017. "Rootkit." June 2. Accessed June 2, 2017. https://www.techopedia.com/definition/4088/rootkit.

———. 2017. "Router." July 15. Accessed July 15, 2017. https://www.techopedia.com/definition/2277/router.

———. 2017. "Scripts." August 23. Accessed August 23, 2017. https://www.techopedia.com/definition/10324/scripts.

———. 2017. "Security Incident and Event Management (SIEM)." July 2. Accessed July 2, 2017. https://www.techopedia.com/definition/4097/security-incident-and-event-management-siem.

———. 2017. "Security Incident." July 15. Accessed July 15, 2017. https://www.techopedia.com/definition/15957/security-incident.

———. 2017. "Server." August 22. Accessed August 22, 2017. https://www.techopedia.com/definition/2282/server.

———. 2017. "Service Set Identifier (SSID)." July 6. Accessed July 6, 2017. https://www.techopedia.com/definition/2973/service-set-identifier-ssid.

———. 2017. "Service Set Identifier (SSID)." August 22. Accessed August 22, 2017. https://www.techopedia.com/definition/2973/service-set-identifier-ssid.

———. 2017. "Session." July 10. Accessed July 10, 2017. https://www.techopedia.com/definition/5392/session-computer-science.

———. 2017. "Software." August 22. Accessed August 22, 2017. https://www.techopedia.com/definition/4356/software.

———. 2017. "Spyware." June 2. Accessed June 2, 2017. https://www.techopedia.com/definition/4125/spyware.

———. 2017. "SQL Injection." July 10. Accessed July 10, 2017. https://www.techopedia.com/definition/4126/sql-injection.

———. 2017. "SQL Injection." August 22. Accessed August 22, 2017. https://www.techopedia.com/definition/4126/sql-injection.

———. 2017. "Static Web Page." July 10. Accessed July 10, 2017. https://www.techopedia.com/definition/5399/static-web-page.

———. 2017. "Structured Query Language (SQL)." July 10. Accessed July 10, 2017. https://www.techopedia.com/definition/1245/structured-query-language-sql.

———. 2017. "Switch." August 22. Accessed August 22, 2017. https://www.techopedia.com/definition/2306/switch-networking.

———. 2017. "Trojan Horse." June 2. Accessed June 2, 2017. https://www.techopedia.com/definition/5484/trojan-horse.

———. 2017. "Virtual Machine (VM)." August 22. Accessed August 22, 2017. https://www.techopedia.com/definition/4805/virtual-machine-vm.

———. 2017. "Virtualization." August 22. Accessed August 22, 2017. https://www.techopedia.com/definition/719/virtualization.

———. 2017. "Virus." June 2. Accessed June 2, 2017. https://www.techopedia.com/definition/4157/virus.

———. 2017. "Vulnerability." July 2. Accessed July 2, 2017. https://www.techopedia.com/definition/13484/vulnerability.

———. 2017. "Web Browswer." July 10. Accessed July 10, 2017. https://www.techopedia.com/definition/288/web-browser.

———. 2017. "Web Server." July 10. Accessed July 10, 2017. https://www.techopedia.com/definition/4928/web-server.

———. 2017. "Web-Based Application." July 10. Accessed July 10, 2017. https://www.techopedia.com/definition/26002/web-based-application.

———. 2017. "Whitelist." July 2. Accessed July 2, 2017. https://www.techopedia.com/definition/1728/whitelist.

———. 2017. "Wi-Fi Protected Access (WPA)." August 22. Accessed August 22, 2017. https://www.techopedia.com/definition/4166/wi-fi-protected-access-wpa.

———. 2017. "Wi-Fi Protected Access II (WPA2)." July 9. Accessed July 9, 2017. https://www.techopedia.com/definition/24488/wi-fi-protected-access-ii-wpa2.

———. 2017. "Wired Equivalent Privacy (WEP)." July 6. Accessed July 6, 2017. https://www.techopedia.com/definition/4170/wired-equivalent-privacy-wep.

———. 2017. "Wireless Access Point (WAP)." July 6. Accessed July 6, 2017. https://www.techopedia.com/definition/13538/wireless-access-point-wap.

———. 2017. "Wireless Fidelity (Wi-Fi)." July 6. Accessed July 6, 2017. https://www.techopedia.com/definition/10035/wireless-fidelity-wi-fi.

———. 2017. "Wireless Local Area Network (WLAN)." July 6. Accessed July 6, 2017. https://www.techopedia.com/definition/5107/wireless-local-area-network-wlan.

———. 2017. "Workstation (WS)." August 22. Accessed August 22, 2017. https://www.techopedia.com/definition/5140/workstation-ws.

———. 2017. "World Wide Web (WWW)." July 10. Accessed July 10, 2017. https://www.techopedia.com/definition/5217/world-wide-web-www.

———. 2017. "Worm." June 2. Accessed June 2, 2017. https://www.techopedia.com/definition/4171/worm.

———. 2017. "Log Management." August 22. https://www.techopedia.com/definition/29394/log-management.

———. 2017. "Virtual Local Area Network (VLAN)." August 22. https://www.techopedia.com/definition/4804/virtual-local-area-network-vlan.

Techtarget. 2017. "Secure Container." July 28. Accessed July 28, 2017. http://whatis.techtarget.com/definition/secure-container.

The White House. 2015. "Executive Order—Imposing Additional Sanctions with Respect to North Korea." January 2. Accessed July 3, 2017. https://www.whitehouse.gov/the-press-office/2015/01/02/executive-order-imposing-additional-sanctions-respect-north-korea.

———. 2013. *Presidential Policy Directive—Critical Infrastructure Security and Resilience PRESIDENTIAL POLICY DIRECTIVE/PPD-21.* February 12. https://www.whitehouse.gov/the-press-office/2013/02/12/presidential-policy-directive-critical-infrastructure-security-and-resil.

Thielman, Sam, and Chris Johnston. 2016. "Major Cyber Attack Disrupts Internet Service across Europe and US." October 21. Accessed July 2, 2017. https://www.theguardian.com/technology/2016/oct/21/ddos-attack-dyn-internet-denial-service.

Trahan, Jason. 2017. "Cockrell Hill Police Lose Years Worth of Evidence in Ransom Hacking." January 25. Accessed January 25, 2017. http://www.wfaa.com/news/local/cockrell-hill-police-lose-years-worth-of-evidence-in-ransom-hacking/392673232.

Trammell, Joel. 2014. "Lead from the Top: 5 Core Responsiblities of a CEO." May 1. http://www.entrepreneur.com/article/233354.

Trend Micro. 2016. "Millions of Amazon Users Targeted with Locky Ransomware via Phishing Scams." May 27. Accessed November 2, 2016. http://www.trendmicro.com/vinfo/us/security/news/cybercrime-and-digital-threats/amazon-users-targeted-with-locky-ransomware-via-phishing-scams.

US Department of Homeland Security ICS-CERT. 2016. *Advisory (ICSA-16-224-01) Rockwell Automation MicroLogix 1400 SNMP Credentials Vulnerability.* August 11. https://ics-cert.us-cert.gov/advisories/ICSA-16-224-01.

———. 2016. *Advisory (ICSA-16-194-02) GE Proficy HMI SCADA CIMPLICITY Privilege Management Vulnerability.* July 12. https://ics-cert.us-cert.gov/advisories/ICSA-16-194-02.

———. 2016. *Advisory (ICSA-16-196-01) Schneider Electric Pelco Digital Sentry Video Management System Vulnerability.* July 14. https://ics-cert.us-cert.gov/advisories/ICSA-16-196-01.

———. 2016. *Advisory (ICSA-16-215-02A) Siemens SINEMA Server Privilege Escalation Vulnerability (Update A).* August 2. https://ics-cert.us-cert.gov/advisories/ICSA-16-215-02.

———. 2015. *Alert (ICS-ALERT-15-041-01) Microsoft Security Bulletin MS15-011 JASBUG.* February 10. https://ics-cert.us-cert.gov/alerts/ICS-ALERT-15-041-01.

US Department of Justice Office of the Inspector General. 2003. *A Review of the FBI's Performance in Deterring, Detecting, and Investigatiing the Espionage Activities of Robert Philip Hanssen.* Washington DC: US Department of Justice Office of the Inspector General.

Ungureanu, Horia. 2016. "Stagefright-Like iOS, OS X Vulnerabilities Allow Remote Code Execution: Update Now." July 23. Accessed July 9, 2017. http://www.techtimes.com/articles/171045/20160723/stagefright-like-ios-os-x-vulnerabilities-allow-remote-code-execution-update-now.htm.

US Attorney's Office for New Jersey. 2011. "Former Shionogi Employee Sentenced to Federal Prison for Hack Attack on Company Computer Servers." December 9. Accessed July 12, 2017. https://www.justice.gov/archive/usao/nj/Press/files/Cornish,%20Jason%20Sentencing%20News%20Release.html.

US Attorney's Office Northern District of Georgia. 2016. "Two Major International Hackers Who Developed the 'SpyEye' Malware Get over 24 Years Combined in Federal Prison." April 20. Accessed July 13,

2017. https://www.justice.gov/usao-ndga/pr/two-major-international-hackers-who-developed-spyeye-malware-get-over-24-years-combined.

US Attorney's Office Southern District of New York. 2016. "Manhattan US Attorney Announces Charges against Seven Iranians for Conducting Coordinated Campaign of Cyber Attacks against US Financial Sector on Behalf of Islamic Revolutionary Guard Corps-Sponsored Entities." March 24. Accessed July 2, 2017. https://www.justice.gov/usao-sdny/pr/manhattan-us-attorney-announces-charges-against-seven-iranians-conducting-coordinated.

US Department of Defense Joint Chiefs of Staff. 2017. "Cyberspace & Information Operations Study Center, What Are Information Operations." July 3. Accessed July 3, 2017. http://www.au.af.mil/info-ops/index.htm.

———. 2014. "What are Information Operations?" November 20. Accessed July 3, 2017. http://www.dtic.mil/doctrine/new_pubs/jp3_13.pdf.

US Department of Health and Human Services. 2018. "HIPAA For Professionals." February 11. Accessed February 11, 2018. https://www.hhs.gov/hipaa/for-professionals/index.html.

US Department of Health and Human Services. 2018. "Resolution Agreements." February 11. Accessed February 11, 2018. https://www.hhs.gov/hipaa/for-professionals/compliance-enforcement/agreements.

US Department of Homeland Secuity. 2017. "Defense Industrial Base Sector." July 9. Accessed July 9, 2017. https://www.dhs.gov/defense-industrial-base-sector.

———. 2017. "Advisory (ICSA-16-194-02) GE Proficy HMI SCADA CIMPLICITY Privilege Management Vulnerability." July 7. Accessed July 7, 2017. https://ics-cert.us-cert.gov/advisories/ICSA-16-194-02.

———. 2017. "Advisory (ICSA-16-196-01) Schneider Electric Pelco Digital Sentry Video Management System Vulnerability." July 7. Accessed July 7, 2017. https://ics-cert.us-cert.gov/advisories/ICSA-16-196-01.

———. 2017. "Advisory (ICSA-16-215-02A) Siemens SINEMA Server Privilege Escalation Vulnerability (Update A)." July 7. Accessed July 7, 2017. https://ics-cert.us-cert.gov/advisories/ICSA-16-215-02.

———. 2017. "Advisory (ICSA-16-224-01) Rockwell Automation MicroLogix 1400 SNMP Credentials Vulnerability." July 7. Accessed July 7, 2017. https://ics-cert.us-cert.gov/advisories/ICSA-16-224-01.

———. 2017. "Advisory (ICSA-17-166-01) Cambium Networks ePMP." July 7. Accessed July 7, 2017. https://ics-cert.us-cert.gov/advisories/ICSA-17-166-01.

———. 2017. "Advisory (ICSA-17-171-01) Ecava IntegraXor." July 7. Accessed July 7, 2017. https://ics-cert.us-cert.gov/advisories/ICSA-17-171-01.

———. 2017. "Advisory (ICSA-17-180-01) Siemens SIMATIC Industrial PCs, SINUMERIK Panel Control Unit, and SIMOTION P320." July 7. Accessed July 7, 2017. https://ics-cert.us-cert.gov/advisories/ICSA-17-180-01.

———. 2017. "Advisory (ICSA-17-187-01) Siemens OZW672 and OZW772." July 7. Accessed July 7, 2017. https://ics-cert.us-cert.gov/advisories/ICSA-17-187-01.

———. 2017. "Advisory (ICSA-17-187-04) Schneider Electric Wonderware ArchestrA Logger." July 7. Accessed July 7, 2017. https://ics-cert.us-cert.gov/advisories/ICSA-17-187-04.

———. 2017. "Alert (ICS-ALERT-15-041-01) Microsoft Security Bulletin MS15-011 JASBUG." July 7. Accessed July 7, 2017. https://ics-cert.us-cert.gov/alerts/ICS-ALERT-15-041-01.

———. 2016. "Alert (IR-ALERT-H-16-056-01) Cyber-Attack Against Ukrainian Critical Infrastructure." February 25. Accessed July 3, 2017. https://ics-cert.us-cert.gov/alerts/IR-ALERT-H-16-056-01.

———. 2017. "Chemical Sector." July 8. Accessed July 8, 2017. https://www.dhs.gov/chemical-sector.

———. 2017. "Commercial Facilities Sector." July 8. Accessed July 8, 2017. https://www.dhs.gov/commercial-facilities-sector.

———. 2017. "Communications Sector." July 8. Accessed July 8, 2017. https://www.dhs.gov/communications-sector.

———. 2017. "Critical Manufacturing Sector." July 8. Accessed July 8, 2017. https://www.dhs.gov/critical-manufacturing-sector.

———. 2017. "Dams Sector." July 7. Accessed July 7, 2017. https://www.dhs.gov/dams-sector.

———. 2017. "Emergency Services Sector." July 9. Accessed July 9, 2017. https://www.dhs.gov/emergency-services-sector.

———. 2017. "Energy Sector." July 9. Accessed July 9, 2017. https://www.dhs.gov/energy-sector.

———. 2017. "Financial Services Sector." July 9. Accessed July 9, 2017. https://www.dhs.gov/financial-services-sector.

———. 2017. "Food and Agriculture Sector." July 9. Accessed July 9, 2017. https://www.dhs.gov/food-and-agriculture-sector.

———. 2017. "Government Facilities Sector." July 9. Accessed July 9, 2017. https://www.dhs.gov/government-facilities-sector.

———. 2017. "Healthcare and Public Health Sector." July 9. Accessed July 9, 2017. https://www.dhs.gov/healthcare-public-health-sector.

———. 2017. "ICS-CERT Advisories." July 7. Accessed July 7, 2017. https://ics-cert.us-cert.gov/advisories.

———. 2017. "ICS-CERT Alerts." July 7. Accessed July 7, 2017. https://ics-cert.us-cert.gov/alerts.

———. 2017. "Information Sharing." July 3. Accessed July 3, 2017. https://www.dhs.gov/topic/cybersecurity-information-sharing.

———. 2017. "Information Sharing." July 16. Accessed July 16, 2017. https://www.dhs.gov/topic/cybersecurity-information-sharing.

———. 2017. "Information Technology Sector." July 9. Accessed July 9, 2017. https://www.dhs.gov/information-technology-sector.

———. 2017. "National Cybersecurity and Communications Integration Center." July 3. Accessed July 3, 2017. https://www.dhs.gov/national-cybersecurity-and-communications-integration-center.

———. 2017. "Nuclear Reactors, Materials, and Waste Sector." July 9. Accessed July 9, 2017. https://www.dhs.gov/nuclear-reactors-materials-and-waste-sector.

———. 2017. "Sector-Specific Agencies." July 2. Accessed July 2, 2017. https://www.dhs.gov/sector-specific-agencies.

———. 2017. "Transportation Systems Sector." July 9. Accessed July 9, 2017. https://www.dhs.gov/transportation-systems-sector.

———. 2017. "Water and Wastewater Systems Sector." July 9. Accessed July 9, 2017. https://www.dhs.gov/water-and-wastewater-systems-sector.

US Department of Justice. 2015. "Major Computer Hacking Forum Dismantled." July 15. Accessed July 13, 2017. https://www.justice.gov/opa/pr/major-computer-hacking-forum-dismantled.

———. 2016. "Seven Iranians Working for Islamic Revolutionary Guard Corps-Affiliated Entities Charged for Conducting Coordinated Campaign of Cyber Attacks Against US Financial Sector." March 24. Accessed July 3, 2017. https://www.justice.gov/opa/pr/seven-iranians-working-islamic-revolutionary-guard-corps-affiliated-entities-charged.

———. 2014. "US Leads Multi-National Action Against 'Gameover Zeus' Botnet and 'Cryptolocker' Ransomware, Charges Botnet Administrator." June 2. Accessed July 13, 2017. https://www.justice.gov/opa/pr/us-leads-multi-national-action-against-gameover-zeus-botnet-and-cryptolocker-ransomware.

———. 2017. "US Charges Russian FSB Officers and Their Criminal Conspirators for Hacking Yahoo and Millions of E-mail Accounts." March 15. Accessed July 3, 2017. https://www.justice.gov/opa/pr/us-charges-russian-fsb-officers-and-their-criminal-conspirators-hacking-yahoo-and-millions.

US Department of Justice Office of the Inspector General. 2003. *A Review of the FBI's Performance in Deterring, Detecting, and Investigatiing the Espionage Activities of Robert Philip Hanssen.* Washington DC: US Department of Justice Office of the Inspector General. Accessed July 12, 2017. https://oig.justice.gov/special/0308/final.pdf.

US Federal Trade Commission. 2018. "Enforcement." February 11. Accessed February 11, 2018. https://www.ftc.gov/enforcement.

US Federal Trade Commission. 2018. "Legal Resources." February 11. Accessed February 11, 2018. https://www.ftc.gov/tips-advice/business-center/legal-resources?type=case&field_consumer_protection_topics_tid=249.

US National Institute of Standards and Technology. 2015. *NIST Special Publication 800-82 Revision 2 Guide to Industrial Control Systems (ICS) Security.* Gaithersburg, MD: US National Institue of Standards and Technology. Accessed July 13, 2017. http://nvlpubs.nist.gov/nistpubs/SpecialPublications/NIST.SP.800-82r2.pdf.

US Securities and Exchange Commission. 2016. "About the SEC." November 27. Accessed October 3, 2017. https://www.sec.gov/about.shtml.

US Securities and Exchange Commission. 2017. "SEC Announces Enforcement Initiatives to Combat Cyber-Based Threats and Protect Retail Investors."

September 25. Accessed October 3, 2017. https://www.sec.gov/news/press-release/2017-176.

US Securities and Exchange Commission. 2017. "SEC Chairman Clayton Issues Statement on Cybersecurity." September 20. Accessed October 3, 2017. https://www.sec.gov/news/press-release/2017-170.

US Securities and Exchange Commission. 2017. "Statement on Cybersecurity." September 20. Accessed October 3, 2017. https://www.sec.gov/news/public-statement/statement-clayton-2017-09-20.

US Securities and Exchange Commission, Division of Corporation Finance. 2011. "CF Disclosure Guidance: Topic No. 2." October 13. Accessed October 4, 2017. https://www.sec.gov/divisions/corpfin/guidance/cfguidance-topic2.htm.

w3schools.com. 2016. "HTML Basic Examples." October 28. http://www.w3schools.com/html/html_basic.asp.

———. 2016. "Try Html Basic Document." October 28. http://www.w3schools.com/html/tryit.asp?filename=tryhtml_basic_document.

———. 2016. "Try HTML Basic Headings." October 29. http://www.w3schools.com/html/tryit.asp?filename=tryhtml_basic_headings.

———. 2016. "Try HTML Basic Link." October 29. http://www.w3schools.com/html/tryit.asp?filename=tryhtml_basic_link.

———. 2016. "Try HTML Basic Paragraphs." October 29. http://www.w3schools.com/html/tryit.asp?filename=tryhtml_basic_paragraphs.

———. 2016. "Try Js Intro Inner HTML. October 29. http://www.w3schools.com/js/tryit.asp?filename=tryjs_intro_inner_html.

———. 2016. "Try Js Intro Style." October 29. http://www.w3schools.com/js/tryit.asp?filename=tryjs_intro_style.

Winter, Michael. 2014. "Home Depot hackers used vendor log-on to steal data, e-mails." November 6. Accessed September 13, 2017. https://www.usatoday.com/story/money/business/2014/11/06/home-depot-hackers-stolen-data/18613167/.

Winton, Richard. 2016. "Hollywood Hospital Pays $17,000 in Bitcoin to Hackers; FBI Investigating." February 18. Accessed July 3, 2017. http://www.latimes.com/business/technology/la-me-ln-hollywood-hospital-bitcoin-20160217-story.html.

Wrangham, Martha and Gretchen A. Ramos. 2016. "Calls for Federal Breach Notification Law Continue After Yahoo Data Breach." October 5. Accessed September 17, 2017. https://www.natlawreview.com/article/calls-federal-breach-notification-law-continue-after-yahoo-data-breach.

www.w3schools.com. 2016. "Try Css Default." October 29. http://www.w3schools.com/css/tryit.asp?filename=trycss_default.

———. 2016. "Try HTML Basic Img." October 29. http://www.w3schools.com/html/tryit.asp?filename=tryhtml_basic_img.

———. 2016. "Try Js Intro Lightbulb." October 29. http://www.w3schools.com/js/tryit.asp?filename=tryjs_intro_lightbulb.

———. 2016. "Try Js Intro Hide." October 29. http://www.w3schools.com/js/tryit.asp?filename=tryjs_intro_hide.

———. 2016. "Ty Js Intro Show." October 29. http://www.w3schools.com/js/tryit.asp?filename=tryjs_intro_show.

Zetter, Kim. 2016. "Inside the Cunning, Unprecedented Hack of Ukraine's Power Grid." March 3. Accessed July 3, 2017. https://www.wired.com/2016/03/inside-cunning-unprecedented-hack-ukraines-power-grid/.

Made in United States
North Haven, CT
30 January 2024

48073803R00163